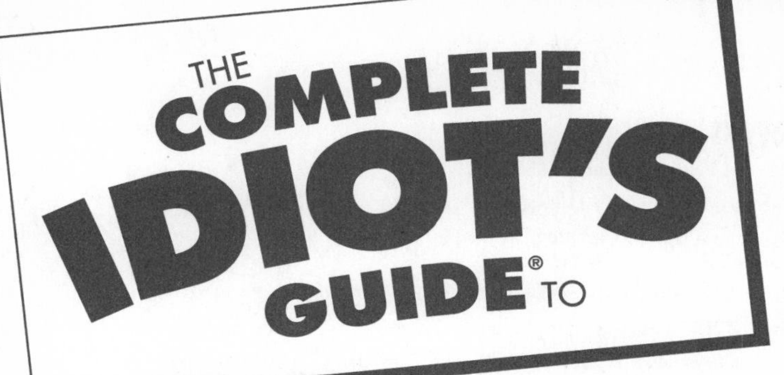

Reading with Your Child

by Helen Coronato

A member of Penguin Group (USA) Inc.

This book is dedicated to my friends in the Holistic Moms Network who are committed to making the world a better place one child at a time. Thank you for all you do.

And of course, to my mother, Priscilla Grimm, who shared her love of reading, and of life, with me. I miss you very much.

ALPHA BOOKS

Published by the Penguin Group

Penguin Group (USA) Inc., 375 Hudson Street, New York, New York 10014, USA

Penguin Group (Canada), 90 Eglinton Avenue East, Suite 700, Toronto, Ontario M4P 2Y3, Canada (a division of Pearson Penguin Canada Inc.)

Penguin Books Ltd., 80 Strand, London WC2R 0RL, England

Penguin Ireland, 25 St. Stephen's Green, Dublin 2, Ireland (a division of Penguin Books Ltd.)

Penguin Group (Australia), 250 Camberwell Road, Camberwell, Victoria 3124, Australia (a division of Pearson Australia Group Pty. Ltd.)

Penguin Books India Pvt. Ltd., 11 Community Centre, Panchsheel Park, New Delhi—110 017, India

Penguin Group (NZ), 67 Apollo Drive, Rosedale, North Shore, Auckland 1311, New Zealand (a division of Pearson New Zealand Ltd.)

Penguin Books (South Africa) (Pty.) Ltd., 24 Sturdee Avenue, Rosebank, Johannesburg 2196, South Africa

Penguin Books Ltd., Registered Offices: 80 Strand, London WC2R 0RL, England

International Standard Book Number: 978-1-59257-661-6
Library of Congress Catalog Card Number: 2007922830

09 08 07 8 7 6 5 4 3 2 1

Interpretation of the printing code: The rightmost number of the first series of numbers is the year of the book's printing; the rightmost number of the second series of numbers is the number of the book's printing. For example, a printing code of 07-1 shows that the first printing occurred in 2007.

Printed in the United States of America

Publisher: *Marie Butler-Knight*
Editorial Director: *Mike Sanders*
Managing Editor: *Billy Fields*
Executive Editor: *Randy Ladenheim-Gil*
Development Editor: *Nancy D. Lewis*
Production Editor: *Megan Douglass*
Copy Editor: *Jan Zoya*
Cover Designer: *Bill Thomas*
Book Designer: *Trina Wurst*
Indexer: *Tonya Heard*
Layout: *Brian Massey, Eric S. Miller*
Proofreader: *Mary Hunt*

Contents at a Glance

Contents

Appendixes

Introduction

I have loved books since I was a kid and have spent most of my adult life trying to get other kids, including my own, to love them as well. As an English teacher, children's librarian, and author, I have always surrounded myself with books; they are as much a part of my life as eating or exercising and a constant source of entertainment. My intention when writing this book was to offer suggestions and strategies for making reading a natural part of your family's life, as it is mine. No expensive products, no gimmicks, no promises, just simple, straightforward ideas for enjoying books in your home with your children.

Because, for me, that has always been the trick. I enjoy reading, and I always have. I don't ever remember having to "log" my reading minutes, count pages, or ask a parent to sign my "reading journal." But the more parents I talk to, the more concern (frenzied fear) there seems to be about reading the right way. Even parents have been duped into thinking kids would benefit from "accelerated reading" programs or early reading intervention workbooks endorsed by medical experts. The only reading doctor I ever saw went by the name of Seuss and I turned out just fine. Because of that, I did not want this to be just another authoritative opinion on the shelf scaring you with stats and requirements. Reading shouldn't be scary; it should be a pleasure. And that is what we will focus on.

Whether you are an avid reader or wince at the thought of cracking open a novel, whether your kids love reading or roll their eyes the minute you suggest turning off the TV to read, the suggestions and strategies in this book can help you build a literacy-rich home. Don't feel obligated to try every idea or read every book recommendation; in fact, I encourage you not to. I have tried to give enough detail about activities and stories so that you may pick and choose those which sound most appealing. You are the expert on your child's needs; look for ideas that suit your family. It's never too soon, or too late, to start a reading routine. This is not a competition and there is no finish line. Start small, go slowly, and above all else, enjoy the process. Reading with your children is as much about your enjoyment as it is theirs. The only way to raise a reader for life is one book at a time. Jump in—the reading is just fine!

How This Book Is Organized

This book is organized into five parts:

Part 1, "Literacy Begins at Home," rolls out the reading welcome mat for you and your family. Everyone is invited to come to the reading party, and I hope you stay for a long while. Part 1 is intended to help you assess where you are as a family of readers, where you want to go, and the best way to get there. Because we are interested in building a literacy-rich home and raising readers for life, I want to make sure you are as comfortable and confident in this endeavor as possible. Part 1 can help set you up for success.

If you are fortunate enough to be reading this book with a baby in your arms or a toddler at your feet, congratulations! **Part 2, "Crib Notes—Introducing Books to Your Baby and Toddler,"** is designed with new parents in mind. Here we will take a look at effective ways to introduce your children to books by creating an accessible reading environment and establishing a firm, but always fun, reading routine.

Part 3, "I Think I Can, I Think I Can: Encouraging Emergent Readers," focuses on the reader who is just coming into her own. Excited about all of the things she can do by herself, she is anxious to add reading to the list. This is a wonderful opportunity to encourage emergent readers to actively participate in their learning process with hands-on games and family-focused activities geared toward reading fun.

Part 4, "The Independent Reader: Leap Into Literature," can help you lighten the reading load. When your reader moves from the Children's Room to the Young Adult section, his independent spirit can be disarming. Capable of making, or refusing to make, reading choices on his own, you'll want to re-evaluate your current reading routine and look for ways to continue sharing reading, and your values, without cramping his newfound style.

Part 5, "Tweens, Teens, and the Reading Scene: Young Adult Audiences," takes a final look at ways to keep reading together and talks about the all-important transition from required reader to reader for life. Hopefully, with all of your hard work and dedication you can truly call books a good family friend.

The appendixes include a compilation of all of the titles spotlighted throughout the book, a separate list of book that can be enjoyed by parents, and online resources for further reading recommendations.

Extras

The sidebars found throughout this book contain are extra nuggets of information:

Success Story

These boxes offer tried-and-true reading recommendations and pointers for building your literacy-rich home.

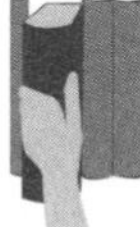

Quick Picks

These boxes are intended for busy families and suggest fast-and-friendly tips for meeting your family's reading goals.

Bookworms Beware

These boxes caution you to avoid common reading routine pitfalls, which can derail your good intentions.

Acknowledgments

I must first thank my friend and agent, Jacky Sach, who recommended me for this book, answered all of my beginner questions, and has talked me off of a ledge more than once; thank you for everything. The first "real" adult whoever told me I should, and could, be a writer was my eleventh-grade English teacher at Kellenberg High School, Ms. Hughes. I hope a copy of this finds you.

I am eternally grateful to Karen and Joni Templin and Kira and Anya Campbell who gave me the time, and peace of mind, I needed to complete this book. Kim Bohn, Wendy DeSarno, Elise Cosenza, and Anna Tillinghast have been endless sources of support, as have Patty and Heather Hopkins; thank you for your friendship and please feel obligated to buy many copies of this book (yes, you read that the right way).

Most sincere thanks goes to my family, especially my in-laws Mike and Kathy Coronato who haven't stopped bragging about me since the day we met, and my brothers-in-law, Bob and Dean, who just keep making it harder and harder to be the star in this family. For my two sons, I hope reading is a gift I can give both of you, as you both have given me too many gifts to count. And of course, my amazing husband Tom, who hasn't seen a home-cooked meal, an ironed shirt, or a day off since I took this project on, but still keeps telling me that I'm doing everything right. You are the best part of my day.

Trademarks

Part 1

Literacy Begins at Home

When parents think about their children's reading levels, they are usually associating reading with education. As reading is the foundation for all formal learning, better readers will do better in school. And what parent doesn't want their child to do better in school? But what you might not realize is that by reading with your children now, you can create an interest in reading that will last far beyond their school years.

Many of us have thought of reading as a mere means to an end. Read the book, pass the test. Read the directions, get to the party. Instead of viewing reading as just a vehicle to get from point A to point B, we should start to think of reading as the medium that transforms us from employee to entrepreneur, from wallflower to public speaker or from self-conscious child to self-empowered adult. A strong reader does more then excel in school, he excels in life. By using my age appropriate activities, suggested reading materials and common sense approach in this part, you can expect to maximize reading fun while minimizing reluctance and eye rolling.

Chapter 1

Who's a Qualified Reading Teacher?

In This Chapter

- The power of the reading parent
- You don't have to go it alone
- You can't rush a reader for life

Admit it, you've had the fantasy. You know the one. Lights down low, soft music in the background. Perhaps a crackling fire. You, a soft blanket across your lap. Your husband, dreamingly lying across the couch. Junior, sprawled out on the floor. What kind of daydream is this? It's the one where everyone in the family relaxes together in the company of a good book. Don't be embarrassed; you're not the only one with this grandiose vision. In fact, whether we care to admit it or not, most of us wish we had quieter homes, better communication among family members, and more downtime to just be together. So what can we do to turn this fantasy into a reality?

For most of us, the idea of gathering in the living room for anything other than a movie night is probably completely foreign.

While we want to make time to turn off all the distractions in our lives and make reading a priority, we can feel nervous, anxious, and even embarrassed about suggesting such an idea. But you need not fear these uncharted waters any longer. In the following chapters, I'll give you several reasons why you will want to make reading with your family a priority and begin to introduce some of the tools that will make this possible.

First, lets take a look at everything you have to offer your child when it comes to reading; and then I'll offer ideas and suggestions for making all of your child's caregivers part of the reading equation. Many parents are concerned that they will "mess up" reading instruction; but rest assured, our focus on recreational reading and raising readers for life will leave you feeling enthusiastic and empowered about your expertise.

Your Child's Most Important Reading Teacher

It seems as if everywhere we turn, we're being bombarded with expert advice. Advice on what to eat, what to wear, where to work. Somehow this expert advice has infiltrated the parenting community and made us feel like we are ill equipped to instruct our own children. Especially when it comes to reading. A lack of formal training has convinced parents that they should leave reading to the experts, lest they ruin their child. Well, I say it's time to take back our library cards, put away our checkbooks, and trust our own instincts. In fact, we're not even going to talk about "teaching" reading; we're going to talk about things we can do to encourage our children to want to read.

What is the difference between teaching reading and encouraging reading? The first relies on results while the latter emphasizes a process. After we teach our children a skill, we expect that they will be able to perform that skill on their own. But just because you have a skill, doesn't mean you are going to use it. I know plenty of children—and adults—who can read and choose not to. On the other hand, when we encourage reading, through routines, rituals, games, and guidance, then mastering the skill of reading becomes a byproduct of reading enjoyment. It makes perfect sense: the more you do something, the better you get at it. Read more = read better. But read better does not necessarily mean you'll read more. And that is our goal: children who read more, and children who grow up to be readers for life.

Meet the Parents

You are your child's first caregiver. The one who walks the halls in the middle of the night humming nursery rhymes until you develop a strong disdain for Mother Goose. The cooing voice, calming hands, constant lap. Long before your child ever meets a single, solitary, certified teacher, you will make every decision regarding his health, environment and education. A pretty huge responsibility, wouldn't you say?

Yet when it comes to reading with our children, a lovely and enjoyable experience, many of us shy away, afraid we'll "mess it up." While we may read a bedtime story to our children, we become nervous when they start to squirm, convinced that we must be doing something wrong. We quickly finish the book, say goodnight, and get out of there, lest the reading police find out we had a close call. Or we have older children who once loved to read, but now prefer to do anything else but open a book. Exasperated with fighting over reading, and fed up with having a sullen middle-schooler roll her eyes at us (yet again), we opt to let it go; worried that we're not doing enough, but stumped about what action to take. Reading with our children is a task that must be done, but not one that we look forward to. We are in a tough spot. But there is a way out.

Yes, *You* Can!

No one is going to care more about your kids than you. Yes, there will be extended family members, memorable coaches, and great teachers along the way; but you are always going to be your kid's biggest fan, advocate, and enthusiast. Since signing on for this 24/7 job, you have wiped noses and bottoms, kissed bruises and bellies and watched as your wardrobe went from hot dish to potluck. At best, you have been paid in kisses and cuddles. You do all you do because you have a genuine interest in your child. From the moment they arrive to the day that you depart, your kids will occupy the biggest piece of your heart. Because you have such energy and enthusiasm about their well-being hardwired into your heart, why not tap into this wealth of wisdom and share the fun of reading together?

I know, I know, you are thinking, "But I'm not a reading expert." I'm here to tell you, you are. You do not need to be a master linguist, have scored an 800 on your verbal SATs, or have read *War and Peace* for pleasure. You are interested in reading with your children, building a literacy-rich home, and enjoying the fruits of your effort. For that, all you need is a vested interest in your children, an open mind, and a few deep breaths coupled with the recommendations in this book. But because some of you will still be reluctant to believe me, I have included this extremely formal, one-of-a-kind certificate of expertise for you to fill out. This way, if anyone questions your credentials, or when you doubt yourself, you will have this helpful reading certificate at your fingertips.

"This document certifies that ________ is an expert at reading with his/her child, and therefore, need not purchase any expensive programs, register for any accelerated classes, or memorize the Complete Works of Shakespeare. ______ has all the credentials necessary to build a literacy-rich home, and can enjoy the process using practical suggestions, great reading materials, and common sense. This certificate is effective immediately and has no expiration date."

> **Quick Picks**
>
> Give yourself a good dose of confidence by listing three obstacles you have already addressed as a parent. Baby finally sleeping through the night? Found a babysitter you trust so you could enjoy a romantic night out? Remind yourself that you can successfully face new challenges.

There you go—an official reading certificate for the record. I assure you, the rest of this journey will be just as painless.

Easy, Affordable, Accessible, Fun

I know it's hard to believe that you already have everything you need to begin reading with your child, but it's true. All of the suggestions I am going to make will be easy to follow. There are no complicated forms to fill out, no extensive research to complete. This is a strictly low-maintenance approach to running a reader-friendly home. And it is affordable. The materials you need can be borrowed or bought, new or used. Your public library has almost everything you will ever need. And garage sales, eBay, discount subscription programs, and used bookstores can help you round out your reading needs.

Reading materials are one of the most accessible childhood supplies you will ever carry around. (Just wait until he signs up for hockey. Ugh!) Light, compact, and spill-proof, reading materials come in all shapes and sizes and can easily fit into diaper bags, glove compartments, and kitchen cabinets. Once you get started, you really won't believe how much fun you will have. Aside from the numerous advantages you'll be giving your children, you will reap rewards you didn't even realize were there for the taking.

Why You Must Do This

Reading increases our comprehension skills, varies our vocabulary, and broadens our base knowledge. Those qualities alone are enough to make a strong case for encouraging reading in our homes. But an even stronger case can be made for one of the most overlooked, and most advantageous, benefits of reading: communication skills.

While you probably already appreciate that strong readers know a lot of words, you may not have realized that strong readers are actually more fluent in their own language. The more we read, the more exposure we have to how language works. Through dialogue, description, and characterization we learn the nuances of our language: the subtle difference between cry and weep; the important distinction between dislike and disdain. Mastering these subtleties can make an individual a much more compelling speaker and a more skilled listener.

Individuals who exhibit strong communication skills are seen as excellent problem solvers—capable of always thinking on their feet. These are the people who fast become the company's rising stars. And don't think that these skills are only useful in the boardroom. Parents who consider themselves competent communicators are more likely to be an advocate for their children, their pets, and themselves.

While you may not be offered a raise for your work with the PTA, you could be instrumental in getting that playground built, having those funds allocated to the library or addressing the need for added school security. Reading skills do not discriminate based on age, gender, or vocation. Reading knows no boundaries. Whether you are climbing the professional ladder or insisting the town's fire department invest in a new one, reading can help each member of your family get the things that are near and dear to your heart.

Considerations for Parents

It feels like there are a million things you must accomplish each day. How, then, can you be expected to fit in another activity? Because it's just too important not to. I'll help you figure out a way to build a manageable reading routine with your child, one you will both look forward to, despite your work schedule, school commitments, or your general reluctance to do this at all. There is no magic pill, no magic program (despite what advertisers may try and tell you) that will help your child become a reading machine overnight. It takes time and commitment to raise a reader, but the social, economic, and educational advantages are tremendous. Making reading a priority in your home will help build your child's self-confidence, intelligence, and social skills.

Bookworms Beware

While you may become very excited about trying the ideas in this book, remember to take your time. Raising a reader for life is a long and steady process. You don't want to burn out before the interest is ignited.

Perhaps you are an excellent reader and want to share that gift with them. Maybe you hate to read and you're worried about what that will mean for your kids. If you are reading this book as a new parent, congratulations! You are setting your child up for success. And if you feel like you are coming late to the reading party, don't worry; your commitment to reading now can set your family on a track to success.

The Weight of Your Influence

Because we know our children so well, we intimately know how impressionable they are. We know that we are constantly being watched, studied, followed. What we do, good or bad, will be impersonated … usually in public. Yes, having a constant audience is a huge responsibility; but it is also a huge asset when wanting to influence our children.

We use our manners and expect them to use theirs. We follow the rules, and so do they. We read for pleasure, and so will they. What we do will be mimicked, and what we don't do will also be mimicked.

If one parent smokes while the other preaches no smoking, what will happen? If one parent eats healthfully while the other parent gorges on junk food, what will happen? In both cases, smoking and junk food become realistic options. In the same way, if you do not read, not reading becomes an option. There are no sidelines in reading participation, either you are in, and making it happen, or you are out, hindering the play. Therefore, it is imperative that both parents take an active role in reading with the children.

If mom is the only one who makes reading a priority, the children, especially boys, will start to see reading as a "girly" activity. If daddy doesn't read, why should they? When mom doesn't read, experts note disturbing statistical data. A mother's literacy level is one of the greatest predictors of a child's literacy level. Meaning, if you're a strong reader, your children will be, and if you're not, they may be at a disadvantage. But for you moms and dads who just swallowed a lump in your throat as you recognized yourselves in those last sentences, relax. You have in your hands an excellent guide to help not only your children, but also help you, become more enthusiastic readers, readers for life.

Success Story

What you say in front of your children is as important as what you say to them. If you are a reluctant reader, refrain from stating, "I hate to read" and try a more proactive phrase like, "I'm look-ing for something good to read."

Your Area of Expertise

Reading with your children is an excellent way that you can all get to know each other better. Remember how before you had children you would spend time making homemade holiday presents, tinkering on a classic car, or downloading your favorite music? Remember how people used to know you by your first name, and not address you as "Michael's Mom" or "Emily's Dad"? Now is the time to reclaim your lost identity and rediscover your adult selves.

There are books on every possible subject under the sun, and quite a few about what exists beyond it. Reading with your child does not mean that you are locked into stories about lions, tigers, and bears (oh my!). You can read about things that also interest you, or are important in your family. If you are a yoga enthusiast, check out a yoga book from the library and narrate the pictures yourself.

Working full time? Your job is most likely a complete mystery to your kids. Bring home books about the office, lab, or schoolroom. Love to craft? Check out craft books for adults or kids and wow your family with your ribbon-curling abilities. You have so much to offer. We already know you make a mean casserole and can find the lost toy pieces in under a minute flat. Take this opportunity to share your own interests with your children and introduce them to all the things that make you, wonderful you. When you read about subjects that interest you, you are far more likely to read for longer durations of time, with greater joy and passion.

How You'll Benefit

After a day spent washing hands, returning calls, working, cleaning, cooking, and refereeing, don't you deserve a little R & R? Reading and relaxation, that is. Reading with your children is the milk and cookies of parenthood. It can be a well-deserved treat for all of you. Soft couch, feet up. A park bench. Five minutes of downtime while you wait for your next appointment. Yes, of course, we want our children to learn the benefits of unwinding and finding solace in a good book; but nobody said we couldn't do the same for ourselves, at the same time.

The wonderful thing about reading with your children is that while you are helping them to achieve fantastic marketable tools, you also get to enjoy the pleasure of their company; and they can enjoy yours. What kid doesn't want more time alone with her parents? Even those hard-to-handle tweens and teens look forward to one-on-one time with a parent (although most would just as soon die as admit it). But shared reading, either with a little one perched in your lap or with an older child during a book club meeting, bridges a gap between family members. When we stop associating reading with work, and start associating it with pleasure, we are able to tap into an endless supply of enthusiasm.

Family reading takes very little preparation, is hardly intrusive, and, when approached appropriately, weighs in pretty low on the embarrassment scale. While not every idea will work for your family, many will. Build on the book experiences that work best for you and your family and you'll all benefit mentally, emotionally, and socially.

I have wonderful memories of childhood reading. I have endearing anecdotes about sharing books with my mother and grandmother, made especially heartwarming as they have both passed away. I don't remember every Christmas present, every family vacation, or every toy I ever begged for, but I absolutely remember the three of us scared out of our wits when we all simultaneously read a Stephen King bestseller. Who knew, years later, that a terrifying story about something merely called It would have such a lasting, joyous effect on me. I am constantly surprised by the magic books have brought into my life. These same surprises are waiting for you.

When Parents Hate to Read

I know that some of you who are reading this book are carrying this deep, dark secret around. This unforgivable, never-mention-this-to-the-neighbors shocker: you hate to read. I mean, after all, it's one thing to not be able to read because you don't have the time, but it is simply unacceptable to be a parent and hate reading. The shame! The horror! The misconception.

Quick Picks

For those parents whose careers demand excessive reading, it may be even more difficult to view picking up a book as a pleasurable activity. So don't. Try magazines instead. Reading a short, high-interest article may help you to remember that reading can be recreational, instead of only required.

Chances are, you don't hate to read, you just haven't found what you like to read yet. When I outline some of the struggles reluctant readers have, I'd be surprised if you didn't see yourself there. And with such a busy schedule, who could begrudge you not being able to find something you like? We often compare ourselves to others, thinking that parents all across town are diving into Pulitzer Prize Winning novels after their Harvard-bound children are tucked into bed. Well, maybe some are, but certainly not most.

For instance, I consider myself a voracious reader of literature, but often prefer lighter fare: chick-lit, bestselling commercial fiction, and, Pulitzer Prize winners forgive me, *People Magazine*. Instead of dwelling on what you aren't doing well enough, think about what you do read. Do you love short, punchy articles? Are you a sucker for sudoku? Do you comb your cookbooks, looking for just the right Sunday-night special? You do read; you are probably just discounting what you read. Cut yourself a break. I give you permission to pick what you want to read, when and for how long. Hate the idea of rhyming picture books? Read an article from *Sports Illustrated*, *Money Magazine*, or *Photography Magazine*. Love antiques and collectibles? Flip through a Sotherby's catalogue together and look at clay pots that are big, bigger, and biggest! A quick board book before work, great. An article from the paper in the evening, super. The Sunday comics, awesome.

More important than the content is the communication. As your child grows and his reading skills mature, you can look for beginner books in the subjects you introduced to him as a baby. There are no hard and fast rules for reading together, just this highly successful suggestion: read what you like. Throughout this handbook, I'll show you how valuable every type of reading can be to your children, including those Style Watch pages.

When English Is Not Your Dominant Language

Parents who speak a foreign language at home will have specific concerns about raising proficient readers. Like all parents, we want our children to obtain a useful education, succeed in school and go on to lead productive and useful lives outside of our homes (but still live close enough where we can drop by unannounced to check up on them). For parents whose dominant language is not English, concerns are compounded. How can we teach something we don't know how to do ourselves? Fortunately, I can help dispel a lot of the second-language learning myths that may be intimidating you.

Children have an amazing capacity for learning, and languages are no exception. While we struggle as adults to learn a second language, wrestle with pronunciation, and become frustrated at our slow progress, children's brains welcome new sounds and are quick to digest the material. You need not decide between speaking your native language and English. You can help your child learn to speak both, celebrating your ancestors' heritage and your current community simultaneously.

Unique Challenges

When reading with your children, no one says it has to be in English. In fact, experts agree that reading with your children in your dominant language, reading with control, emphasis, and pleasure is much more desirable than struggling through a foreign language. When it comes to reading, you want to model good, clear communication skills; the language you choose to use is merely the vehicle by which you do that. Instead of putting pressure on yourself to read the right things in English, look for opportunities to read right now. A parent's influence on raising a reader translates into any language. Practice these recommendations in the language you are most comfortable with, and reap the benefits of creating a literacy-rich home in any language.

Success Story

A wonderful picture book about the benefits of being bilingual is *The Barking Mouse* by Antonio Sacre and Alfredo Aguirre. Based on an old Cuban tale, this hilarious story about a mouse family saved by a bilingual mother is sure to become a fast favorite.

While we tend to focus on the challenges facing ESL families, we often forget to celebrate the huge advantage a child has to being bilingual. The earlier you introduce a child to a foreign language, the more successful that child will be at mastering accents and nuances. Don't worry that a child will become confused or develop language-comprehension problems; in fact, it is now believed that learning languages simultaneously as a young child is better than trying to learn a second language after age 12. While it is perfectly natural for you to want your children to be proficient in English, there is no denying the advantages of knowing multiple languages.

Embraceable Opportunities

Public libraries have long been a friend to any and all who wish to learn. Storytimes are an excellent introduction to fabulous books, especially when read with enthusiasm and inflection by an engaging adult. Most library Storytimes are offered to town patrons at no cost. Scheduled once a week at the same time, these professional read-alouds can make a welcome addition to your family calendar. Children are most often grouped by age, and the books are chosen with their interest level and attention spans in mind. Sometimes, an easy craft is included in the program. They are a great chance for both adult and child to learn a second language, while associating books with fun, socialization, and enlightenment.

After Storytime, foreign-language adults can continue to learn English right along with their children. Books on tape or CD, which can be borrowed from the library, are an excellent way to hear a new language spoken with confidence. Tones or bells signal when to turn the page, making it simple to follow along and learn together. Parent can look for simple bilingual picture books or wordless books that they can narrate in English. As many popular titles have been reprinted in foreign languages, especially Spanish, parents are encouraged to check out the many different formats available. Here are three different styles to get you started:

My First Farm Board Book: English/Spanish by DK Publishing. Clearly labeled, bright photographs introduce readers to farm life, including the animals, workers, and machinery. All items are named in English and Spanish. Part of the My First Series. Other titles available.

Brown Bear, Brown Bear, What do you see? Author Bill Martin and illustrator Eric Carle's classic board book loses nothing in translation, in the Spanish version, *Oso pardo, oso pardo, ¿qué ves ahí?*

Green Eggs and Ham, the immortal Dr. Seuss title, is cleverly translated into *Huevos verdes con jamón* by Aida E. Marcuse. What is interesting about this Spanish version is that Marcuse has maintained the "Seussism" by not relying on a verbatim translation, but concentrating on capturing the essence of the story. The result is a rhyming, rhythmic good time.

Family Fluency

The important thing to remember is that you are fluent in a language: your own. You can take all the tips and recommendations in this book and apply them to your own dominant language. Raising a reader in English is the same as raising a reader in Spanish, German, or French. The strategies don't change. As you build your confidence as a reading expert in your own language, you can be working on incorporating a second language, at your own pace and comfort level, with the help of bilingual teachers.

Quick Picks

Looking for children's books in your native Japanese, Russian, or Thai? Check out the American Library's Association's bilingual recommendations at www.ala.org/ala/alsc/alscresources/booklists/bilingualbooks.htm. These titles represent high-quality literary fiction for children published from 1995–1999 or currently in print.

When looking for a good place to begin learning English as a second language, your best bet is your local public library. For starters, adult books on tape are an excellent resource for learning how a language truly sounds and can be checked out the same time you check out your children's books on tape. Libraries also have on hand, or can get, recorded English lessons so you can learn at home. Many towns offer free ESL classes to their patrons, or the library staff can put you in touch with your area's continuing education/community education coordinator, where ESL classes are offered. If no such classes exist in your area, ask the librarian about local student volunteers who would like to work with an ESL family, or contact your local school district and ask to be put in touch with the ESL teachers. Introducing yourself and your family to your school district can help you get an early start on formal materials, and they may be able to set your family up with a volunteer tutor.

Caregivers

Never underestimate the power of a home-field advantage. In your house, your rules go. While little Johnny down the street may be allowed to watch TV all day and all night, under your roof your rules reign supreme. But that does not mean these rules will be welcomed with open arms. To help minimize resistance, try soliciting the help of the caregivers your child has come to known as her extended family. The more people who are on your reading team, the more successful your efforts are apt to be.

The wonderful thing about wanting to create a literature-based home is that you do not have to do it alone. You can invite all the special people in your child's life to join in building this environment. This approach has many benefits. First, it's nice to know that you are supported and that your ideas are carried out by the other caregivers in your child's life. With you spending so much time working to create a literate environment, you will want others to fall into your groove, not create waves. Second, as your child grows, he is apt to question your priorities and decisions, comparing your house rules to that of his friends and neighbors. But by coordinating your reading routine into your daily life, and by including all of your child's caregivers in that mix, you'll have broadened his ideas about reading. This isn't just something his parents do; this is something all the people who care about him do.

Bookworms Beware

There is no guarantee that your caregivers will love reading or have access to great materials. You can always keep a small backpack of parent-approved titles in the car to bring with you to Grandma's, on playdates, or for show and tell. Just remember, in someone else's home or classroom, their house rules apply. Be positive, not pushy.

Softer Touches: Grandparents

Grandparents have an excellent sense of timing; everything else can wait when they are with their grandchild. Instead of having a reading quota to meet, they can meander through the book basket, picking and choosing what captures their eye, talking about the pictures and listening to the many, many, many (many) interruptions from their little audience with beaming love. Grandparents especially are interested in the process, the experience, not the goal. Whereas I have to go flip a load of laundry, get dinner started, and return phone calls, grandparents have no place else in the world they have to be. And there is a quiet contentment that most grandchildren have when they know they are in the presences of such rapt attention. Encourage your parents and in-laws to read to your child. You may be surprised how long the experience lasts.

This can also be an excellent area to give grandparents a little room to rule. Grandparents are probably used to checking in with you when it comes to acceptable snacks, appropriate clothes, and safety measures. But when it comes to reading together, different styles can complement instead of clash.

I am so happy that my in-laws enjoy reading books with our 15-month-old son. But how they read aloud and how I read aloud is completely different. They play more with books, flipping back and forth, finding and naming animals, rereading the same page. I tend to be all business, read from cover to cover, and then go back and discuss the content. Our son just likes to be close to those who love him and hear them read. And while I do have a habit of letting my family know when they have deviated from my well-orchestrated plans in other areas ("You let him eat what?!"), in this area it's the grandparents' show. You, too, can benefit from this kind of exciting exchange, confident that your children are in capable, though different, hands.

You're Paying Them: Babysitters

When you hire a babysitter for your children, you probably cover snack schedules, emergency contacts, and general house rules. During this discussion, be sure to mention reading. Babysitters are a wonderful asset when it comes to associating reading with fun.

For starters, most children love their babysitters and cherish this unique playtime. No errands, no vacuums, just fun and games. One of my favorite things about our babysitter Amanda was her enthusiasm for books. I would come home to find her and my son sharing picture books. After reading aloud, Amanda would hand off the book to Michael, choose another one for her, and then each would settle in with his and her own book for a few minutes. What a natural, relaxed way to spend time away from mom. Combining books and babysitters is a winning situation.

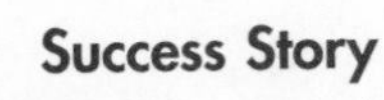

Success Story

Many parents leave a checklist for their babysitters with emergency numbers, snack schedules, and nap times. Add a book title or two to this list to emphasize that reading aloud is also a part of the job.

I know families who save special toys for when the sitter comes, making the transition from parent to caregiver easier. Why not apply this same theory to books? Keep a book or two stashed away for when you will be out. A musical push-button book or lift-the-flap books are great sources to hold in reserve because they are highly entertaining. Have the books ready for when the sitter arrives and take a few moments to all get excited over this special treat. After the day is over, take back the book and save it for next time. Remember, you are paying for your sitter's services. Expecting some reading time is absolutely appropriate.

Do Your Homework: Day Care

If you have your child in day care, or are considering one, I encourage you to ask them about their reading program. There are three main program points to look for. First, children should be read aloud to throughout the day. The typical read-aloud times are first thing in the morning, before meals and/or naps, and at the end of the day. Stories can be used to introduce a new concept, soothe children before sleep, and signal the end of a day. Second, books should always be within reach. Books should be accessible so that children may choose to "read" to themselves during free play. Third, books should be kept in nice condition, be age-appropriate, and be rotated. For instance, in the fall there should be books on leaves, and in the winter, books on snow. When the bulletin boards change, so should the books. Caregivers who treat books and storytime as an important commodity will have these systems in place.

Children who spend formative years in day care adopt the values of their program. Clearly established routines will give your child a rhythm he can depend on. Part of this rhythm should be reading. It should be valued as an integral part of the day, not a peripheral, sporadic activity. Make sure that books are part of the routine, and you and your child will be much happier for it.

Hooked on Commercial Products

Up until now, we've discussed the importance of reading with your children, why you are your child's most important teacher, and ways you can include other caregivers in this important endeavor. But I'm pretty certain some of you may still doubt your own abilities and consider purchasing a "real" reading program—one that is endorsed by the proper experts and tells you exactly how to go about this reading stuff. It can be comforting to sit among dittos, worksheets, and comprehensive directions that are packaged and priced accordingly. But these supplies are just not necessary.

Trust me when I tell you, your child will have a ton of formal written material pertaining to reading when she hits school. You do not have to give her a head start on paperwork. And while I appreciate the many means of encouraging children to enjoy reading, this is not one of the design goals dominant in these products. Most commercial merchandise is geared toward improving a reader's skills, not fostering a love of reading. While I don't dispute that some children do need extra attention to become enthusiastic, capable readers, I hardly think drier drills are the answer. Our purpose in this handbook is to find activities that nurture and engage all the readers in our home, most likely when we focus on finding the right the process, not the right product.

Packaged Programs and Parental Fears

We all want what is best for our children, especially when it comes to something as important as reading. Maybe you are an avid reader and want to share that gist with your child. Perhaps you read only when you absolutely have to, and you're afraid of what that will mean for your kids. Whether you are at one extreme or the other, chances are you have toyed with the idea of helping the reading process along with a nicely packaged program. After all, why not give your children an edge in this competitive society? You can give your children a huge edge in school, socialization, and business, just by reading with them. Reading books, magazines, mail, recipes, and directions will cover every phonics sound, consonant blend, and irregular verb tense known in the English language. Then how come we are convinced we need more?

> **Success Story**
>
> If you are convinced that a pre-packaged program is advantageous, I encourage you to borrow a program before buying one. Many libraries have different materials available to their patrons, giving you an opportunity to test the waters before diving in with your own dollars.

It is very hard to believe that something as simple as reading with your children could be so effective. In today's consumer-savvy market, it defies logic. Manufacturers know this, and spend lots of advertising money reminding you that what is bigger, brighter, faster, and more expensive might just be better. And that is the number-one culprit compromising parents' faith in themselves: advertising. In fact, many parents often feel guilty if they do not "invest" in their child's reading future. Unfortunately we have come to equate investing in our children's future with opening up our checkbooks. This is all crazy talk. Expensive crazy talk.

You Cannot Buy a Better Reader

The well-advertised benefit behind consumer products on reading is that you can hurry along the reading process. I have seen several commercials that feature beaming parents looking at their Harvard-bound pre-schoolers, workbooks in hand, explaining to the camera, "We're just so happy we could give him this 'advantage.'" What is the advantage, though? Being able to parrot back a handful of trite sentences may impress the neighbors, and it may even get you on TV, but it is a far cry from establishing a lifetime love of reading. What strikes me as ironic is that these commercials all lead to the same conclusion, "Their favorite part is when we read the book." Then why not just read the book?

What I think the children in these programs probably most enjoy is spending time with their caregivers, not gaining an early advantage on reading skills. I want all parents to spend more time enjoying books with their children. These pre-packaged programs probably have merit, but they are just not necessary to meet your goal of raising a reader for life. Why not read a favorite picture book together and look for all of the words that begin with the first letter of your child's name? If you want, write them down on individual index cards. Draw a picture that complements the word. Do it twice and play a quick game of memory.

Keep the cards in a shoebox marked, "My Letter 'T' Words." Decorate the shoebox. Tomorrow, choose a word from the box and try to rhyme it with another word. See where I'm going with this?

Phonics skills are important, when studied in conjunction with reading books. Phonics done in isolation can be frustrating, mundane, and often ends up turning the reader off. Throughout this book, I'll offer some fun, kid-friendly letter and word games that can help children learn about the function of letters and language. But I truly believe that these exercises should be done for fun only, not as a pivotal part of your day. Reading is the priority, not programs.

Quick Picks

Children value their one-on-one time with you. With your busy schedule, would you rather have your child sitting across the table from you reciting vowel sounds or curled up in your lap listening to a story chock full of every vowel-sound combination possible? You can't go wrong by choosing the reading situation that brings you closer together.

Keep It Simple

Yes, reading is the cornerstone of all formal education. Yes, reading is one of the most important things you will ever learn to do. Yes, your reading level has direct correlations to your level of education, your career opportunities, and your family's financial security. No, you do not need to worry about all of these things while you make dinner tonight.

While it's true that reading is an important part of our lives, it is only one part. It has been my experience that when we are obsessing on one aspect of our lives, we are out of balance. Instead of taking small steps toward an attainable goal, we become frozen in fear, incapable of doing anything. Overburdened with curriculum options, a slew of best-selling titles, and a laundry list of reading requirements, we just don't know where to start. As parents, we have started taking reading way too seriously.

I want you to do what you can, when you can. Read in the morning or at night. Read for 15 minutes, or 50. Read classics or comics. But whatever you do, enjoy yourself. And the best way to do that is by keeping things really simple. Stop comparing your child to the neighbor's kid. Stop watching the clock. Start reading for pleasure, not results.

While it may feel safer to trust experts and wait until school starts before trying any reading activities, or just buy expensive software, simple really is better. As you begin this new journey with your own children, whether you are just starting out or sensing that it's time for a change, I promise you that you can do this, you can enjoy this, and you can build a literacy-rich home.

The Least You Need to Know

- Everyone in your family will benefit from a literacy-rich home.
- Reading routines can work in any language.
- Parents must be personally engaged in the reading experience if a routine is to take root and grow.
- Reading is a process, not a product. Customizing your family's reading routine helps to promote long term reading success.

Chapter 2

Assessing Your Audience by Age and Stage

In This Chapter

- A literacy-rich home is not built in a day
- Enjoy what you are doing
- Be realistic about your expectations

There is a lot of useful information in this chapter regarding reading routines, catering to your reader's needs, and enjoying the process of redesigning your reader-friendly home. But what you won't find is a one-size-fits-all formula. It just doesn't exist. There is no list of mandatory books that will guarantee your child learns to love reading, nor is there a particular time of day that will trigger an instant affection for the written word. What I can offer you are valuable suggestions for looking at your own family dynamic and deciding what paths to pursue.

Interestingly enough, what works with one child may not necessarily work with another. But as these recommendations are intended to be incorporated into your day, not dictate it, you'll be better able to manage individual needs and still get dinner on the table. If at any time you feel overwhelmed or underqualified, refer to your reading certification from Chapter 1. I have all the faith in the world in you. And so do your kids.

Getting Started

Now that you are jazzed about bringing more reading into your home, you are probably wondering where to start. Is there an ideal age, season, or occasion to begin a reading routine? What are the best resources to use? How will you know if it is working? Hopefully you are beginning to realize that you can trust yourself, that you are the premier expert on your own child, and that reading can be enjoyable and educational at the same time. Somewhere between requesting early acceptance to Harvard and throwing up your hands in frustration lies a happy medium. Together, we can find out where that is and encourage your family to embrace reading as a part of their daily lives.

Maybe you've already read *War and Peace* to your newborn. Maybe you're not sure if your town even has a library. Rest assured, wherever you are, you can jump in at any point in your child's reading development. You do not have to wait for the moons to align, nor do you have to feel that the reading ship has sailed. If you are headed in the right direction, my recommendations can help you enjoy smoother sailing. If you feel like you are up a creek without a paddle, these same recommendations can help bring you safely to shore. When is the best time to begin focusing your family on reading? Right now.

Is It Too Soon?

It is never too soon to begin reading with your children. If you are reading this book with one hand and cradling your newborn in the other, start reading these chapters out loud. There is nothing as comforting to an infant than the sound of a parent's voice. Parents have often told me that they feel silly reading to their babies, as there is no interaction. They feel like they are talking to themselves. Well, they're not. And while your newborn may not sit up and say, "I really think the author made a compelling argument in that last chapter," her peaceful breathing and relaxed posture accompanied by occasional gurgles and arm flairs are an indication that she is enjoying herself. The sooner you make reading an integral part of your daily routine, the better off you will both be. Remember, both of you will benefit from the soothing sounds of a read-aloud.

Why would you want to put that off?

Is It Too Late?

It is never too late to bring a reluctant reader around. It is, however, often harder. If reading resources have never been available in your house, or if they have sat unused, it may feel awkward getting into the swing of things. If your child is frustrated with reading "boring" books, has a packed schedule, or avoids discussing the problem altogether, you may get easily discouraged. The trick here is this: slow and steady wins the reading race.

Consider approaching reading with an older child the same way you would approach a new weight-loss diet. It is really easy to make over the top claims about your expectations, looking for a quick fix, only to get burnt out before you make any progress. Insisting that your children read for 1 hour a day, turning the TV off forever, or making them hand in parent-prescribed weekly book-reports makes as much sense, and will last as long, as committing yourself to a daily 3-hour exercise routine complemented by a grapefruit-only diet. Both scenarios are going to fail. Miserably. This is a process and one that you can enjoy together, if you learn to pace yourself and lower your expectations.

> **Bookworms Beware**
>
> Do not use TV as a reward or punishment for reading, especially with reluctant readers. TV is TV. Reading is reading. If you have decided to limit television time in your home, do so because you do not want your children watching so much TV. Plain and simple.

When it comes to winning back a reluctant reader, it is important to remember the three Cs:

- **Consistency** It takes time to build a habit; especially when your efforts are met with opposition. Remember that readers aren't made overnight. You'll need to gently push and prod a bit in the beginning.

- **Customized** I will offer a slew of different tactics, but only you know your children as well as you do. Take what works and leave the rest, even if that means editing expert advice. Trust yourself.
- **Cooperation** This process is truly a two-way street. You want your kids to read novels. They want to read comic books. Try alternating days and materials, try extending bedtimes for their reading preferences, try finding comic books that are not offensive to you. Try to find a middle ground so you can both get what you want.

Is There a Right Way?

You will find the right way for your family. And don't be surprised when it turns out to be an approach you never would have thought would work. In a million years I never would have assumed my son's favorite time to read would be when he first wakes up in the morning. But there we are, me with my cup of coffee, him with his cup of milk, making our way through numerous titles. I noticed that by the end of the day, we were both spent, and a quick story or some page-flipping was all that either one of us was up for. But in the morning, well rested and rejuvenated, talking cows, roaring lions, and chugga chugga choo choos are just our style. Who knew? Watch what is happening under your own roof and go with the flow.

Success Story

Don't be surprised if your routine reader wants to take a break from the norm and turns down reading in lieu of puzzles or stacking rings. Everybody, including children, needs a change every now and again. Taking a morning, afternoon, or evening off is not cause for panic. Just try it again tomorrow.

Common Denominators

So what should you be looking for? There are common strategies that successful reading families share. And all of these different roads lead to one common place: pleasure. I know of no avid reader who hates reading. All the devoted readers I know, children and adults, associate reading with pleasure. Yes, there are times we must read dense college textbooks on subjects that bore us to tears, but these experiences really are few and far between. A good rule of thumb throughout your reading activities with your children is to check everyone's interest level. When engaged in reading activities, are you constantly checking the clock, or do you lose track of time? Are you all able to focus on the activity at hand, or are you mentally compiling your grocery list? Is the experience energizing or exasperating? While reading won't rival a trip to the circus, it should be fun. If it's not, check the **TIME** (Time, Interruptions, Motivation, Eating).

Time What time is it? Is everyone worn out after school and soccer practice? Are you rushing to get out the door? Keep track of what time of day your reading seems to go most smoothly. And drop the times it seems to crash and burn. If your middle-schooler drags his feet between dinner and bedtime, why push reading then? Look for different areas of opportunity. The morning paper is delivered first thing in the morning, after all.

Interruptions Do you have an ear out for the doorbell? Do you keep getting up to stir the tomato sauce? Is the TV on? You may be surprised at how distracting background noise can be. We are so used to constantly talking on cell phones, driving with the radio on, and multitasking our multi-tasking, that many of us have forgotten, or never learned, how to sit quietly and focus on one activity. Try limiting the interruptions.

Motivation Why are you reading this particular book, article, or brochure? Is anyone actually interested in this subject, or is it on your list of "things good parents should make their child read even if she is bored to tears"? Of course, there will be reading materials that are mandatory (ever try submitting an insurance claim?) but in our quest to rediscover the pleasure of reading, let's try to stick with things that are actually pleasurable.

Success Story

The next time you are in the car, turn the radio off. Keep it off for 3 days. Give yourself and your children the gift of calm while driving from one activity to the next. We owe it to our children, and ourselves, to learn to live without background noise so we may better concentrate on the tasks at hand, including reading.

Eating Honestly, trying to do anything with your kids when either one of you is hungry is an experiment in torture. My sugar level is in direct proportion to my patience level. When either one drops, watch out. Have a snack, and then read, or better yet, try reading and snacking together. If you are reading *If You Give a Mouse a Cookie* by Laura Numeroff, have a cookie. When has a cookie ever made things less enjoyable?

If you're right on TIME, keep it up. If things seem out of balance, try a new TIME. And keeping trying new things until you find a rhythm that runs like clockwork.

Bookworms Beware

When our children hold the book, we can often become frustrated because they are going too fast or too slow. Instead of correcting their pace, respect their turn and wait for yours. You go at your pace, modeling how to read each page in succession, and give them a chance to practice what they have seen. The more uninterrupted practice they have, the better their timing will become.

Living by the Pleasure Principle

There is absolutely no denying a simple truth: when we like what we do, we do more of it. Instead of looking for the one right way to do things, have fun exploring a series of interesting approaches. You'll probably find that there is a particular time of day when you can all read for a block of time. But even here, feel free to try something new and interesting. Maybe one day you and your first-grade son will read several different books together and another day you'll concentrate on only one. Perhaps you and your middle-school daughter would like to spend an afternoon wandering through a bookstore independently, and then meet up to compare what you've found. Reading materials are still a mainstay of your day, but the experience is fresh and engaging.

Routine doesn't have to mean mundane. Check in with yourself throughout this process. If you are not having any fun, this venture won't last much longer. Concern yourself with your pleasure, and theirs, and you'll all be happier for it.

Is There a Wrong Way?

Since we have just determined there is no "right" way to read with your children, it would make sense that there would also be no wrong way to read with your children. And there is not; what there is, really, is a wrong emphasis when reading. Since more than one person has approached me about their baby's "reading career," I have good reason to believe that we are taking reading way too seriously. Our over-emphasis on the standards movement in education and our misconception that our children must always be "challenged" has far removed us from associating reading with pleasure. Let's take a look at the direction our emphasis has gone in and see why this detour is so troublesome.

Quick Picks

If you feel like you are in the minority because you favor the outdoors over accelerated programming for your children, you may enjoy *Reclaiming Childhood: Letting Children Be Children,* by Dr. William Crain, who encourages parents to let their children play and learn in natural settings to achieve optimum development.

Misinformation

A friend of mine recently told me about her reading routine with her son. She was beaming as she spoke about picking out new books together, rereading favorites, and trying some of the activities they had learned about in a science book. It was immediately obvious that reading is a source of joy for both of them and a means by which they are developing their relationship while learning about the world around them. So imagine my surprise when she asked, "So am I doing it right?" Why the self doubt? Because we no longer trust that what we enjoy has enough validity. I really think, and will show with examples like these, how reading in real time, using real resources, can inspire your children to be readers for life. Reading together does not have to be painful. But one of the reasons it may be perceived as an agonizing activity is the aggressive language associated with it.

When I hear words like "must," "required," and "absolute" associated with reading, I tend to cringe. Why take such a hard line with such a pleasurable activity? There seems to be a return to the school of hard knocks with reading, meaning, if it's fun, you are doing something wrong. Let's move away from this ridiculous idea and start using words like "encourage," "support," and "promote." We don't need to get bogged down in serious jargon to convince ourselves that reading is important. We know it's important; that is why we want to encourage, support, and promote reading in our homes.

Misguided Attempts

I have to refer back to my diet analogy here: making unrealistic demands on ourselves, our schedules, and our families is a recipe for disaster. When I taught middle school, each student would write down his or her goals for the year in September. Without fail, each one said, "Study every night, get straight A's, and be an excellent student." Needless to say, I did not have a straight-A class. Life happens. Reading will need to be balanced with all of the other activities in your life. If you are a dual-income family, with both parents walking through the door after dinnertime, I hardly think a 2-hour evening reading marathon is realistic. Know your limits and you'll approach reading from a much more realistic perspective.

Do you have to read every day? It would be best if you could. But most frustrated families approach reading from this perspective, "If I don't have time to read for the recommended 30 minutes a day, why try reading at all? Let's just skip it today." Unfortunately, today turns into tomorrow, which turns into the week, the month, the routine of not reading. If your schedule makes you look at daily reading like an overwhelming task, try scaling back the materials and time, instead of eliminating it. Maybe Tuesdays are just the day from hell. Maybe it's the day when you drop off early, dad picks up late, and 9 out of 10 times, an orange-headed clown welcomes you through golden arches for dinner. Everyone has this day in the week. It's not just busy, it's almost unbearable. This is not the day to crack open a 32-page picture book that is heavy on words and light on

Quick Picks

For those days that you spend more time in the car than out of it, try lightening up the mood with a joke book. Keep a pocket-size, kid-friendly joke book in the car and have your children take turns reading from it. Yes, this counts as reading. And it might just help ease the tension of all that travel.

illustrations. This is the day for a poem, a page from a chapter book, or maybe it's the morning drive where you retell a favorite story with your child as the hero. Cut yourself a break. Habits are not made in a day. And they're not broken in a day, either.

Sorting Through the Stacks

There are thousands of books, magazines, and reading resources to choose from. If you have heard of a subject, I'll bet you there is a book, or 10, on it. While it is wonderful to have such a wide array of choices, it can deem a daunting task to find the best book for you and your child's needs. But you are not alone. If you have not already done so, get to know your town's librarians. They are a wealth of knowledge and help. Good librarians can make recommendations, suggest what you may like to read next, give you their reviews of books and almost always have an area of expertise they would love to share. As a former children's librarian, there was nothing I loved more than helping a child find just the right book. And how this is done is no secret, but there are several tips I think might help.

Success Story

As soon as your children meet the age requirement, they should have their own library cards. Make them responsible for taking care of their cards and the items they borrow. And it goes without saying, if you do not have a current card, now is the time to get one.

All Books Are Not Created Equal

As a book lover, I hate to admit this, but there are a ton of bad books out there. Books that are boring, pointless, or condescending are all turnoffs. And with my time, and your time, being so precious, how can you weed through such an enormous amount of material and make a good book choice? In each section, I'll pinpoint the book attributes that can set you on the right path. Each age and reading level will have different specifications, but these common approaches can be applied to all:

High-Interest = High-Impact Whether you are picking out a picture book on zoo animals or searching the periodicals for articles on inline skating, if you have an interest in the subject matter, you are much more likely to stick with it. Having a book that caters to children's individual likes is a great way to keep them engaged in reading and is instrumental in heightening their comprehension skills. Since it is true that the more you read the more you know, having a child become an expert in his desired "field" will give him the added confidence he needs to choose more reading material. Also you may find that his comprehension level rises. The more comfortable we are in a subject, the more familiar we become with its jargon and nuances.

Bookworms Beware

Once a library book is in your possession, it is your responsibility. If a page should become ripped, help your child repair it. If it is the victim of overzealous coloring or spilled juice, return the book with an offer to replace it. Do not slip it in the overnight slot and hope to get away with it. Books are valuable, whether owned or borrowed. Help your children learn this lesson from the start.

Aesthetically Inviting There is nothing worse than trying to read a book that is hard on the eyes. I have seen children's beginner books with sentences that wrap around the pictures, making it awkward to read aloud, and young adult novels with print so small and close it is headache-inducing. Before you even read a word of the content, flip through the pages and scan the book. If it looks like trouble, it is.

One Size Does Not Fit All What type of reader are you? Do you like short articles with numerous sidebars? Brief, fast-paced chapters? Or do you prefer to get caught up in a long chapter and linger over lengthy articles? What type of reader is your child? Shorter works can provide a much-needed sense of satisfaction for the struggling reader, while longer works can help take an advanced reader to the next level. The purpose of reading is not to read the biggest book, or to read the most books, but to find a means by which to read pleasurably. Choose a book whose size will keep your child's attention, give her a sense of satisfaction, and keep her coming back asking for more.

Discover Treasure

Once you have an idea of what you are looking for, tap into the many resources available to readers. Librarians are a great place to start your search, as they have dedicated their careers to the written language.

But don't underestimate the power of a knowledgeable bookstore staff person. While this may not be the dream job of their lives, chances are they have an innate interest in books. Plus, they will be familiar with what sells, meaning they can make recommendations that can have a real impact on your family.

While you may not love every popular choice, there is a reason that some books do well and others fail. Great-selling books usually have a story that moves along, compelling characters, and a satisfying ending. Who could argue with that? Plus, in major chains, staffers tend to "work" a section and have an intimate idea of what is happening in that genre. It is great to have someone in your corner who knows the latest and greatest works on your favorite subject.

Abandon Ship

If something is broke, fix it. I have seen children try to explain to their parents, "I don't want to read about that. I don't like that anymore," bullied into checking out the book anyway. And I know adults who hate what they are reading, who plug along anyway, compelled by some imaginary force to finish what they have started. This just doesn't make sense, although it does explain why so many people say they hate reading. There are bestsellers that bombed with me, and recommendations that I quickly rejected.

If your child is no longer interested in a subject, move on. If they hate biographies, choose science fiction. If you are reading a book that stinks, go get another one. There is no Reading Police that is going to revoke your library card because your son doesn't want to read mysteries or you return a book after chapter two. Let it go. There are too many great books to waste time on the stinkers.

Quick Picks

Before choosing a book, take a minute to read the first few pages and see if the story sounds compelling. If it doesn't catch your attention right away, skip it. We have to be in the mood for the books we read. If you don't make an immediate connection with a character, try it again at another time.

Loan or Own?

Really, the answer is loan and own. In an ideal situation, we will have a balance between the two. Libraries are a critical part of our community and provide the ultimate lesson in sharing. Owning books are a wonderful way to reinforce how valuable they are and can become a source of great sentimental value.

Try to make the library part of your reading routine. Help each child acquire her own library card, give each one her own library book bag, and talk about what a privilege it is to have access to so many books. Even if we could give our child everything, we wouldn't. It's important to learn to share, to take care of someone else's items with the same sense of dedication as you take care of your own. Help your children keep track of due dates on the calendar, return books in proper condition and get to know the library staff. Borrowing books gives you access to a wealth of materials; it is a privilege, and it should be treated as one.

Success Story

Sometimes your family will have to wait for a new book or popular title. While you may be tempted to run out and buy it, put your name on the list and wait. Libraries offer a nice lesson in delayed gratification and help build anticipation about the expected story.

All Access Books

Café Lattes aside, one of my favorite places is a bookstore. I love all kinds of bookstores from the mega-giants to the mom-and-pop shops. I love how fresh and clean the books appear, how the inventory is rotated with the season, how well lit the store is, and the great reader-friendly music playing in the background. But what I love most is that you are allowed to touch all the books. In fact, display shelves encourage you to touch the books, soft chairs invite you to read, and great coffee makes you want to stay.

I used to treat my books like some sort of revered artwork. Nice to look at, but please don't touch. I enjoyed having all of my titles lined up on the shelf, in size order, proudly standing at attention. And while they looked nice, they just weren't inviting. Then my husband happened to purchase a few books for the coffee table and I noticed our friends looking through them. I noticed I was looking through them. Not one person I know of has ever taken books down off the shelves, but many have picked up the books lying out. A connection had been made. Instead of setting my home up like a library, I would set it up like a bookstore.

Now our guest room has books stacked on the nightstands. Our coffee table plays host to a rotating selection of titles. And current magazines are found in just about every room in the house. Let's face it, we are not going to pick something up unless it looks inviting. Until we can actually get a book into our kids' hands, we don't stand a chance. So let's look at ways to get books off the shelves and into some hands.

Quality, Not Quantity

The first lesson I learned from the bookstore is about quality. No books on the shelves are damaged. There are no dog-eared pages, crayon markings, or coffee stains. Since I do not have a million-dollar book budget to replace books as needed, I became much more committed to preserving a book's looks. I invested in bookmarks and use them. I invested in beverage coasters and use them. I hang pictures using a hammer, not the spine of a good hardcover (I can't be the only one). You don't need a lot of books, but you should have some nice books. And nice doesn't have to mean expensive. I opt for softcover savings any day of the week. But we are a visual species. When things look better, they are much more appealing. I want my books to be more appealing, don't you?

If you are going to encourage children to handle your books, buy books that can withstand being handled. Our toddler son struggles with the concept of "gentle"; he does much better with the concept of "bang this object as hard as I can on the floor until whizzing it against the wall." So when it comes to books, we opt for board books. And we treat his books with care and respect. Children must be taught how to handle books. Teach your children to use bookmarks to save their spot, help them clear off their nightstand so books can be stacked neatly, and help them repair torn pages when accidents happen. While well-worn books with frayed edges are an unavoidable battle wound, jelly stains and coffee rings should be remedied.

Fostering a Sense of Ownership

Perhaps the most important lesson from bookstores is about ownership. Although I am currently waiting for a call from our library, I admit it, I love instant-book gratification. I love going to the store, finding a great new book, taking it home, and reading it at my leisure. I like that it is mine. Of course, I now own more books than I know what to do with, but I love them all. I use books I own for reference, as rereads, for inspiration, and for pleasure. People own what is important to them. You wouldn't consider renting your television; it is too central to your house. The same should be true of books. While books on loan are a great way to try out new authors, gather a slew of information on one particular subject, or explore new genres, invest in the books that mean something to you.

Quick Picks

Keep your children's books in good condition by wiping them down with a safe solution of vinegar and water. Freshen up covers and disinfect board books with this kid-friendly homemade cleaning agent, easily kept in a handy spray bottle.

Children like to own books, too. There is something comforting about being surrounded by favorite books. It's a great idea to teach children to take care of their books, to watch their collection move from picture books to chapter books. Since we decide what our son owns, buying him books lets him know that books are important. We keep track of all the books our son has read in a marble notebook, and it's really rewarding to see how much we've all read together. This little keepsake has also prompted us to go find that title we haven't seen in a long time. We own what we value. And we value what we own.

Success Story

Help your child learn to earn the book of her choice by playing Pennies for Pages. Empty your pennies and other loose change as you wish, into a see-through container. When you have acquired a bit of money, count up the loot and use it to buy a new book.

No matter how young or old your children are, you can make reading together an enriching, exciting part of your daily lives. When you focus on enjoying each other's company, keeping the focus on progress rather than perfection, and finding a system that works best for you, you can be sure you are on the road to reading success.

The Least You Need to Know

- Find the right formula for your family by trying different strategies and suggestions until you find what works best for you.
- When we like what we do, we do it more, so make reading enjoyable for both you and your child.
- The value in borrowing and owning books is complementary. Have both on hand to build a personal collection while rotating inventory.

Chapter 3

Reading Is More Than Just Books

In This Chapter

- Reading resources worth revisiting
- Home is where the heart of reading is
- Variety is the spice of reading

Magazines, cookbooks, comics, and correspondence have long been disregarded as "real reading," making many a parent believe that these kinds of resources don't count. Convinced that real reading only means books, parents could be missing out on a great chance to deepen their children's interests while engaging them in reading. For the record, here is an easy, tangible definition of reading that is accepted by the literacy community: different letters combine to make various words that when strung together make sentences that convey meaning. Here is what the definition of reading is not: critically acclaimed epic works of fiction that look good on a resumé but that did, in fact, put you to sleep after six sentences. Now that we have clarified what reading means, let's take a look at why all reading counts.

Reading is a necessary part of our day. So much so, that as adults we take for granted how much reading we actually do in a day. On any given day we read calendars, date books, recipes, directions, instructions, road signs, store signs, advertisements, cards, newspapers, articles, books, television guides, medicine boxes, shampoo bottles, and mail—just to name a few. What we want to do now is include our children in all of this reading and help them to learn how useful reading really is.

Special Delivery

We've talked about loaning or owning books, and the benefits to each. We can consider these two methods the layers of a cake. The icing, then, is reading material that is delivered right to our doorstep. As adults, we can share with our children the magic that is our mailbox. Whether you're waiting for the next issue of your favorite magazine or anxiously expecting a bestseller from Amazon, there is a great satisfaction in having reading materials delivered. You know how much you love getting the mail (sans bills); why not introduce your children to this curbside Christmas?

Success Story

Looking for a gift that keeps on giving? Purchase a magazine subscription in your favorite reader's name and give that child a personalized periodical to look forward to every month.

If magazine subscriptions are not in your budget, consider what you can accomplish for the price of a stamp. Help your child begin a letter-writing relationship with grandparents, neighbors, or friends from playgroup. Homemade cards, crayons, and a message written by you works for the youngest set, while glitter, magic markers, and stickers can keep older children interested in this activity.

Precious Periodicals

Covering a variety of topics from mainstream money and business markets to obscure lapidary journals (the art of cutting precious stone), magazines can help readers develop a hobby, perfect a niche, or learn more about an area interest. Magazine articles are written to convey a lot of useful information on a succinct and entertaining format. Since the editorials are short and fast paced, readers can move through the material as they see fit—either spending time reading an issue from cover to cover, or squeezing in an article here and there. If you have an interest, you can find a magazine that specializes in it.

Why do readers of all ages love magazines? For starters, they look good. Major magazine labels are chock full of great photos, fun fonts, and catchy title phrases. Even small-budget periodicals are nicely laid out with an eye toward detail. Second, they provide a great sense of accomplishment for readers at all levels. Almost anyone can finish an article in a reasonable amount of time. Instead of staring at that book that just seems to be getting bigger, magazines can be absorbed quickly and painlessly. Third, they are a great source of entertainment, making the critical connection between pleasure and reading.

When can you start a subscription for your kids? As soon as possible! For the smallest set, there is *Babybug*, full of short stories and simple rhymes, and constructed on heavy-duty paper resembling a board book. For the three- to seven-year-old range there is Your Big Backyard, a great magazine about animals and nature. Then, there are the heavy hitters like *Sports Illustrated for Kids*, *National Geographic for Kids*, and *Highlights*. Your best bet is to check out each magazine's website to review the content and see which content would best suit your child's interest.

Quick Picks

Check out some of the following kid-friendly sites with your children and together decide which magazine subscription you would like to welcome into your home: www.nationalgeographic.com/kids, www.cricketmag.com, www.highlights.com, www.sikids.com.

Magazine subscriptions cost a fraction of the newsstand price, are delivered to your doorstep and provide a variety of uses after they have been read. Namely, magazines are a great resource for projects. Who among us hasn't cut out a recipe, torn out a picture of a great haircut, or made a collage out of old issues? After reading your magazines, try one these activities with your children:

1. Cut favorite pictures out and make a collage with a unifying theme. Make sure to leave room to title your project, such as "Skateboarding tricks I will learn this summer."
2. Go on an advertising treasure hunt. Give your child a common advertising adjective like "great" and a slew of different magazines. See how many times they can find the word.
3. Ask your child to cut out their favorite article and mail it to a grandparent to share their interests. Ask the grandparent to do the same.
4. Find a new recipe in a magazine and try it together.
5. Help your child write a letter to the editor what she likes or doesn't like about the magazine.

The list of ideas could go on and on, but you get the point. When you own magazines, they are yours to do with as you see fit. While I know there are parents who will worry that magazines aren't literature, may I suggest viewing magazines as appetizers. What interests your son in an article can lead to researching a topic further in a book, the main course. Encourage your children to whet their appetites with these tasty treats and work up a hunger for something heartier.

After you are done, keep special issues, like holiday or birthday party ideas, in a three-ring binder for future reference. You can cut out relevant articles, three-hole punch the papers and keep them in a handy binder. Mark the binder "rainy-day ideas" and turn to it when foul weather threatens to turn your mood sour.

Sunday Comics

When I was a kid, we did not have a dozen channels dedicated to broadcasting cartoons 24/7. We had Saturday mornings. Cartoons were on from about 7 to 11 A.M., and then, without fail, Abbott and Costello or King Kong or an Elvis movie would come on, and it was time to go out and play. Imagine my delight when I discovered that I could have cartoons on Sundays, too! Reading the comics was one of the best things about Sunday mornings then, and is still one of the first things I reach for now.

Since we have already decided that all reading counts, let's not discount comics or comic books. There are a few things these mediums have that you'll be hard pressed to find elsewhere. First, they are funny, silly, and entertaining. Insert pleasure principle here. Second, they rely heavily on dialogue, giving your child a quick example of how sentence structure, body language, and tone affect a conversation. Third, they are witty. A sure sign of advanced intelligence is a well-developed sense of humor. Introduce your children to humor early on and encourage them to flex their own funny bone.

For those of you who have visions of male-dominated bloody comic books with grotesquely disproportionate women, I want to assure you that child-friendly formats are available. While many do incorporate mild violence, it is reminiscent of cartoon violence, not late-night movie violence. The magic and mysticism used helps the heroes fly, disappear, and rid the world of evil, not conjure up dangerous potions or poisons. If you are a stranger to this genre, try the following suggestions:

- **"Teen Titans"** Presented by DC Comics, these young superheroes are the sidekicks to such legends as Batman, Wonder Woman, and Aquaman. These characters can also be seen in their own cartoon series and are available on DVD.
- **"The Incredibles"** Based on the blockbuster movie, these comics retell the story of a family of superheroes who must hide their identities from the neighbors while trying to make the world a better place.
- **"Spider Girl"** Marvel Comics longest-running comic featuring a female as a lead character, it tells the tale of Peter Parker's daughter, Spider Girl.

Bookworms Beware

When searching for comic books online or at the library, make sure to target "children's comic books." General comic books and graphic novels are intended for older audiences and have material and situations most parents would object to.

Letters, Postcards, and Packages

Is there anything more exciting than reaching into the mailbox to find an invitation with your name on it, a postcard addressed to you, or a birthday card from your best friend? While e-mail has made communication a lot faster, it has not necessarily made it more meaningful. A hand-written note, personalized and custom tailored for you often makes its way into a scrapbook, keepsake box, or onto the refrigerator. I have never printed out an e-mail and put it in my scrapbook. But I do have several birthday cards that I hold onto because they are near and dear to my heart. Help your children be both the provider and recipient of such treasured materials and you'll help them make the connection between reading, writing, and joy.

> **Quick Picks**
>
> If you often return from work after your children are in bed, consider mailing them a letter to let them know you are thinking about them. This midday message might not be a goodnight kiss, but it's sure to warm little hearts.

Room with a View

Here are three reading strategies that I encourage parents to try with their children, if they want to raise read readers for life. In no particular order they are as follows:

1. Read to your children.
2. Read to your children.
3. Read to your children.

By following this three-step formula, you will expand your children's vocabulary, elevate their communication skills, add to their knowledge, and provide a pleasurable activity.

The easiest way to make this formula happen is by having plenty of reading materials on hand. We can nurture the budding artist, sing along with the music, discover the past, and begin a collection.

While the formula may be simple and straight-forward, the method works best with variety. I love pizza as much as the next person, but I don't want to eat it everyday. Nor do I want to read the same things everyday. By providing children access to a variety of materials, we can help them find their favorite materials, while still providing opportunities to find new resources.

Art and Artists

Every child is an artist. And every artist needs encouragement. Kids should have access to blank paper, colored paper, lined paper, crayons, markers, and pencils as much as possible. There is something magical about creating something from nothing. Unfortunately, we may not always understand our artist's vision; that's where reading and writing come in. Helping your children to articulate their thoughts and see them represented on paper is an excellent way to encourage them to share their ideas.

There are dozens of activities that combine reading and art, which can help children of all ages tap into their creative sides. Here are seven ideas to get you started.

1. Choose a new book and read only the title, without showing the book to your child. Ask her to draw a cover based only on the title.
2. When your youngest artist tells you about his picture, write down his words and attach them to the picture. When friends and family come over, read what it says, validating your artist's efforts and making for a great conversation piece.
3. Tell your children stories from your childhood and ask them to draw what you've shared.
4. Before reading a farm book, draw pictures of all the farm animals you are likely to see. As you read, pull out your homemade pictures and match them to the text.
5. Design a dream mobile based on your favorite bedtime story. Draw and color the best parts of the story, attach to string, and hang near your child's bed to inspire adventuresome dreams. Talk about why she chose those particular pictures.

Quick Picks

If your artist's creations are starting to take over the house, consider buying a box of 9x12 envelopes and turning the work into homemade cards. Write a message, help your child sign his name, and mail the treasure off to friends and family.

6. Have older children draw a picture for each chapter they read and paperclip it onto the chapter page, making a nice reminder of the book.
7. Check out a book of famous paintings from the library and use it for inspiration. Copy a picture that is particularly moving or get ideas to come up with your own creation.

Music Appreciation

I cannot carry a tune in a wheel barrel. While my son enjoys my singing, I know it is only a matter of time before he realizes that this is not my strong suit. And that's okay. Whether your voice rivals Pavarotti or the Chipmunks, music appreciation is about just that: appreciating. For those of us who struggle with music, we can turn to reading to help us bridge the gap between melody and mayhem.

Liner notes come in almost all contemporary CDs. Read the words out loud, and then play the music. Don't the words sound better when accompanied by music? Songs are meant to be sung, not merely read. Hearing words performed adds a whole new dimension to reading, and this can be the perfect place to introduce poetry. Keeping time with rhythm and rhyme works with music and poetry.

Success Story

If you or your kids think poetry is stuffy and boring, *The Simpsons'* "Treehouse of Horror" Halloween special may change your mind. Guest star James Earl Jones narrates Edgar Allen Poe's "The Raven" while Homer and Bart act out the poem. You'll never look at poetry the same way again. Available at www.amazon.com in *The Best of The Simpsons, Boxed Set 2* (1989).

Many adults can become uncomfortable with poetry, again seeing it as a school tool used to complicate simple subjects. But poetry, especially children's poetry, does not require a doctorate in metaphors and similes. It can be fun, silly, and, thank goodness for small miracles, short.

Where the Sidewalk Ends, *A Light in the Attic*, and *Falling Up*, all by author and illustrator Shel Silverstein are light, lovely, and laugh-out-loud funny.

If you are looking for a nice anthology of poetry that offers classic and contemporary selections, try *Sing a Song of Popcorn: Every Child's Book of Poems*. Various authors and award-winning illustrators make this a beautiful children's collection.

Reading poetry can be poignant, powerful, and pleasant. And that is music to everybody's ears.

History's Mysteries

When thinking of reading history books, most of us probably conjure up images of dense, dilapidated European History textbooks with numerous pictures of soldiers killing one another. Not a real page-turner. It wasn't until well after college (no need to take anymore of those history courses in college, thank you very much) that I learned history could be exciting, rewarding, and relevant. But I would hate for kids today to have to wait until they were adults to learn about this great land of ours.

So why not try *Discover America State by State: Alphabet Series* published by Sleeping Bear Press. Get to know the ins and outs of your own great state with these beautifully illustrated books chock full of interesting facts. Kids will discover that history lives right around the corner. *We Were There, Too! Young People in U.S. History* by Philip M. Hoose is a great read for children ages 10 and up. Do your kids ever wonder what all the children were doing as Columbus sailed to America and wars broke out on the home front? This book explains in compelling detail the exciting contributions of children to American history.

History becomes much more engaging when we find that we live today because of what happened yesterday. These history books can be read aloud and shared together, helping everyone to better understand the world we live in today.

Success Story

An easy way to introduce the concept of the past to children is with photo albums. Look back at pictures together and reminisce about your favorite memories.

Antiques and Collectibles

Every kid should have his own collection. Whether it ends up being worth a fortune someday is beside the point. In the meantime, becoming an expert in an area of interest encourages concentration, commitment, and conversation. Helping your children build a collection is one of the most valuable skills you can give them.

First, it teaches respect for their own precious things, making it more likely that they will respect others' things. Next, it can give everyone in the family a source of education and pleasure, as you are apt to learn more about whatever subjects your children become interested in. A great way to model "you are never too old to learn a new trick" is to keep learning new tricks. Third, collections require research, which is a difficult concept to introduce and an even harder one to master. In our information age, how do you decide whose word you can trust? How do you find reliable resources? What makes someone an expert? Instead of arbitrarily trying to introduce the importance of solid research skills, you can give your children a tangible means to practice these skills.

Bookworms Beware

The Internet has made information more accessible than ever before; but that does not mean you can trust everything you read. When you do research online, point out the sites you use, and explain to your child why these choices can be trusted. Pull up a site you would not count on and explain the differences.

Heart of the House

We recently finished building a new home. It is a large, center-hall colonial with plenty of living space. We have a comfortable family room and a lovely playroom space. And I still can't get people out of my kitchen. There is no denying that the kitchen is the heart of the house. Say what you will about plush couches and big screen TVs, but around here, we are huddled around the center island, catching up on our day, making plans for the weekend, and stirring the sauce on the stove. The kitchen is where the action is. What better place to participate in the activity of reading?

Inch for inch, I'd venture to guess that more reading is done in the kitchen than anywhere else. All the pre-packaged programs in the world can't compete with the resources you have available in your kitchen; you just need to know where to look.

Everything, Even the Kitchen Sink

You have more reading material in your kitchen than you will ever have time to take advantage of. You just don't know it. Take a moment to visualize your kitchen. Section by section, you'll find everything you would ever need to encourage reading. The trick is acknowledging that these materials are useful, and then working them into your reading day. In fact, just stand at your kitchen sink and see how many reading resources you have within reach:

- At the sink: dish soap, hand soap, vegetable wash, and a colorful supply of cleaning supplies tucked underneath.
- Refrigerator: On your fridge you will find one or more of the following reading resources: print, script, black and white newspaper print, magazine articles, recipe cards, photos, magnetic letters, calendars, invitations, postcards on holiday greetings.
- Pantry Closet: a colorful array of all different sizes and shapes with different kinds of writing from directions, to nutritional values, to varying parts of speech.
- Counter tops: opened and unopened mail, daily planners, coupons, recipe books, school books, library books, ingredients for tonight's dinner, and appliances with trademark names.
- Window sill: cards, homemade gifts, knick knacks.

Bookworms Beware

If the cabinets underneath your sink are home to various cleaners and detergents, move them to higher ground. Fill that space with a basket of books. Instead of having to worry that your son or daughter has gotten into a dangerous situation, you can turn this high-traffic area into a reading haven.

Let's take a look at how you can take advantage of your kitchen reading collection.

Magnets and Magic

On our refrigerator is a running grocery list. Next to that is a business card dated for my son's next check-up. Below that is a magnet that reads, "With enough coffee, you can do anything." Scattered across the middle are party invitations, photos, art projects, and reminder notes. At the bottom of the fridge are brightly colored alphabet magnets, arranged in absolutely no particular order. Does our refrigerator sound a lot like yours? Probably. We already have a fabulous focal point in the most popular room in the house. Let's take advantage of this treasure and build on the opportunity.

In addition to your running grocery list, keep a "Library List" with titles to check out on your next visit. You can use the titles recommended here, write down subjects you liked to read more about, like "apple picking," or jot down titles you hear promoted by morning talk shows or Oprah. If your children come home raving about a story they heard in school, add it to the list. Why should the teachers have all the fun? Read it again at home and talk with your child about why they liked this title so much. Look for other books by this author and read those, too. Keeping a list on the fridge makes it easy to grab on your way out the door.

Quick Picks

Magnetic letters are a great tool to introduce letters to your young children and leave little messages for your older children. Since they are inexpensive, buy multiple sets so you can make even more words.

Relative Recipes

Cooking is one area that lends itself to reading; yet we are so used to reading recipes silently that we take for advantage the rich vocabulary associated with reading. I have hardly ever used the words "whisk," "pre-heat," "yield," "strain," "combine," "slow-roasted," or "substitute" anywhere other than my kitchen. What a shame to neglect this delicious language!

When you are cooking, get into the habit of reading your recipes out loud. Directions words like "step one," "first," "next," and "finally" are easy ways to introduce sequential order. Collecting all your ingredients and grouping them according to liquid and dry introduces classification. Plus, everyone can help in the kitchen. Yes, it will get messy. Yes, it will take longer. But if you were looking for a neat, time-saving method of going about your day, you probably wouldn't have become a parent in the first place. Help the youngest hand stir the ingredients and encourage older children to read the recipe cards while you follow the directions you are given. Putting children "in charge" of the recipe card builds reader confidence.

Quick Picks

Do your children usually have dinner with a babysitter or alone? Have some reading fun with them from a distance by writing a joke on their dinner napkin. Even if you can't share a meal, you can share a reading smile.

Cooking brings families together. And not just around the dinner table, but around the world. When we share a favorite recipe, we are really sharing a piece of ourselves. If grandparents live far away, ask that they send a weekly or monthly family recipe. Prepare this gem while talking about grandma and grandpa. If this idea takes off, start a special recipe box with grandma's picture on it and look forward to adding to the collection.

Daily Planners

Whether you choose to sport a PalmPilot or a spiral-bound calendar, daily planners are a necessary part of organization. We have a family calendar for appointments, late-night meetings, and family outings, as well as my pocket planner for playdates, due dates, and upcoming events. Sharing these tools with your children is an excellent way to introduce the days of the week for the youngest set, and to model time-management skills for your older children.

When your children ask, "What are we doing today/tomorrow/next weekend/next Christmas?" take out your handy calendar and show them. How many more days until the weekend? Count 'em up. When is that birthday party? On Saturday. Today is Thursday. Tomorrow is Friday and then comes Saturday. See here?

Daily planners also provide a great means by which to read numbers, again emphasizing sequential order. When your children become old enough, help them fill out their own daily planner, highlighting important holidays, school events, or special occasions. Many schools actually distribute daily planners, more commonly called student agendas, to help children keep track of their assignments. Share your schedules with each other. This is a great way to keep track of your kid's busy life and check in on what she thinks so most important it had to be written down.

Bedrooms

While the rest of the house is common ground, our bedrooms are our own. Our sanctuary, our solace, ours to call our own. After a day spent sharing space, we can retreat to our bedrooms where we are surrounded by a few of our favorite things. Today's bedrooms have become mini-media centers, complete with stereos, televisions, and computers. In our desire to give our kids the best of everything, we may be overlooking what is really best for them: uninterrupted downtime.

Reading materials in the bedroom should rival all other entertainment. Bedrooms are where we keep our favorite things, things we don't necessarily want to share, things that are personal and precious. Add reading materials to this list.

Prized Possessions

Did you have a diary as a kid? Or secret journals that you kept under lock and key? Journaling is an excellent tool to keep track of the important events in our lives, highlight our favorite (and not so favorite) outings, and learn more about ourselves. As soon as you can, introduce this introspective device to your children who will love writing and reading about their favorite subject: themselves.

Beginner writers and readers may need some direction to get going, and will probably do best with a blank, spiral-bound journal that encourages creativity. At a time that works well for you both, be it before dinner or before bed, talk to your kids about their day and offer suggestions for what they may like to draw about. Depending on their age and ability, they may ask you to write for them, to help them spell, or prefer only to draw. There is no right or wrong approach, just another means to lovingly encourage language development.

Older children will appreciate being given privacy and are most likely to write in their journals before bed. While you should not expect to be privy to every (or any) entry, offer to listen if they would like to read to you. Always encourage your children to look back at what they wrote. A problem that seemed larger than life 2 weeks ago may have been resolved without crisis, or a great birthday party may help to bring back pleasant memories. And who doesn't like to read about themselves?

Bookworms Beware

If you give your child a journal in hopes that he will use it as a trusted diary, resist the temptation to read it while he is away. If you want to know what is going on in there, offer to share your own journal writing first in hopes of paving the way for this special communication.

Guilty Pleasures

My nightstand reveals the type of reader I really am. Away from prying eyes, protected from inquiring passers-by, I am able to indulge in the kind of reading I feel like. Not the kind of reading that is required. I have never curled up in bed with my Biology textbook from college, the financial section of the newspaper, or the coupon circular. When the day is done, you can find me catching up on the latest issue of *Vanity Fair*, scanning the pages of *People* for the current Hollywood gossip, or diving back into a bestseller that I have been thinking about all day. Since bedrooms are a place of rest and relaxation, I make sure my reading reflects that. We can help our kids learn to do the same.

Reading at night is a wonderful way to settle down for a good night's sleep. But this can also be prime time for making the pleasure connection between child and reader. Instead of just looking at bedtime as a necessary, quick reading routine, try tapping into your Pillow Power!

Here are five Pillow Power points:

1. "Five More Minutes Please!" Children will do anything to stay up later. Stick to your regular bedtime routine, but let them know they can stay up 5, 10, or 15 minutes later to enjoy reading.
2. "Leave the Light On!" Bed lamps are wonderful assets to encourage nighttime reading, but why not also try a flashlight? Reading a favorite story, especially a not-so-scary story by flashlight, adds to the experience.
3. "Read to Me!" While your child my have a favorite book that suits her reading level, you can read to her at a higher level. This increases her vocabulary and comprehension levels while giving her some anticipated insight into what to look forward to next.

4. "Show Stopper!" Read an adventuresome story with your child but substitute his name for the character's name. Who doesn't want to be the star of the show?
5. "Children's Choice!" Do you hate comic books? Do you think Teen People is a waste of time? Do your children love them? Let your kids indulge in reading materials that suit their tastes. Consider this material the reading dessert of their diet. It may not be nutritionally sound, but it's always satisfying.

The Special Shelf

In every child's room, at every age and reading level, children can benefit from a special shelf. This shelf will have a very specific focus and hold only valuables, like a framed family photo, a first-place ribbon, and a few chosen titles. These will be books that do not have to be shared with siblings, are usually owned, and change with your child to fit her needs. The shelf can be painted plywood or engraved mahogany, depending on your personal décor. The important thing is what goes on it.

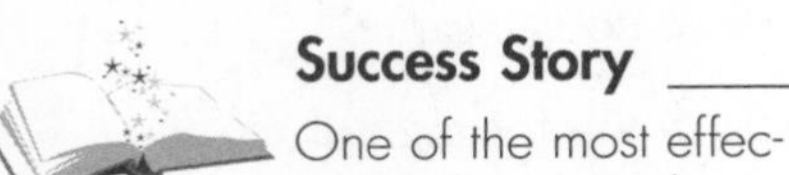

Success Story

One of the most effective parenting techniques we have is modeling. Design your own Special Shelf in your bedroom and display some of your favorite valuables and treasured book titles in plain sight. Everyone deserves his or her own individual place, even moms and dads.

Think of this shelf as you would a shelf in your formal living room—a place where you might display a wedding photo, a Lenox vase, or an antique collectible. You don't want just anybody touching it, because it is special. It deserves to be treated with respect and reverence.

I'll offer suggestions for how you can best target your child's special shelf and help her make it a purposeful and entertaining asset to every bedroom.

At first, you will choose the items for your children; but as they mature and begin to appreciate the value of the shelf, they will be able to maintain it with your help, and then, independently. You will initiate its use, and they will take it over. In each section, I'll offer ways in which the Special Shelf can grow with your child.

Twenty Great Titles to Try Together

In each part, I'll supply you with a list of books geared toward that chapter's reading level. These selections cover a wide spectrum of tastes and preferences, so there will be something for everyone. In addition, I'll suggest helpful Internet sites, recommend additional reading materials, and offer ideas on how best to introduce these resources to your family. My best advice is this: take what works and leave the rest.

Quick Picks

As you read this handbook, always keep a pad and pen handy to write down the books that pique your interest. Keep a running list of titles in your car, so that when you find yourself at the library or stumble upon a used-book sale, you have a recommendation at your fingertips.

A Look Back: Five Timeless Tales

From Dr. Seuss to Judy Blume, these are the books we grew up with—and the books I want my children to grow up with. I've chosen the term "timeless" over "classic" for several reasons. The most important is this: classic implies required, bored classroom reading, while timeless implies, well, not classic. Because whether or not you consider *One Fish Two Fish Red Fish Blue Fish* a literary masterpiece on par with *The Grapes of Wrath* isn't really the point. These books are still selling for a reason. We'll discuss the reasons and enjoy the chance to introduce a whole new generation of readers to the magic that was once ours to discover.

Hot Off the Press: Five New and Improved Stories

As much as I love some of my childhood books, you cannot believe the amazing advances made by children's literature. Picture books with brilliant illustrations, captivating stories, and multicultural themes grace the pages, while young adult lit is smart, sassy, and, yes, sometimes even sexy. The recommendations you'll find here have all been written within the last dozen years or so and represent the freshest voices and most exciting developments this side of Go-Gurt.

Playground Picks: Five Mom Approved Titles

I am a true believer in kitchen table wisdom. While mini-van-driving soccer moms often get a bad rap, I'm apt to choose a reading recommendation from a woman who can simultaneously fold laundry, make dinner, and check homework. After all, if a children's book has made an impression on this busy parent, you can bet it will make an impression on the rest of us.

Award Winners: Five Critically Acclaimed Books

There are dozens of awards given for children's and young adult's books, and loads of notable lists that spotlight great works. The recommendations here can be considered a professional referral, as these works have been voted on by a slew of reading enthusiasts, including actual children (what a concept!). While I haven't loved every award-winning book ever written (and in fact I have actually cringed over a couple of choices), think of these books as Oscar winners. Other people find them worthy of attention. You can decide for yourself whether or not they deserve the red-carpet treatment.

As you begin to build your reader-friendly home, be sure to take advantage of the rich resources available to you. Once you realize how much you are already reading, it becomes easier to build upon your family's foundation. You are not starting from scratch, but simply renovating your reading routine.

The Least You Need to Know

- You already have everything you need to encourage reading, so start with an idea that interests you as excitement is contagious.
- Reading is relevant in every subject because you never know when you are going to discover the topic that launches a reader for life.
- Bedrooms and bedtimes provide special opportunities to bond over books. Make it a special place for both of you to enjoy.

Part 2

Crib Notes—Introducing Books to Your Baby and Toddler

Until recently, babies were most generously regarded as cute vegetables. While they demanded some attention to grow, their needs were predominantly physical and not much attention was paid to their mental or emotional development. The emphasis on child care was on meeting the basic needs of food, water, and shelter. Today, however, the pendulum has swung in the opposite direction and we are strongly encouraged, i.e. pressured, to "challenge" our newborns and toddlers so they might "excel" at an "accelerated" rate. This approach considers the development of the whole child (good) but it is making parents a bit "crazy" (bad).

In this part, we will look for ways to begin building a literacy rich home; a place where reading is a natural part of our day, new experiences are welcomed, and familiar favorites are celebrated.

Chapter 4

The Benefits of Reading Aloud to Newborns

In This Chapter

- Little brains, big gains
- Nursery necessities
- Setting the stage for read-alouds

We can talk and talk and talk and talk about the importance of read-alouds, the necessity of read-alouds, the do's and don'ts of read-alouds, but until we actually do it, it is just talk. Read-alouds must be experienced, like a great meal. You can tell someone all about thanksgiving dinner, with the centerpiece bird cooked for hours, all the fancy trimmings, enough dessert to send you into sugar shock, the need to pass out on the couch afterward; but until you enjoy the meal with family and friends, it's just another recipe you haven't tried. The same holds true for read-alouds.

Getting started with any new routine often feels awkward. We may want to make reading an important part of our day, but not know how to go about doing so, especially when it seems that our main participant is incapable of telling us whether or not what we are doing is working. In this chapter, I hope to convey that your baby can communicate with you, reading aloud will have a positive effect on her growth (and yours), and that instead of worrying about whether or not you are doing this "right" you can start to find a routine that is right for your family.

The recipe for a successful read-aloud with your newborn is simple enough: mix parents, baby, and simple books with energy and enthusiasm; let reading relationships thrive. The best time to try this winning recipe? Right now!

All Babies Are Created Equal

If you were to walk past a hospital nursery, you'd find striking resemblances among all the newborns. And I'm not just talking about the cute hats. You would see babies sleeping, crying, or waving their legs and arms spastically. What you won't see is a newborn sit up and ask for something to drink or pass a note to the cute baby in the next bassinet, or complete a list of things to do.

That's because, despite our personal bias, all babies are born with the same communication skills. None can speak, read, or write; these are all learned skills. But babies are all hard-wired with the capacity for learning much faster than we usually give them credit for. Despite their helplessness, newborns can communicate much more effectively than we may think.

We don't wait until our newborns hit a certain growth milestone before we begin speaking to them. As soon as they appear, and oftentimes before, we tell them how much they are loved, who we are, and what we'll be doing throughout the day. Since we start talking right away, it follows suit that we can start reading right away.

Books and the Bump

Expectant parents have asked if there is any benefit to reading to babies while they are in utero. There have been some interesting studies done that seem to reveal a connection between hearing repeated stories while in the womb and being able to recognize those same stories as newborns. So it is plausible to believe that in utero babies can hear you. While it sounds a lot like speaking under water, a baby in utero is learning the sound of her mother's voice. Talking, singing, and reading to your baby can make that connection even stronger. But much of this research is still in the infant stages, literally. My recommendation: any reason for a pregnant woman to put her feet up, relax, and read, I'm all in favor of. Whether or not you're giving your child a head start on education is inconclusive, but you'll definitely be giving yourself a much-needed break.

Quick Picks

If fetal development is an area you are interested in researching further, you may enjoy "In the Womb" presented by National Geographic. This program uses cutting edge 3-D and 4-D ultrasounds to explore an embryo's amazing nine-month journey. It is available for purchase at www.nationalgeographic.com.

Fathers can benefit from reading to the unborn child, too. Pregnancy takes over a woman's life, but fathers can feel a bit like outsiders, hanging around waiting for the big event. Dad can read to the baby and enjoy some active participation in the pregnancy. And remember, we're not limited to picture books and nursery rhymes. It's never too early to share with your child your affection for baseball stats or your love of history. Choose what you like to read and share it with your little love.

A Little Lesson on Language Development

Once they make their grand appearance, babies begin to communicate with others. They turn toward loud sounds, look toward the voice that is speaking to them, and "talk back" with coos and babbles when being spoken to. From about 6 months on, babies will begin to learn to recognize the biggest word in their day, "no," and try to talk with longer babbling sentences that range in pitch. After about a year, your child will start to point, consistently making the same sounds for objects (although it may have limited resemblance to the actual pronunciation), and try gestures as accompaniment to words.

From 18 months on, children will say about 8 to 10 words consistently, exhibit that they understand common words like "time to eat" by walking toward their highchair, begin pointing at their belly or nose when prompted, and imitate favorite animal sounds, like "moo." From 2 years on, the communication floodgate opens, with children stringing together simple sentences, including questions like "more juice?" that sound like a question, learning adjectives like "big" and plurals like "balls."

The more language a child hears, the more language a child will learn. We can compare language exposure to a buffet table. If you only feed your son or daughter white toast and milk, they will have nourishment, but it will be rather bland. If you feed your child a vast variety of foods, foods with different smells, tastes, and textures, you will provide more enriching nourishment. We want to select our language from the buffet table whenever possible, and reading can help make this happen.

The Value of Vocabulary

As of 2005, the *Oxford English Dictionary* has over 300,000 main entries, and yet I still can't figure out what to write in our Christmas cards. The English language, obviously, has a lot of words. How many of those words 300,000 entries are we actually using? It's impossible to nail down an exact number, but experts estimate that we rely most heavily on the 5,000 words that comprise the Basic Lexicon of the English Language—the high-frequency words used in everyday language. So how do we move past "more milk" and tap into the rich resource of words available to us? By reading books.

Children's books are rich with rare words, words we do not rely on in our everyday lives. In our New Jersey neighborhood, I have never seen an armadillo, hippopotamus, rat, or moose. Yet I have introduced all of these colorful creatures to my son, courtesy of Sandra Boynton's *But Not the Hippopotamus.* Friends of ours have a son who devours books on dinosaurs and now recognizes words like Stegosaurus, fossil, and extinction. Would these words have come up while preparing mashed bananas? Probably not. But books can be a wonderful resources to tap into rare words and make them part of our daily language. Is the basic lexicon necessary? Absolutely. Are we limited by it? Absolutely not. We can add all sorts of words to our repertoire.

Bookworms Beware

While it may be tempting to speak to your newborn in baby talk, using words like "ba ba" for bottle, it is much more advantageous to always model appropriate pronunciation.

A good way to get into the habit of expanding your own basic lexicon is by looking for the most appropriate word for the occasion. Try this: when your child falls down, resist using "boo boo." Use bruise, bump, scrape, or cut. When you're outside collecting nature's spoils, talk about the difference between a twig and a stick, a rock and a pebble. You already have the words; why not use them?

Sounds Familiar

As much as we want to vary our reading materials and use different words when we speak, it is repetition that helps to drive the point home. I have never had this conversation with my son, "Michael, 'more' is an adjective used when you would like additional snacks, games or attention. When you say 'more', and follow it up with a noun, like "juice" you are letting others know that you are not finished and would appreciate further beverage attentions." Has anyone ever had this conversation with their toddler? Yet one of the first words a toddler masters is "more." Why? Because the child has heard this word over and over again and knows that he can (usually) get more of what he wants by asking for it.

We use the words we need most often. With our children this will most likely be these: more, no, love, mommy, daddy, _____(the child's name), hot, good job, milk, all done, bath, book, bedtime, and clean up, to name a few. When I talk to other moms I usually hear the same thing, "I feel like I'm having the same conversation day in and day out." That's because you are. Repetition is necessary for teaching your children about the world they live in, safe boundaries, etc. With the 14 words I listed you are teaching your children who their primary caretakers are, safe boundaries, when they have followed directions, when they are in danger, how to get more, and how to finish. Not bad for 14 words. What we want to do is build on the words and expressions we use most frequently to expand our children's worlds.

If you are thinking this information is starting to sound contradictory, hang in there. As we go through this chapter you'll begin to see how repetition and variety are complementary and both are needed for language development.

Motherese

First, motherese is not baby talk. Baby talk is that nails-on-a-blackboard, shrill way of speaking to babies that makes most people want to run screaming from the room. Motherese, on the other hand, is the sing-song voice of mothers that relies heavily on exaggerating sounds. Usually spoken in a higher pitch than your regular voice, speaking motherese seems to be an almost automatic reaction to holding a baby. It is not the voice you use in the boardroom. It is the voice you use in the baby's room.

Reading in this voice changes the sentence from "Look at the ball" to "Loook at the Ballll." After every sentence you'll be apt to hum. Why is this important? Well, since we do this instinctively, it's bound to be important. So studies aside, instinct is pretty valuable in and of itself. But if you're looking for some more solid thoughts, consider the sound and pace of motherese. When you are learning any new skill, isn't it better received in a pleasing tone? The sing-song voice sounds pleasant and draws babies in. Its pace is slower, giving little ears extra time to absorb these new exaggerated sounds.

Success Story

Despite the name, motherese is not the exclusive right of mothers. Fathers, grandparents, siblings, and day care workers can all tap into this sing song voice that provides comfort and console.

Voice Recognition

Your baby was introduced to mom's voice in the womb and it will be the first voice recognized once born. Soon after, other caregivers like dad, siblings, and grandparents will make a memorable impact on these tiny ears. From all of these different people babies will come to learn the inflection of their native language, the syntax, and the nuances; but at first, familiar voices reign supreme as a comfort. I mean, imagine being wrapped in a warm, safe environment your whole life and then suddenly being thrust into a world of ever-changing elements. What happened to the consistency? Parents can offer some reassurance by talking to their children. But narrating your whole day and asking, "How's baby?" 500 times may not be realistic.

Turning to a reading resource can give you a medium by which to find the right words. Motherese is especially tailor-made for babies. If anyone else spoke in this exaggerated manner we'd be quick to end the conversation, but this calming voice is immediately recognizable and puts a newborn at ease. When we are at ease, we are more open to learning. Again, this is why parents are a child's most important teacher. Parents are the first ones on the scene and set the tone for associating language with pleasure.

Success Story

I know there are adults reading this book who are worried because they love reading and their children don't. I hope I can shed some light on why that may be, in the reluctant-reader sections. But chances are, if you start reading aloud to your baby, she will want to imitate you.

Are You Sure This Really Works?

When my husband and I decided to try to start a family, I had absolutely no idea what I was getting myself into. I was absolutely shocked that the licensed professionals at our hospital were letting me take home our son. I mean, he was so little and needy and I was so clueless. What was I going to do? I did what most new parents do:

1. Panic.
2. Yell at my husband because he is not panicked.
3. Ask for help.

With the help of parents who had previously walked in my shoes, the wonderful women in my Holistic Mom's Network, and half a dozen parenting books, we survived. As I sifted through advice and suggestions, I found that what worked for me was a combination of expert theories and good, old-fashioned kitchen table wisdom. Luckily, when it comes to reading aloud with our children, both camps are in agreement. Here are both sides of the story.

Experts Agree

It's probably safe to assume that you would not be reading this book if you didn't already think that reading with your children was important. But even when we are confident that we are on the right path, it can be comforting to have the backing of those in the know. And what the experts seem to know is that reading aloud is beneficial for promoting literacy, and life skills.

- According to the U.S. Department of Education, "reading aloud helps children acquire the information and skills they need in life, such as knowledge of printed letters and words, the relationship between sound and print, the difference between written language and everyday conversation."
- According to the National Network for Child Care, reading aloud, "stimulates imagination; sharpens observation skills; enhances listening skills; promotes self-confidence and self-esteem; contributes to the child's problem-solving skills; satisfies and heightens curiosity; encourages positive social interaction."
- According to the nonprofit literary organization, Reading Is Fundamental, Inc., "A child whose day includes listening to rhythmic sounds and lively stories is more likely to grow up loving books. And a child who loves books will want to learn to read them."

Kitchen Table Wisdom

Until you are a new parent, you can only guess at the meaning of sleep deprivation. Exhausted at waking up throughout the night, I read (bleary-eyed) several expert opinions on how to help my son sleep through the night. Nothing worked. But when I started talking to experienced mothers about what to do, I was given a solution that worked: "Send your husband in with water instead of milk, and your son will realize the gravy train has derailed." After two nights of this, our son started sleeping through the night. There is a lot to be said for ideas based on "Been there, done that."

The common consensus about reading aloud with newborns and young children is that these same children learn to love reading. These kids tend to watch less TV, be more involved with creative projects, and do well in school. They are less restless and more focused than their nonreading friends. Can I offer you a statistical graph to back this up? Nope. All I know is, these parents read to their kids and the results were positive. I'm willing to try a common-sense approach that is working well for others.

Quick Picks

If you are a stickler for stats, you may enjoy Jim Trelease's *The Read-Aloud Handbook,* which is chock full of statistical research and professional resources and yet still remains parent-friendly.

Attitude vs. Aptitude

You will not see any immediate signs that reading aloud is preparing your child for early acceptance to Harvard, but it will be obvious that they are enjoying it. And we are more likely to continue doing the things that we enjoy. It will take some time before your child walks over to the book basket, selects a worn-out favorite, and hands it to you while getting comfortable in your lap. Until then, there are other signs to be on the lookout for.

Babies wear their hearts on their sleeve and have no qualms about letting you know what they like and don't like. When reading aloud to babies, you can tell they are enjoying themselves by the way they kick out their legs, wave their arms, gurgle, and look toward you. It is not necessary that a newborn look at the book. She is much more likely to follow the direction of the voice.

Since you have a captured audience, stay with the reading activity as long as your little listener seems interested. Reread the same book or just flip through the pictures and point out the names of the colors you see. Find those same colors in the room you are sitting in. Talk to your baby about your favorite colors. Reading aloud can be a great springboard for conversation, even at this young age. When your daughter has had enough, she will look away from you, wiggle in your lap, or begin fussing. Until then, enjoy this one-on-one time.

Routines, Rituals, and Relaxation

One of the nicest things about reading aloud is that it helps to give structure to a baby's day. Books can be used to settle someone down for bed, used as a transition between activities, or as a means of easing into the day. Finding the routine that works for your family is a personal journey. Maybe your baby has his days and nights confused and you need to get him on track. Reading can help. Maybe your baby has a time of day when nothing can soothe him except your undivided attention. Reading can help. Find the routine that works best for your family. In this section, I'll outline some popular methods, but don't be afraid to go your own way.

Once you decide on your routine, you'll begin to develop your rituals. How is a routine different from a ritual? A routine focuses more on the time of day and the length of the activity whereas the ritual is the spiritual side of reading. Rituals for a baby are sacred. Which light do you read by? What blankets and pillows do you snuggle up with? What is the order of the books you read? Rituals are what personalize the routine.

The result of a well-appointed routine rich with familiar rituals is relaxation. Both baby and parent can relax when reading. There has been many an afternoon, with laundry piling up, breakfast dishes still crowding the sink, and beds unmade, that I sat down to read to my son frazzled and frustrated. Having just been so keyed up with housework, I struggled to get comfortable and get into our reading groove. But as soon as our farm-animal friends made their appearance, my jaw unclenched, my shoulders softened, and I started to breathe a little easier. You can benefit from your routines and rituals as much as your children.

Lights Out

How important is the lighting really? Well, picture a romantic dinner for two at a favorite restaurant. Do you see candles or spotlights? Lighting helps to set the mood. Turning particular lights on and off can help to trigger transitions.

Soft lighting will also help set the tone for you. When it's time to sleep, you'll probably be choosing books that are best read in a hushed voice. Stories like *Guess How Much I Love You* by Sam McBratney and *I Love You as Much* by Laura Krauss Melmed are excellent bedtime choices that read like lullabies; and who yells a lullaby?

A reading lamp can really help do double duty, as we found out with our newborn. Our reading lamp became our "quiet lamp." When middle-of-the-night feedings roused me from sleep, I would turn on this softer light, signaling that we are were quiet mode. In the morning I turned on the big light, signaling the start of a new day. While this all may sound a bit like wishful thinking, we have had peaceful nights around here for a long time, and a big part of me believes it's the lighting.

Bookworms Beware

Don't confuse a reading lamp with a nightlight. A reading lamp, while softer, should still provide enough illumination to make the pictures and words easily visible and prevent eyestrain. A nightlight need not meet such criteria.

Rise and Shine and Read

If bedtime is not your cup of tea, try looking at another part of your day. Since my husband works late many nights, I was often spent by the time bedtime rolled around. My enthusiasm for all things small and cute was waning, and quite frankly, I just wanted to go pass out on the couch. But I wanted to read, also. So our bedtime routine became two short stories accompanied by our end-of-evening rituals, and morning became our favorite time to explore many books together.

I like to ease into the day. I hate having to be anywhere first thing in the morning, and would much rather laze around in pajamas with coffee until the caffeine kicks in. It turns out, minus the caffeine, my son is the same way. Since he was old enough to sit up in my lap we would spend the first part of our morning investigating the book basket together. For as long as his attention would dictate, we would read different books, reread favorites, and enjoy each other's company. A lovely way to start the day.

Bookworms Beware

More important than watching the clock to see how long you have been reading is watching your baby to see if she is still engaged. Ten minutes of interactive enjoyment is more productive than 30 minutes of fussing and fighting.

Creature Comforts

Since we spoke about wanting to vary vocabulary, you may be tempted to introduce a host of new books at every seating, under the impression that different means better. Instead of making yourself crazy trying to always bring in new inventory, try varying familiar favorites with new titles. Babies thrive in familiarity. Having one or two titles you always turn to at transitional times can be just the kind of comfort and consistency your little one needs to settle down. Don't be surprised if the books you reread to your newborn become the ones your toddler asks for over and over again.

Our friends the O'Rourkes have a wonderful routine that balances the idea of introducing new stories with tried-and-true choices. At bedtime, mom and dad would take out three board books to read to baby Colin. Books one and two would rotate, but book three was always the same. Before long, baby came to expect this reading routine, with book three always signaling that it was time for bed. Without fuss or fret mom and dad would say goodnight and Colin would go to sleep. The O'Rourkes appreciated Colin's need for consistency, but still managed to read some new stories, too.

Education is serious business, for adults. For babies, learning is just another natural part of their day. Eat, sleep, play; and play includes listening, talking, touching, smelling, experiencing, recalling, exploring, and digesting, to name but a few. All of this play is made possible with books. Reading aloud to your newborn is a wonderful way to bond with your newest family member while introducing him to the wonderful world that is his home.

The Least You Need to Know

- Babies are not too young to benefit from books. Begin reading with them as soon as possible and know that you nourishing their heads and hearts.
- Your voice is a source of comfort and counsel, so find books that you enjoy and help your child get to know you a little bit better.
- Repetition and variety are two sides of the read-aloud coin. Repetition helps to establish the rhythm of how language works; variety helps by introducing new and diverse words.

Chapter 5

Little Learners: Toddler Time

In This Chapter

- All hands-on books
- What great read-alouds have in common
- The ABCs of read-alouds

My toddler is my shadow. Everywhere I go, he goes. That means I have constant companionship at the grocery store, around the garden, in the bathroom. What is so amazing to me is that my son makes no distinction between work and play. Whether we are emptying the dishwasher together or chasing a ball in the yard, he is happy to be participating in any activity I throw his way. Instead of having to occupy him while I try to get chores and errands done, or bribing him to help, he just comes along on the adventure. What I have, what all parents of toddlers have, is a captive audience.

As I said before, children want to learn. They want to explore and engage in their environment. But as much as I try to do with my son, I must admit that due to financial restraints, work schedules, and daily commitments, our days do tend to be relatively routine. Yes, we pick pumpkins in the fall and hunt for eggs in the spring, but we have never traveled to the Rainforest, petted a polar bear, or explored the inside of a volcano. Luckily for us, and for you, we have books to help us round out our experiences. The sooner you introduce your child to the wonders of reading and the adventure they provide, the easier it will be to keep your captive audience captivated.

Thank Heaven for Little Read-Aloud Books

As you and your toddler are just getting to know each other, books are a great medium to find out what truly interests her. Up until now, you have pretty much decided what she will wear, eat, watch, and play with. But your once-docile newborn is starting to develop some very clear ideas about what she likes and dislikes. A variety of reading resources can help her pursue new passions.

We can think about introducing reading materials in the same way we think about planting a garden. With every new subject we present, we plant seeds. As parents, we want our children to blossom, and books are instrumental in that process. Out of all the topics you read together, you will most likely find that it is the same one or two subjects that keep her most engaged. For my son, it is trains and dogs. We read other books, but these two themes have captured his attention. And this is where the pruning comes is. When your son or daughter makes a connection to a type of book or a subject, nurture that interest. Other books can continue to be introduced, but the pursuit of one's passion helps to make that all-important connection to the pleasure principle.

Built to Last

Toddler books are virtually indestructible. Yes, they will look well worn by the time you are through with them, with frayed edges and crayoned pages, but they can take a licking (literally) and keep on ticking. Made from a host of hardy materials, these books are intended to be handled, and not with care. This means, your children can truly call them their own.

Play is how children learn. The more senses they can use while playing, the more apt they are to stay engaged in the activity. This is why children don't just touch things with their hands, but taste, smell, and roll around with everything within reach. While toddlers may only play with these treasured toys for a few minutes at a time, their time with books will grow with their attention spans. Even these limited intervals provide enough time to introduce some wonderful reading skills.

Quick Picks

We want to encourage our children to touch and taste their books, but we don't want to encourage germs. Keep a spray bottle filled with kid-friendly vinegar and water within your reach and give your child's collection a good wipe-down at least once a week.

Board Books

Probably the most popular choice for parents of toddlers is board books. They are exactly as they sound, made with heavy-duty cardboard. Small and compact, these 6 × 6 books are custom-made to fit into little hands. Their pages can be turned without fear of ripping and they can easily be tossed into a basket or box.

Some publishing companies specialize in targeting this particular age group with titles made especially for board-book production. These books are most commonly known as "concept books" and focus on a particular topic like colors, shapes, or numbers. Many other board books were originally published as traditional story books, and then repackaged as board books to meet the needs of this age group. A well-loved example of this is *Goodnight Moon* by Margaret Wise Brown.

Cloth Books

Cloth books can be about the same size or a little larger than board books and make wonderful accessories for strollers, car seats, and highchairs. Many cloth books are interactive with different textures and shapes adorning the page, or have bells, whistles, horns, or crinkly material sewn into the construction. Soft cloth books are favorites of young babies and make excellent teething toys.

These touch-and-feel books are light on words, usually one key word or phrase per page, but high on visual effect. They are not intended as story-time material as they usually have only between three and five pages, but they can be a lifesaver when you are stuck online. Despite their short length you can still turn, squeeze, and play with the pages, making them the ultimate book toy.

Elements of the Read-Aloud Story

Toddlers love to have books read to them, but some choices really do work better than others. Keep these suggestions in mind as you choose a story to read aloud, and remember that children may need a couple of readings to warm up to a book. If after reading a book three different times your little guy still seems restless and disinterested, leave this title for awhile and try something else. You can always pick it up again at another time. The name of the game in toddler read-alouds is "simple."

- **Simple Themes** Stories should be focused and easy to follow. A book about farm animals should only have farm animals, not farm animals and zoo animals.
- **Simple Text** Rhyming and repetitive text reads like a nursery rhyme and is most pleasing to little ears.
- **Simple Pictures** If you are reading a sentence about a train, a picture of a train should be on the page so your child can easily make the connection.
- **Simple Size** Read-alouds for this age group should be short. One to two sentences per page, about 16 pages per book.

The Art of Choosing a Beginner Book

Picture books are called such because the illustration is the most important thing on the page. The text complements the pictures, but it is secondary to the illustration. For this reason, it is quite important to appreciate the kinds of artwork available.

When choosing a picture book, consider the aesthetics of the illustration. Pictures should always be proportional. A cat is smaller than a horse, which is smaller than a house, which is smaller than a tree. Also avoid a book whose text wraps around the illustration, or text that is written upside down or vertically. While those styles may be fun for the older reader, they are not read-aloud friendly.

Keep in mind, young children will recognize familiar pictures before they recognize familiar words. My son can pick out cows on different pages of the book, but he can't yet pick out the word. He points at the picture and I point out the word. Eventually, the connection will be made. As most people are visual learners, your best bet is a well-defined picture on a solid background. As your child better understands how books work, the pictures can become more elaborate.

Success Story

Picture books and wordless books are not the same thing. In a picture book, the pictures are the driving force of the story, with the words narrating the pictures. In wordless books, there are no words at all.

If You're Happy and You Know It, Buy This Book

All the parents I know have a favorite picture book they read to their kids. For my husband, it's *Hippos Go Berserk* by Sandra Boynton. For me, it's *What Mommies Do Best* by Laura Numeroff. These were books that we picked out not because we wanted to introduce hippos to our son or emphasize all the wonderful ways mommy loves him, but because we, the adults, liked them. How nice to look forward to a picture book that you enjoy. My husband has a wonderful sense of humor and the idea of a hippo having a big party with 44 of his closest friends cracked him up. I couldn't wait to bake homemade birthday cakes with my kids, and the illustration in that book sold me. If you love it, they will love it.

If you read a book that makes you laugh out loud, hum along, or get misty eyes, buy it. Consider it an instant keepsake. Reading with your children is not just about

Bookworms Beware

Just because you love a book does not mean your child will. If your choice is being met with some reluctance, don't despair. Try reading it at another time of day, putting it in the toy box or reintroducing it at another time.

their enjoyment, but yours. Every time I read the last page of Mommies I feel compelled to kiss the top of my son's head. Every time. And yes, I hope one day my son understands why that book means so much to me. And yes, one day I hope to give it to his wife at her baby shower when they are expecting my first grandchild (like you haven't already thought about this, too). But until then, I'll just look forward to my favorite read-aloud and the top of my son's head.

Sneeze, Cough, Clap, and Snap: The Joy of Sound Effects

Great writing sounds great. Since part of the goal of reading is to convey meaning, we want to do whatever we can to help make the meanings of words clearer to our children. One of the best ways to do this is by taking advantage of all the wonderful sound effects available in children's picture books. There is a huge difference between reading, "Achoo" and throwing your head back and giving the kind of "Aah, Aah AACHOOO!" that leaves your toddler in a fit of giggles. Or prompts her to pass you a tissue. And while sound effects are fun, the effects of annunciating such words are a great lesson in phonics. The more dramatic, drawn-out AACHOO gives little ears the chance to hear every distinct sound in the word. All that and a fit of giggles. What could be better?

Sensory stimulation is definitely the name of the game when you clap and snap. Anytime you can combine senses, you are making a stronger impact on your reading. The more senses you use when learning a new skill, the more directions and information you give to your brain. That's why it is so much more engaging to work in the science lab, rather than just hear about what happens in a science lab. Reading is an inactive activity. The more activities you can incorporate through hand motions, dramatic facial expressions, and body movements, the more meaningful the reading will become.

Quick Picks

Practice flexing your fingers with simple songs like The Wheels on the Bus, Bingo, and The Itsy Bitsy Spider. Toddlers will love imitating your happy hands.

Captive Audience = Energy + Enthusiasm

Words, words, words. Without energy and enthusiasm, all words sound the same. When reading aloud, don't be afraid to be silly! A cow does not say, "moo," a cow says, "MOOOOOO!" Imitating farm animals is a great way to exhibit energy for reading.

Enthusiasm does not always have to be loud and bold, either. If you are reading a bedtime story, try lowering your voice as you move through the book, with the last few sentences being read close to a whisper. If you are going to bed, you want to read more slowly, more quietly. Enthusiasm and energy are about looking at your reading and deciding how to best make that reading appeal to the listener.

If there is a story about a race, or if the characters are in a hurry, read faster, huffing and puffing along the way. Tell your child, "Quick, we must turn the page!" Races are fast, after all. Your reading speed should reflect the speed of the book's action. This is especially helpful when reading action verbs. If a character is quickly running up the stairs, you should be reading quickly to help illustrate what running quickly actually means. Your child will take her cues from you. If reading is fun and engaging to you, it will be fun and engaging to your kids.

A Successful Strategy: Storytelling Suggestions

As I stated in the first chapter, there are no hard and fast rules to reading with your children. But I can offer you suggestions to make the experience more enjoyable for everyone. Some of these suggestions may sound like I'm encouraging you play with books. Well, good, because I am. Remember play is how children learn, and books are toys with words. Set yourself up for success and enjoy this playtime.

Get ready, get set, read:

- Sit comfortably. Sit close together. Make sure you have enough light.
- Invite your child to read with you. Instead of, "I'm going to read this story," try, "Would you like to read together?"

- Don't panic if your son seems distracted or your daughter is more interested in her pajama buttons. Try asking your child a direct question to refocus their attention.
- Talk about the cover. Introduce the author and illustrator. Use the words "author" and "illustrator" and describe what each person does.
- If this is the first time you are reading a new book together, read from beginning to end without questions or comments so that your child can appreciate the story line.
- If it is a well-worn favorite, ask questions based on age and interest level.
- Leave enough time after finishing the story to flip back through the pages and find favorite pictures.
- Say thank you.

In addition to planning your actual reading time together, setting yourself up for success can help make your routines go more smoothly. Knowing what to expect from a book; anticipating opportunities to invite your child to become part of the action, and finishing reading on a positive note also strengthen the reading relationship.

Preview

It may seem silly to pre-read a baby book; after all, you are not likely to find material that has to be censored, right? But we preview board books not to look for things we may want to take out, but to look for things we want to emphasize. Since these books are going to be short, we can give them a quick scan before sharing them with our children. There are universal things to look for, and things that are going to be unique to your family. Both are worth discovering.

If you don't preview the book, you may miss out on an opportunity to give a good sneeze, speed up your reading pace, or lower your voice to a whisper. While you could always do these things later on, why not try to make each read-aloud session as meaningful as possible? "Start strong, finish strong" is the motto here.

Look for ways to make connection between the book and your toddler's world. Pointing out relevant facts like, "We have a blue car, too" or "That dog looks just like Roscoe" can make the reading more meaningful.

Participate

When you empower your children and make them active participants in the reading activity, you are much more likely to keep them engaged. As you move through the book, ask questions like, "We have seen two cows already. Do you think we will see more cows?" Although your toddler will probably not give you a coherent answer, you are modeling a wonderful skill of reading, retaining information and using it to make predictions. If you should find another cow, enthusiastically point it out, "Another cow! I can't believe it! Three cows in this book. Three cows that say 'MOOOOO!'"

Success Story

In your quest to keep your child involved in the read-aloud, he may try to take over. If your son is grabbing the book, let him have a crack at it first. Chances are, after he has had an opportunity to touch it, he'll be more likely to sit and listen.

Participation usually means that you will "get off track." When my son and I read *Barnyard Dance* by Sandra Boynton, we must first find all the cows in the book. This means that his pudgy little hands get to hold the book and flip around the pages finding cows. We see other animals along the way, and sometimes we talk about them, but our cow-finding mission has become part of our routine.

And for the parent who is asking, "But does this count as reading? This back and forth and pointing?" I say yes. We have books that we read from front cover to back cover, left to right. And then we have Barnyard Dance. Instead of insisting on a militant approach to reading, with my always holding the book and directing the action, Michael is able to take charge of reading.

Yes, it takes longer when you do it this way. Sometimes we just read one story from beginning to end. Sometimes we just play with books. But as we do not have only one time of day when we use books, we can afford to get off track. It's like our evening walks after dinner. I set out to make it down the block and back. Michael sets out to collect pebbles. Along the way we have discovered ants, grasshoppers, grass, leaves, cracks in the pavement, and puddles. Take a walk through reading with your children and see what you can discover.

Praise

Who doesn't appreciate a kind word? Who doesn't like to have their efforts acknowledged? There are a couple of different ways to bring a note of gratitude into your reading.

Acknowledge the author. Did you love the book? How about saying out loud, "I really enjoyed that story. I'm glad the fish made friends." Giving specific reasons for your opinion will help your child learn to make similar assessments. If you hated the story, express that tactfully. "That book was a little longer than I like. I'm glad it rhymed, though. I like reading rhyming books. But next time, I'll look for a book that has fewer pages."

Raising a reader for life takes honesty. You are not going to love everything, and neither are your children. No one needs to pretend that they do. Chances are you can find one thing about the book that was agreeable and mention that. And talk about what you can do in the future to make better choices. Not liking a book does not mean you don't like reading. It's important to model that distinction.

Bookworms Beware

Even if you hate a book, remember not to say, "I hated reading that." Your child will hear "I hate reading." Give reasons for disliking a particular story, but always emphasize that you enjoy reading together.

Make sure to acknowledge the illustrator and recap what her contribution to the book means. A simple definition like, "The illustrator draws the pictures" is all you need. Point out your favorite picture and ask your child to do the same.

Most important, acknowledge your child. How lovely to hear from a parent, "I really enjoyed reading that with you. Thank you for sharing that story with me. I look forward to reading more together tomorrow." It's always nice to have your presence acknowledged.

Print Awareness

Before you know it, your toddler will begin to make the connection between words on the page and the words coming out of your mouth. Instead of looking at you while you read, she will look at the book. While it will be quite some time before she picks up a crayon and writes her name, she is beginning to understand the concept of print.

As I said earlier, children recognize pictures before they recognize words. In a book, for example, a picture of a cow represents a real cow. Next comes early print concepts, which involve understanding that letters make up words, and words represent something, too.

You can encourage print concepts by continuing to do what you are already doing: reading aloud. While you are doing this, try to incorporate the following recommendations into your routine.

- Point out the title on the cover and talk about what to expect from the name of the story.
- When you open up the book, show your child that you are starting at the beginning, on the first page.
- Point out the first word in the first sentence as you begin to read.
- Use your finger to trace the words as you read them. Talk about how you are reading from left to right.
- When you come to the end of the sentence, keep your finger there and take a deep breath to signal an intentional pause.
- When you come to the last word of the book, tell your child you are at the end. When you run out of words, you stop reading.

Quick Picks

The next time you are on a walk with your child, look for collectibles that begin with her name. Help Pam find pebbles and Suzy find sticks. Opportunities to discover language are all around us.

The techniques I just mentioned sound so obvious to us, the proficient reader, but they are all learned skills. Because we do not want to become bogged down in the lessons of reading, but, rather, have these skills develop as the opportunities present themselves, I would encourage you to practice one suggestion each time you read. Remember, we want to enjoy the story. Print concepts can be reinforced a little bit at a time so you don't lose your listener in the lesson.

Now I Know My ABCs

Probably one of the first songs you ever learned to sing as a kid was the alphabet song. Singing this song with your own children is a wonderful tool, but it probably won't have much meaning until they start to associate it with actual letters. For this reason, singing the song while reading an alphabet book makes for a more meaningful connection.

There are a ton of great alphabet books available and the best ones utilize the standards we talked about when choosing a great picture book: clear pictures, no complicated text, and easy to follow. Look for alphabet books whose letters are right side up, have one letter per page, and pictures of familiar everyday items that represent the highlighted letter. When beginning a story book, begin to point out the differences between capital and lowercase letters.

Success Story

An easy way to explain the difference between capital and lowercase letters is by using your own family. If you have a daughter, explain that both mommy and daughter are girls, but mommy is a big girl, and daughter is a little girl. Just like the capital H and lowercase h are both the letter h, but one is big and one is little.

Have fun manipulating letters with magnets or foam cut-outs for the bath tub. Toddlers are starting to understand that words are made by combining different letters. Use your child-friendly toys to make simple words on the fridge and in the tub. Have crayons and blank paper available so your kids can practice their "writing."

What's in a Name?

Here is a secret that I did not know for a really long time: when introducing letters, you do not have to start with the letter "a." Really, you don't. You can start with any letter you choose. Like all the other reading ideas I'll talk about, I think the most important criteria for introducing any new concept is relevance. So why not focus on your child's name?

You can start to write your child's name on the inside cover of his books, on his art projects, and on his belongings. A nameplate on your daughter's bedroom door is a great reading addition to her favorite room. If you have a label maker, you can pretty much tag everything in the house including "Joni's toothbrush" and "Anya's hairbrush," to show possession.

Focus on the first letter of your child's name when you are out running errands. Look for signs that begin with the same letter and point them out. On your next trip to the library, check out books whose titles match this featured first letter. All of these simple games will help reinforce that letters combine to make words, and words have meaning.

Number Recognition

Just as your toddler will begin noticing individual letters and frequently used words, she will begin to notice numbers. Again, a similar connection will be made: numbers represent something. You can point out the number of the page you are reading, count how many numbers are in your book, and count down how many books you are reading during one sitting.

In addition, you can help your son or daughter understand grouping. Children will start to group toys, blocks, and books according to shape, size, or color. You can put all your books about farm animals in one pile, and all your books about zoo animals in another pile. Then, talk about which group has more or less. These early math concepts don't require memorization or "lessons" but develop naturally out of your read-alouds.

Reading aloud with your toddler does more than just help bring the two of you closer together; it also provides an excellent springboard for introducing the world beyond your backyard. You can travel to great places and meet different faces every time you open a book. Not only will you get to know more about what is happening around the world, but you'll also get to learn important reading skills along the way.

The Least You Need to Know

- Toddlers make no distinction between learning and playing, so don't be afraid to get loud, messy, or silly. The enjoyment lesson is lesson enough.
- Preparing for your reading routine can help make it more engaging for everyone; try setting the stage for reading enjoyment by practicing your performance.
- Reading skills are a natural byproduct of a healthy reading relationship; make sure you annunciate the words, pace yourself, and treat books with respect they deserve.

Chapter 6

Building Your Home Library

In This Chapter

- Keeping reading materials at an arm's length
- Why the same stories are so satisfying
- What your read-alouds have to look forward to

When you think of a library, you most likely conjure up visions of neatly stacked bookcases situated along a quiet wall. But the kind of home library we're looking to build has your children in mind. Instead of using a typical library for our mental picture, let's use the supermarket. Advertisers pay a premium to rent shelf space at eye level because you are more likely to choose what you can easily see and reach. Why not apply this same theory to reading with your toddler? Let's take the books off the shelves and put them in inviting containers that can be accessed at all times. Like the supermarket shopper who is drawn to a brightly packaged product in her direct line of vision, let's reel in our kids with strategically placed reading materials that beg to be touched.

Once we have our materials set to go, we will take a look at taking advantage of reading-ready moments and building a reading routine that everyone looks forward to. Keep in mind that you are under no obligation to try every recommendation on this chapter tonight. By taking small steps and making small changes, you will see big results.

Positive Play

There are several lines of safety items designed to keep a toddler out of danger. From electric socket covers to safety gates, no child's home is complete until it is outfitted with anti-exploring devices. But as we've spent so much time planning how to prevent our kids from getting into the bad stuff, we may have unconsciously forgotten to help them get into the good stuff, too. Luckily, this is a quick fix, and one you have probably already set yourself up for.

Take a mental walk around your home, taking notice of where your child's toys are. Are toys confined to one room, tucked neatly in a shelf in size order? I'm guessing no. You probably have toys everywhere: in low toy chests, in corner storage bins, on a play mat. Would you dream of putting toys up high and waiting for your child to request each and every one he wanted? Of course not; how could you return phone calls? Could you imagine lining up every one of her toys on a high shelf each time she was finished playing? Of course not; when would you make dinner?

Yet, when it comes to books, we are more apt to keep them safely preserved, out of reach, and therefore, out of bounds. We want to bring books onto the playing field and encourage their use throughout the day. Remember, books are our most treasured toys. Let's play.

A Tisket, a Tasket, My Very Own Book Basket

While a beautifully stacked book shelf provides a lovely focal point, designing mini-book centers throughout your house sets you up for sudden success. For this reason, I love book baskets. We have baskets of books stashed all over the house. Big baskets with handles, little baskets in bathrooms, old laundry baskets in the playroom. You can also recycle holiday baskets, shoeboxes, or storage containers into little libraries, ensuring that you'll be covered during unexpected downtime. Waiting for the oven timer to go off? Laundry still not dry? Dishwasher on its last cycle? Reach into your ready-made book nook and slip in a 5-minute story. Rotate your story collection throughout the house and add some unexpected fun to your routine chores.

Success Story

Turn a toddler hot spot into a reading opportunity. Use the cabinet under your kitchen sink to hold a favorite basket of books. Instead of shooing your kids away, they can camp out at your feet and bond with you, and books.

Sure, book baskets make cleaning up a cinch, but they also make reading a cinch. Does your child hand you his favorite toy as an indication he wants to play? Does she lead you toward her favorite blocks on the carpet in hopes you'll stack them together? This same initiative can be expected when books are readily available. Now, instead of having to find additional time to read, you can make it a part of your regular routine.

Try putting your reading materials in book baskets, too. I have a subscription to Family Fun magazine that I look forward to reading every month. For a long time I would keep it on the table next to our living room couch with the intention of reading it … later. Well, later never seemed to come. So I got myself my own book baskets and put my magazines and catalogues in them. I keep these fragile materials just out of reach from my son, but within my direct line of sight I remember they exist. When he becomes engaged in an activity, whether rearranging his stuffed animals or flipping though his own books, I can reach for my magazines. Children need to see us reading. It's not enough to talk about the joy of reading: we must set the example.

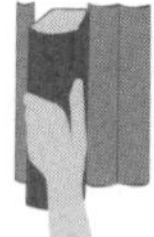

Quick Picks

Book Baskets make a great baby-shower gift for new parents. Choose a pretty, sturdy basket, several board books, and voilà, instant gift!

Stop, Drop, and Read!

There is a great deal of emphasis on the reading routine, which I do not begrudge, but I think it's important to round out the routine with spontaneous reading. When we keep books all around us, this becomes much more natural. And you don't have to limit your books to the house. Keep books in the car, in your diaper bag, in the garage. We have a sing-along book that drives me up a wall; so, of course, Michael loves it. We keep it in the car, under the driver's seat, and pull it out when the ride has gotten too long or the traffic too deep. Yes, it makes me cringe; but having this emergency tool in reserve has seen us through more than our fair share of rush-hour horrors.

Reading material is readily available once you get in the habit of looking for it. For example, when you're stuck in line at the grocery store, grab a magazine and show your daughter the pictures while you wait to check out. Read her the coupons you have in your hand. Show her that you checked off all the items on your grocery list and are now ready to pay for your food. Once you start realizing how easy it is to build reading into your daily activities, you won't be as worried about meeting your daily quota.

While we want to establish a routine because it reinforces that reading is a valued family practice, reading in real time exposes your children to additional vocabulary and reading experiences they might not otherwise have. In fact, in no picture book have I ever seen "Manufacturers coupon redeemable," but I have had plenty of opportunity to read those words. And save 35 cents.

The Zen of Read-Alouds

Reading with your children is a worthwhile activity that can, and should, be enjoyed throughout the day. But like all serious endeavors, be it exercising, attaining a degree, or completing a hefty project, dedication to the endeavor is necessary if you want to see results. What are the results of reading with your children? To recap: greater communication skills, increased vocabulary, better problem-solving abilities, higher achievements in school, and a more financial secure future. So while we will continue to take advantage of the readable moments available throughout our day, we also want to dedicate ourselves to a consistent reading routine.

Reading with your children connects you to them in a way few other mediums afford. Read-aloud routines offer one-on-one time between you and your child, give you a common purpose to focus on, and help smooth out the rough edges of both of your days. Dedicating yourselves to each other's company takes time, patience, and commitment, but remember that you already have everything you need to make this happen: an open heart, an open mind, and open arms. Now we just need to give those assets some structure.

Bookworms Beware

In our quest to set up the perfect reading space, we can often tend to overdo it. Skip the background Beethoven, cancel the chaise lounge purchase, and forgo the fancy new lamp. If you wait for perfect, you'll never get started. Keep it simple and just go for it.

Cooling Off and Calming Down

There was a time when our son's nighttime bath was a calming force in his evening routine. Then he discovered bath toys, splashing, and the magic of blowing soap bubbles, and calm was replaced by chaos. He loves bath time, and it's a nice part of our evening, but I wouldn't call it calming. I would call it wet. Our reading routine has therefore become an indispensable step in our bedtime ritual.

Warm, clean, and quiet, we cuddle among teddy bears and flip through books together. Sometimes we read three or four books from cover to cover; other times he wants to hold onto one book and only flip through those pages. This is a time for rereading favorite stories, searching for our friends the farm animals, and winding down. This routine not only calms him down, but calms me down. As harried as my day has been, as nuts as I got over spilled milk, I can end the day on a kind and quiet note.

Success Story

Feel free to create more than one serene setting in your house. If caregivers are on different schedules, you may want a "daytime" and "nighttime" reading space to accommodate everyone's preferred routine.

Quality Quiet Time

Reading is not a busy, bustling activity. It is interactive, yes, but in a Sunday drive kind of way, not a Monday morning rush-hour kind of way. For our purposes, quiet doesn't mean silent, it means free from distractions. We are used to eating dinner on the way to soccer practice and finishing homework on the ride home. Thanks to cell phones, Blackberries, and instant messenger, we are accessible 24/7. We have become so used to multi-tasking that it may take time to shift gears and feel comfortable focusing our full attention on one activity. But such a practice will yield great benefits.

We give our children a wonderful gift by helping them learn to slow down, be quiet, and remain focused. Your read-alouds are a lovely time to turn off the noise and tune into each other. Since we are talking about toddlers, you may be wondering how long these routines will last. Experts suggest that children be read to for 30 minutes a day. But keep in mind, this does not necessarily mean 30 consecutive minutes. More important than watching the clock is watching your child. Some days, she may be ready to call it quits after 5 minutes, where other evenings she requests another story after 15 minutes. Thirty minutes a day is an average. If we work on establishing our regular routines while taking advantage of reader-friendly moments throughout the day, we can be confident that our time will be well spent, regardless of what the clock says.

Bookworms Beware

If bedtime reading is impossible due to your own demanding routine, establish a reading habit that works with your schedule instead of skipping the recommendation altogether. More important than the time of day is your consistent commitment to this activity. Morning rituals are just as important as bedtime rituals.

Quick Picks

Worried that you're not clocking enough reading minutes? Then "Take Five." At every meal and snack, read for 5 minutes. Considering that the average toddler eats three meals and two snacks, you'll have five chances a day to "Take Five." Then at bedtime, you can concentrate on memories, not minutes.

Repetition, Repetition, Repetition

We own a ton of books for my son and consistently borrow a rotating bunch from the library; yet every day, for as long as I can remember, I have read one particular train book that he loves. This book is not a great book. In fact, I think it's pretty poorly done. But he loves it. So I read it. Again and again. And again. I was hoping that he would outgrow the book, and I'm sure he will, but it hasn't happened yet. Michael doesn't just like this book, he needs this book.

Toddlers are acutely aware that their parents can leave them behind, that older children can do more than they can, and that they can't get everything they want. The bigger a child's world gets, the more uncertain she can become about her place in it. No wonder this is the age when children reach for a favorite stuffed animal to snooze with, insist on traveling with their security blankets, and request a read-aloud that looks, sounds, and feels familiar.

Familiarity Breeds Content

While you may assume that your child would easily tire of hearing the same story over and over again, the opposite is actually true. Children thrive on routine and repetition. It's comforting to be surrounded by what is familiar, for children and adults. For instance, when I am sick, tired, or out of sorts, I am not interested in a gourmet dinner from an exotic restaurant. I am interested in a big bowl of pasta with butter and parmesan cheese. That is my comfort food. Our children have comfort books. After a day spent running errands, attending playdates, and trying to make sense of their ever-expanding world, it's nice to come home to a familiar serving of a favorite story.

And unlike my big bowl of comfort carbs, this reading repetition is excellent brain food. Humans learn by hearing, seeing, and practicing the same routines over and over again. The more times you read, "The cow says moo," the more opportunities you give your child to learn that a cow says moo, or that a policeman helps his community, or a mommy loves her baby. Just think of all the reruns you have watched on TV. Chances are, when you are watching the same program a second time you pick up on a new joke you may have missed, while still enjoying the punch lines you knew were coming. Read-aloud reruns work in the same way.

"When Can We Move On?"

I know, I know. You are willing to give it your all, while you have to, but you really would like to know that there is a light, and another book, at the end of the tunnel. I wish I could tell you when you'll cross that magic finish line and leave this now-memorized book behind. But as every child, and every child's timetable, is different, all I can do is offer suggestions for promoting, not forcing, a smooth transition.

Respect that your child needs his comfort reading, but continue to introduce new books and new topics. The most effective way to do this is by connecting reading to her experiences. Going to the zoo? Take out books on zoo animals and practice talking like the animals together. Is Halloween right around the corner? Check out books on pumpkin picking. Balancing new books with tried-and-true favorites gives each of you what you need: reading enjoyment. Just remember, this won't last forever. Nothing ever does.

Bookworms Beware

Don't try to skip pages. The same toddler who cannot tie her shoes, find the potty, or remember not pull the cat's tail knows exactly how many pages are in her favorite book. She is depending on you to meet her needs. And she'll let you know when you don't.

The Special Shelf

In our home we have our everyday dishes that serve us well for breakfast, lunch, and dinner; and then we have the fancy plates that we use only on special occasions. We take them out for holidays, birthdays, and special occasions, and treasure how special they are. You can bring this same concept to reading.

Book baskets are absolutely fantastic for encouraging children to make reading a part of their day. Easy to access, filled with an assortment of favorites and seasonal selections, these friends in low places are wonderful. Like my everyday dishes. But we want to also teach our children the pride that comes from taking care of "fancy" belongings, too—and this is where the Special Shelf comes in.

Every child's room can have a Special Shelf. Made of mahogany or plywood, the construction is not as important as the content. And it may take awhile for your children to appreciate why it is that this shelf exists, but the payoff will be well worth the preparation. This shelf is where you'll keep treasured items, such as framed family photos, a beloved souvenir, and a few chosen books. Right now, these books must be shared due to reading levels; your toddler needs you to read to him.

Later, we will choose materials that foster shared reading and talk about why children who can read independently can still benefit from shared reading.

When your children are very young, you will be in charge of the shelf, but as they mature, they can take an active part in maintaining this bedroom mainstay. Eventually, they will be the sole proprietor of their Special Shelf, making it special, indeed. For now, we'll concentrate on choosing the books that will help launch a million memories.

Success Story

You should also construct a Special Shelf for yourself. While your nightstand probably holds your reading materials now, having a shelf that matches your children's can provide you with many of the same benefits and will set an excellent example when they are older.

Souvenirs

Buying books while you are on vacation is a great way to add variety to your home library and makes a memorable addition to the Special Shelf. Instead of looking for tee-shirts or key chains, check out local authors, books rich with photography and tales of local history. If a location warranted your traveling there, chances are it has something valuable to offer your children.

Don't miss out on this opportunity, either. Browse area bookstores and boutique shops where you're likely to find books displayed and signed by local authors. Perhaps these authors specialize in an unfamiliar genre or have researched a subject that is completely foreign to you. Great! Modeling for your children that you are interested in new reading materials will help them appreciate that reading is an adventure that even adults enjoy.

What to Read Next

Some of my favorite things to keep on the Special Shelf are books that are just out of my children's reach. These stories are high interest, of course, but their format isn't as reader-friendly as other choices. For the parents of toddlers, these next-step books would have paper pages, more words, fewer pictures, and be less repetitive. This is not to say that the special-shelf books are off limits, but they are titles that will require a bit more maintenance to enjoy.

After reading Jim Trelease's *The Read Aloud Handbook*, I was encouraged to start reading a chapter of the book *Charlotte's Web* with my son. Who knew it was possible? After having introduced the book with mixed success we have now found an ebb and flow that works for us. Every couple of days we try to read about a half a page to one page per night. Obviously we are in no rush. And why should we be? My son gets to hear a host of new words, but I get to read a "real" book; a nice change from singing pigs and dancing donkeys (not that I don't love both). Reading with your children is as much about you as it is about them. Remember to stick stories on the Special Shelf that you can't wait to hear, too.

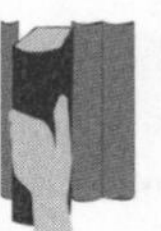

Quick Picks

Open up your souvenir books to the inside cover and trace your child's hand. Write her name, the date of your trip, and where you went. Instant keepsake.

A throw pillow in the corner next to a reading lamp, a book basket under the sink, a short story before heading in to see the doctor. Once we start becoming aware of all the reading opportunities that are available in our homes and throughout our day, we will well be on our way to building a home library whose effects reach far beyond our familiar four walls.

The Least You Need to Know

- Books are purposeful toys. Encourage kids to play with reading by keeping books within reach.
- Reading routines require discipline, so make a realistic commitment that works instead of a grandiose plan that is abandoned and savor the success.
- Look out for new titles to add to your home library when on vacation, when the seasons change, and during the holidays.

Chapter 7

Little Kids with Big Problems

In This Chapter

- Children's books can help smooth transitional times
- Read-aloud suggestions that tackle sensitive subjects
- Activities that can help manage a crisis

When we think about reading aloud to our toddlers, we probably have visions of happily ever after. Stories that make us laugh together, hug one another, and help induce a goodnight sleep. Toddler's books are filled with simple stories because, well, toddlers have pretty simple stories themselves: eat, play, sleep, repeat. Most of the time this pattern will outline your routine, but there are less-than-lovely situations that also color the landscape. For these tough times, you need not wrack your brain thinking of the right things to say; chances are, the words are already available for you.

Children's books tackle uncomfortable subject matter, everything from surrendering pacifiers to giving up diapers. As adults, it's easy to downplay our toddler's troubles or think that they are not yet fully capable of such strong feelings; but when we do that, we exacerbate the situation. It's best to acknowledge that something upsetting is happening, rather than abruptly saying "You'll be fine" without providing support to become fine.

Picture books are a wonderful tool to help your child through a sticky situation. As the parent, you (usually) know what life-altering experiences are headed down the pike. Whether it's time to say goodbye to pacifiers, diapers, or mommy, read-aloud routines can be custom tailored to address the would-be disaster du jour. We have already begun to carve out this sacred one-on-one time, so now let's utilize it further by bringing in some "band-aid" book titles. We can't stop the pain, but we can help the healing along.

Separation Anxiety

At one time or another, all children become anxious about change. Because kids thrive on lifestyles rich with routines and rituals, an unpredictable set of circumstances can throw them into a bit of a tail spin. This is especially true when the primary caregivers must periodically step out of the picture. Whether you are going back to work or going into the backyard, when you are out of sight, you are not out of mind. Children will quickly learn the signs that you are leaving and do what they can to prevent you from going. Usually, this means sticking to you like glue. So what is a parent to do?

What you can't do is stay in the house for the rest of your life waiting for your child to "be ready." We do not always have the luxury of taking more time off from work, postponing daycare, or continuing with diapers. There are situations that demand we move faster than we would like to. Instead of adding guilt onto an already exhausting situation, we can look for ways to help our toddlers, and ourselves, develop coping mechanisms to manage difficult dilemmas. We have the opportunity to lay the groundwork for important life skills. Like many of the other issues that apply to our children, we don't have to do this alone, either.

Easing Transitions

Parent confession time. In the past, when I have had to leave my son with a sitter, I would usually try to sneak out the door. I really thought this would be better for everyone. But it wasn't long before my son made the connection between the babysitter appearing and me disappearing. As soon as she would walk through the door: hysterics. It was time for a change, a change that involved building more time into our transitions. Now, instead of running out the door and leaving my son wondering what just happened, we have devised a routine that has minimized panic and capitalized on the activity we already enjoy doing together: reading. With our babysitter next to us, Michael and I curl up to read a favorite book. When I'm done, our sitter continues reading by choosing stories from the book basket. Less rushing means less fussing. Try implementing this three-part system and get going on your own transition routine.

- **Preparation** It's not enough to know what you want to do during transition time; you must have all of your materials in order. I keep our transitional read-aloud book on the kitchen shelf next to where I hang my keys. It has its own special area so I always know where it is. If you have to go in search of your materials, you will probably skip it.
- **Patience** Despite your best intentions, your child may still panic, knowing that you will be leaving soon. Keep calm and reassure your child that you understand this is hard; it's hard for you, too. At first you may only flip through the book, but eventually she will settle down to listen to a story. Don't give up and run out the door.

Quick Picks

Keep your Transition Time bag well stocked in the car. Things to have on hand: favorite read-aloud stories, a small snack, a drink, a comfort toy. Don't try to add another chore to your morning list; have these things set and ready to go the night before so they are ready for you when you are ready for them.

- **Persistence** Whether you read one book or one poem, decide what works best for you and stick with your routine. Don't read an extra story or start on a puzzle together because your child begs you to stay. This is not about avoiding that you have to leave, it's about making it as smooth as possible.

"Bye, Bye" Doesn't Mean Forever

Children love to wave "bye, bye" to grocery clerks, the mailman, and the bath toys, but saying goodbye to mom and dad is a whole different story. Since toddlers do not fully comprehend the concept of time, an afternoon away can feel like ages. Words like "later," "tonight," and "this weekend" do little to offer any comfort. Instead of trying to make your child understand your time frame, look for ways to use his routine to your advantage. You probably already appreciate a well-established evening routine with warm baths, books, and kisses goodnight; here is where homemade books can come to the rescue. The same concepts can help you get out the door without having to dry any tears, theirs or yours.

When I taught pre-school, we encouraged parents to send their children in with a family photo album. When loneliness struck, the child could go to the album and look at pictures of mom, dad, and kitty. Ideally, you can include pictures of you and your child doing a favorite activity, the two of you at your office, and so on. It is very helpful to have pictures of the family at breakfast, dinner, and bedtime as the caregiver can then narrate the homemade book and talk about the child's day. Talking about breakfast before school and looking forward to a bath after dinner can help a toddler put structure to her day. Knowing that her days have a routine, one that always include mom and dad, and being able to see and hear her story in a photo album, can be a lifesaver.

Quick Picks

Instead of saying "bye, bye" when you have to leave your child, use a special expression reserved for these transitional times. You might try, "I'll be back soon," "See you later, alligator," or "Here's a hug to hold until later." The words "bye, bye" could be triggering the anxiety. Use a different phrase and see if your child is not more settled.

Meaningful Milestones

Just because diplomas and wedding flowers are a million miles away doesn't mean that there aren't any milestones to celebrate along the way. There are many significant moments in our lives that we can celebrate as a family. When it comes to our children, we can address the negative emotions attached to new and intimidating situations by counterbalancing them with positive rituals. Change can be cause to celebrate when we use books to help put reading into action.

More than just pictures on the page, "crisis" stories are relevant to the circumstances at hand and show what happens when the transition is completed. Even as adults, our fear of what might happen is usually never as bad as what actually happens. The "it's never as bad as you think" mantra just happens to be a lot harder to communicate to children. Using a medium they have come to trust, like books, coupled with your own gentle, intuitive touch, can help you guide your toddler through some tough times.

Preparing for Potty Time

Next to, "How do you get him to sleep through the night?" I know of no conversation more popular on the playground than potty training. There are several different theories on how to approach this tender transition; but whether you follow grandma's advice or consult the latest expert recommendation, reading can help.

As I mentioned earlier, connecting reading to real life can help your child understand his world better. Going to the zoo? Check out a book from the library that talks about all the different kinds of zoo animals. Bring the book along to the zoo and look at the picture of the lion while standing in front of the lion cage. Later that night, reread the book and talk about what the lion was actually doing in real life and compare it to the information on the page. Makes sense, right?

The same concepts can be applied to potty training. I suggest browsing through a couple of titles and purchasing the book that you like best. Read the book together for a few days during your regular reading routine. Then move the book into your bathroom book basket and read it to your toddler while you use the bathroom. Take a moment to prop a stuffed animal on the potty and read to teddy. When the time is right and your child is sitting on the potty herself, read the book to her and compare the pages to her actual experience. This is not a theory on potty training (there are enough of those), but a theory on easing the transition from diapers to dry drawers.

Books help us learn how to do something new, like going potty. Here are a couple of popular potty-time titles to try reading aloud the next time you have a captured audience:

A Potty for Me: A Lift-the-Flap Instruction Manual, copyright © 2005 by Karen Katz

The main character could be either a girl or boy, making it a nice home edition if you have more than one child, and it includes having accidents, having anxiety, and then, having accomplishments.

My Big Boy Potty Lap Edition, copyright © 2006 by Joanna Cole and Maxie Chambliss, and *My Big Girl Potty Lap Edition*, copyright © 2006 by Joanna Cole and Maxie Chambliss

These two books share very similar storylines, but are gender specific. Throughout the story, everyone is smiling, regardless of accidents or accomplishments. The emphasis is an encouraging "You can do it!" without being pushy or scary.

Success Story

If you haven't already done so, put a book basket in your child's bathroom. Along with "potty tales," try some titles that will keep her engaged during her stay, increasing your chances of potty success while encouraging reading.

Everyone Poops (My Body Science Series), copyright © 2001 by Taro Gomi and Amanda Mayer Stinchecum

If potty training is starting to become the biggest, most upsetting part of your day, you are probably taking it too seriously. Try a silly pooping book like this to lighten the mood.

Pacifiers and Security Blankets

Many children find comfort with a pacifier, security blanket, favorite stuffed animal, or other familiar object, like a toothbrush (seriously). While there is absolutely nothing wrong with a security item, you may be approaching a time when the item has to be left behind due to changing circumstances, like starting daycare or because your dentist suspects a problem with the pacifier use. When a child has come to rely on an object for safekeeping, you can have a very tough time trying to break him from this inclination. Knowing that others have successfully surrendered their prize possessions can help ease the effects of this challenging transition.

A story like *Little Bunnies Pacifier Plan* by Maribeth Bolts and Kathy Parkinson focuses on stepping down pacifier time until it is no longer needed, but this plan could be used with any security item. Instead of having to go "cold turkey," children gradually wean themselves away from their comfort piece. I would not suggest hiding a pacifier or security blanket, or simply throwing it out, but would encourage you to find a plan that works best. Like any good plan, set clear expectations and time frames. Again, we cannot hope to make every transition a pleasant one, but rather, we can help our children by acknowledging that while life circumstances can be less than pleasant, they can be manageable.

Quick Picks

When it's time to say goodbye to a coveted possession, use a familiar song to help mark the transition. Sing the "Happy Birthday" song, but substitute the words with "No More (insert object)." Smiling and singing "No more pacifier right now," can help make the shift feel less overwhelming.

School Days

Whether you choose a daycare setting or opt for an education-focused environment, bringing your child to another location, dropping her off, and not returning for a substantial amount of time can be difficult for both of you. But you can still build a transitional routine into your morning. No one says you can't arrive at the daycare 5 minutes earlier and climb into the backseat to read a story together. This book can be counted on each morning, creating a few quiet minutes together before going in your separate directions.

You may also want to check on the daycare's "show and tell" policy. Bringing a favorite book from home to be shared with the class can be

Bookworms Beware

While having a moment in the parking lot together can be lovely, coming into the classroom for a lengthy goodbye is not always a good idea. In my experience, once you are with the caregiver in the classroom, a brief, routine "changing of the guard" seems to work best.

a nice way to reinforce your fondness for reading with your child's new friends. Daycare providers and preschool teachers want your son or daughter to enjoy themselves at their facility and are usually very accommodating to simple requests such as these.

One of my favorite books, *The Kissing Hand* by Audrey Penn, is an excellent story to share with your child, whether she is starting daycare or school. A young raccoon is hesitant to leave his mother, but she reassures him that he will have a wonderful time and offers up a family secret, a kissing hand, to keep him company while he's away. A word of caution parents: read this book with a box of Kleenex near by (for you).

A Formula That Fits

Using relevant picture books, both those that are published and the ones that you will create, can help your child cope with changes in her environment. These suggestions work best when you give yourself plenty of time to implement their use. Not only do you want to have time to talk about the book as you are reading it and reflect on it afterward, but you also want to give your child enough time to familiarize himself with the new stories before the actual event takes place. Giving your toddler a chance to "warm up" to these suggestions will make for a much more successful scenario.

When you reach the other side if this challenge, don't forget to commemorate these achievements! We often assume that birthdays, holidays, and popular milestones, like graduations, deserve a congratulatory cake; but taking time to celebrate new underwear, new classrooms, and new independence can be just as meaningful. You probably don't need to have the event catered, but marking the occasion, whether it is a full week of no accidents or several tear-free goodbyes at the classroom door, can go a long way in boosting family morale. After all, it takes a whole family pulling together to make many of these milestones happen. Why not celebrate together?

Shared Fears and Tears

When your child is suffering, so are you. There is not a parent among us who would not want to spare their children any harm and opt instead to take it all on themselves. But since this is not possible, we can talk to our children about our own fears and tears. Relating our own experiences, like starting a new school, and being honest about what we were feeling, can make these unfamiliar feelings of fright seem more normal. Try to always focus on what happened after the fear passed: making lots of friends, playing with new toys, getting to be in the school play. Don't gloss over your fears, but don't obsess over them either.

I know of some parents who think it's best to pretend that they are not scared of anything in hopes that they will raise brave children. But really, fear is a good thing. We want our children to be wary of new people, new situations, and new environments. This is an excellent defense mechanism that helps to keep us safe. What we don't want is for our children to be paralyzed with fear. A happy medium can be struck, one that relies on honesty and experience.

A good tool when relating your own story is a family photo album. Looking at pictures of mom and dad on their first day of school can help make the conversation more comprehensible. This tool is especially helpful if you have pictures of yourself enjoying activities you once feared. A class picture, with you smiling among your friends, with a teacher you came to adore, is a lovely way to help refocus your son or daughter on what they have to look forward to.

Success Story

If you don't have any pictures like the ones suggested, use pictures of your son or daughter instead. You may have pictures of them falling down when they learned to walk or spilling food as they learned to eat. Explain that there was a time, not too long ago, when these things seemed foreign and strange. But now, they are great walkers and eaters. Like anything else, practice helps makes us more comfortable and confident.

Being scared of the unknown is something no one can hide from. If you want to help convey that point, you can also try these not-so-scary stories that amuse and delight, while overcoming fright.

What Was I So Scared Of?, copyright © 1997 by Dr. Seuss

When a little boy stumbles upon a pair of empty pants, he is certain they are out to get him; and they are, but for reasons he never suspected.

Mouse's First Halloween, copyright © 2000 by Lauren Thompson and Buket Erdogan

All things that go bump in the night seem frightening until Mouse bravely discovers that nothing is that scary once you know what it is.

Brave Irene, copyright © 1986 by William Steig

When Irene's dressmaker mother becomes sick, it is up to Irene to deliver a much-needed package despite a terrible snowstorm. A great story about perseverance and courage in the face of danger.

"Just Like Me!"

No one likes to feel that he is the "only one." Relating to familiar faces can help children realize that their experience is not unusual or strange. More than that, it can help toddlers appreciate that lots of people get anxious, scared, or worry when they are about to do something new. Since toddlers don't have the ability to ask their "friends" what they are feeling, it is up to us as parents to take the initiative when it comes to soothing our children's fears. Instead of waiting for a total meltdown, then trying to quick fix the situation, assume that most youngsters will be reluctant to leave you, their security items, or their home. Some will do better than others, but all can benefit from a little extra attention.

Parents may hope that by not talking about uncomfortable situations they will be able to hide them. And some children do move from activity to activity with no sign of alarm. But at the very least, I would encourage you to have a couple of crisis-friendly books on hand in case there is a problem. That way, if trouble does begin to brew, you will have a child-friendly tool at the ready and not have to reach for an empty feel-good fix, like candy or a new toy.

When notable progress is being made with your toddler, try adding photos to the books you relied on during this transition. If you have been working on potty training, take a picture of your child on the potty, flushing, or wearing big-kid underwear. Paste the pictures inside your book and reread the text with these additional illustrations. Talking about the character's accomplishments, and your child's, is a great way to connect the book to her own experiences.

Homemade Books

Picture books that focus on giving up security items or starting school narrate the progress of the event: fear, trepidation, involvement, acclimation, accomplishment, excitement. We respond well to stories that capture the many facets of fearful events. We are especially grateful when things work out, when we, along with the characters, can breathe a sigh of relief. Because children's memories can be unreliable, formatting your own journey books can celebrate your accomplishments and become a valuable reference tool when the next challenge approaches.

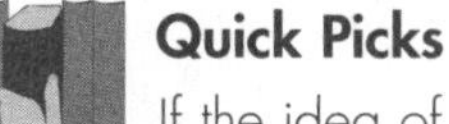

Quick Picks

If the idea of putting together a homemade book sounds too time-consuming, post the pictures on your refrigerator using magnetic frames. Write a couple of quick sentences, tape them to the front of the picture, insert a magnet holder inside, and point them out to your child as you make meals.

Let's say it's time to surrender the security blanket during the day and only use it at bedtime. You could take a picture of your daughter's blanket, pictures of her playing with her toys, eating and bathing without her blanket, and then a picture of her going to bed with her blanket. Slide the photos into a mini album and write simple sentences to accompany the photos. You could try the following idea: Photo of blanket: "This is Sally's blanket." Photo of Sally playing: "This is Sally playing. No blanket." Photo of Sally going to bed: "This is Sally going to bed. Time for blanket!" The finished product should be short and sweet, making it more likely that this visual project will get done.

Just because our children are little doesn't mean that their problems feel that way. Reading is not only a source of joy and pleasure, it is also a tool to help get us there when circumstances detour us from our regular path. Stories that help us find our way are a valuable resource to our reading routine.

The Least You Need to Know

- Toddler's troubles should be taken seriously. Visual aids and simple sentences can help you both pinpoint the issue and address it lovingly.
- Proactive parenting focuses on progress, not perfection. Be sure to keep your eye on the big picture and not throw in the towel when you hit a snag.
- There is a satisfying reading solution for just about any obstacle; and if a book doesn't exist, make your own!

Chapter 8

Simple Solutions for Restless Readers

In This Chapter

- Reading rules are meant to be broken
- Proactive plans and innovative ideas
- Help outside of your hands

It happens without warning. The wind stirs, the air feels different, the hairs on the back of your neck stand up. You know you are helpless against its powerful force. It's your toddler's personality: it's here. Once content to follow in your footsteps and play along with your preferences, your rapidly developing toddler is part infant, part big kid, all emotion. Trying to keep up with your fiercely dependent but self-determined child can keep you constantly guessing, "What is it that you want?"

Toddlers are not trying to make us crazy, they are just trying to make sense of their world; unfortunately, this tends to drive us crazy. Tactics that worked for us yesterday may miss the mark today. This means constantly being on the lookout for new strategies, while staying grounded in our own values. Your reading routine is not exempt from these growing pains. Your once-enamored storytime companion could all of the sudden appear cool and aloof. But don't lose heart (or hope!). A tweak here, a turn there, and you can be right back on the reading track.

He Won't Sit Still!

The world is an increasingly exciting place to your toddler. Everyday is a new adventure filled with bright colors, shiny objects, drawers to open, and cabinets to close. With all of this exploring to do, who wants to sit still? Certainly not your active little learner. Of course we want to encourage our toddlers to play, but we also want them to read. Luckily, you can strategically combine these two activities.

Even if you create a warm and comfortable reading atmosphere, set aside routine times free from distractions, and have several engaging, age-appropriate titles on hand, you may still find that there are times where your toddler wants nothing to do with reading. These phases can last anywhere from a couple of days to a couple of weeks, but you do not have to fear that your reading rituals are failing. Most likely, your children will come around on their own. Until then, you can make minor adjustments in your reading routine without having to abandon your plans. Let's look at ways to entice your toddler back to books, without tears or tantrums.

Break the Reading Rules

As parents, we have certain expectations of how our children's routines should work. At meal time, we expect them to sit in a chair, not walk around the house grazing. At bedtime, we expect them to lie down and relax, not jump and climb in their cribs. At reading time, we expect them to sit with us and snuggle in for a story. But restless children do not make for serene storytime situations. It could be time to rearrange your reading room.

If you have a favorite loveseat you usually sit on, but your daughter is refusing to climb into your lap like she used to, try getting onto the floor and propping a few books up on the couch. Kneeling next to her, open the books to some of her favorite illustrations and talk about the pictures. She may hand you a book—a sign she would like you to read it—or enjoy just looking at the pictures. Stack the books, line them up, or use them to make a tunnel for her toy cars to drive through. Using books in this way can help to reignite the idea that books are fun. Looking at books from a fresh perspective, literally, can help to spark a renewed interest in reading.

Rework the Routine

When it comes to toddlers, routines are never that routine for very long. Just think about how many times your child's sleep habits have changes since you first brought him home. It seems like as soon as we start to schedule our days according to our son's nap schedule, he decides it's time for a change. The same can be said for his eating, playing, and reading preferences. We have finally learned to go with the flow; if something is not working, be it for a day or a week, we adjust, without having to abandon, our routines.

Quick Picks

Since our kids can't tell us what is wrong, it is difficult to know if they are restless because they don't like the book, are teething, or have an upset stomach. Don't take reading rejection personally; address the unusual cranky behavior and try again tomorrow.

An evening bath can last anywhere from 5 to 25 minutes. Lunch can be a couple of bites or a couple of bowls full. Instead of watching the clock, watch your child. If you are used to reading for a considerable stretch of time in the morning, but your daughter is more interested in going outside, go. Take a couple of books with you and head for the playground. Having worked off her excess energy, offer to read a book when she stops for a cup of juice. Tomorrow, resume your regularly scheduled reading program and see how receptive your little listener is. You may find that her inclination to read has returned, or you may see that a lengthy morning storytime is no longer appealing, and opt to extend your bedtime book rituals. As long as books remain accessible and you continue to make yourself available for read-alouds, you will find time to read.

Wordless Books

An often-overlooked storytime solution is wordless books. Our expectations may dictate that reading must involve words for it to "count" as reading; but when it comes to how books work, there is more to learn than just the words on the page. We can use wordless books to reinforce that stories have a beginning and end, pages turn from front to back, and illustrations have a purpose. These are all valuable lessons that do not require written text, just your narration.

The thing I like most about wordless books is the pace at which we enjoy them. When I "read" these stories, I tend to slow down, giving us a chance to note the details of each picture and really digest the images. Instead of rushing to find out what happens next, I am more prone to watch for what my son finds intriguing and respond to what he points at. The text is no longer in charge; his natural curiosity is. Allowing our children to set the pace of our shared time and articulate their interests is not just a good read-aloud practice, but a good parenting practice. Here are two to try:

Black on White, copyright © 1993 by Tana Hoban

Simple black illustrations on white backgrounds are easily recognizable and the familiar objects will be fun for the two of you to name together. *White on Black* is also available from the same illustrator.

Changes, Changes, copyright © 1987 by Pat Hutchins

A wooden couple lives in their block house until it catches fire. Then they must use their wooden blocks to make a fire engine, then a boat, and then a truck, and eventually a new home. This is an excellent inspiration for playing while you read.

Success Story

Instead of trying to separate your children from their toys, try keeping a couple of small, quiet toys on the sacred shelf. Having something special to hold can help reduce fidgeting and increase concentration.

Should I Force Him to Read?

As any parent of a toddler is quick to find out, it is quite difficult to "force" your toddler to do anything. This is a challenging age for every parent, evident in the overwhelming number of self-help books geared toward moms and dads who are trying to make heads or tails of the block-building beast that is their offspring.

As I just mentioned, a lull in your child's reading enthusiasm is probably just a phase that shouldn't be fretted over too much. So if there are a few days when your routine is not well received, remain available and upbeat, and ride it out. Check your own approach to reading and make sure you are coming to the table optimistically. Children tend to adopt our emotions; if our attitudes are apathetic or our approach disengaged, our toddlers will respond with restless behavior. On the other hand, if things still look bleak, despite your best efforts to keep things on track, you can try some of the following suggestions. Remind yourself that you are not "forcing" your child to do something, a concept many parents are uncomfortable with, but rather, you are requiring that your son or daughter respect the values of your home. And one of those values is reading.

Threats Ruin Reading

A close second to bribery is threats. Threats are usually made after you have already lost your patience, after your buttons have been pushed, after a long day that only seems to be getting longer. It is not so much the threat that is the problem, but the timing: "after." During a meltdown, both child and parent lose rationale. When we couple threats with an unrelated or delayed punishment, we do little to foster the reading relationship. Consider this popular comment, "Fine. You don't want to hear your book. You are going to bed right now and no TV/trucks/playdough tomorrow."

I know this kind of frustration. I have made this threat only to find that absolutely no impact was made. While my tone and body-language let my son know I was upset, he had no idea what I was upset about and even less of an idea what "tomorrow" meant. He went to bed confused, I left guilt-ridden, and the next day came and went without playdough, but since he never asked for it, how much of a punishment was it anyway? (And what

Bookworms Beware

Incentives only work if you are realistic and consistent. Don't set the bar so high that your child never meets the goals, and always reward the experience in a timely fashion to help reinforce reading.

in the world does playdough, or TV, or trucks have to do with reading anyway?)

We all lose our patience with our kids; there is no denying that. But setting yourself up for success with incentives really can make a difference in your reading-routine outcome.

Monitor Materials

When I am restless, it is usually because I am bored and need a change. Things that I usually love seem to annoy or frustrate me, and I do well to get out of my rut and take a look at something new. While repetition and routine are usually a comfort to kids, introducing a new piece to your puzzle might be a welcomed twist to a tried-and-true template. The key is to think small and succinct, not big and bold.

For example, I have a favorite quiche recipe that I always make with broccoli and gruyère cheese. But I wanted to freshen it up a bit, so I tried kale and asiago cheese. Delicious! The basic recipe stayed the same, but a couple of substitutes gave it a quick kick. In the same way, bringing in a new story or blowing some bubbles when you've finished, or reading by flashlight can give your reading routines a new flavor. You don't need to revamp the whole recipe, just play around with the ingredients.

Bookworms Beware

Regardless of the crime, never use reading as a punishment. Sending a child to his room to read because he has misbehaved makes as much sense as giving him caffeine because he can't sleep. Reading is a pleasure, never a punishment.

Find Your Own Way

As you were reading this section, you may have been thinking: "How long should I depend on an incentive chart?" "But I want my son to read just for reading's sake, not for a reward," or, "Maybe some kids are just not good readers? Can't we try this at another time?" When our kids don't seem to be acting in the manner we expect, we can become very unsure of what our next move should be, and all advice can seem suspect. Assuming that we have already made mistakes (why else would this be happening?) we are reluctant to try something new, lest we make matters worse. Ah, parent guilt; the gift that keeps on giving us grief.

Success Story

Remember to reward yourself for your own efforts along the way. Take 5 minutes to read that new novel you have been looking forward to, splurge on a new bookmark, or subscribe to a popular magazine you enjoy. Nurture yourself while you care for the kids and you'll be more likely to see the solutions.

I encourage you to trust your own instincts. There is no one way to raise, or ruin, your child. Whatever you choose to do, whether it is ride out the resistance or rearrange parts of your routine, remember that you can always change direction again. Try something else, and if you need to, try something else, again. Nothing needs to be permanent. Incentives are bridges, not band aids, which can help your children connect to reading for the intrinsic reward of enjoying a good story. When they get where they are going, you'll know; and you can then decide if the incentives are still needed or not.

When Should I Start Formal Instruction?

You already have. Formal instruction is a fancy term for focused attention given by an experienced mentor to a novice. As parents, we already have begun to "teach" our children how to read, just by being present and active in their lives.

Before we can learn to read and write, we must hear language spoken. All language learners imitate the sounds of the words they hear long before they actually understand what the words mean. So the more we speak to our children, the more exposure we give them to these sounds. Which means, the more we read aloud to our children, the more exposure we give them to the way oral and written language work together—words on the page represent the words that are being spoken. These are the necessary components in building pre-reading skills, because if you never hear a language, you will never be able to read it. Therefore, it makes sense to believe that the more we read with our children, the more literate they will become in their native language, making them better readers.

When it comes to learning to read, being read to is formal instruction. But because the advertising community is a powerful medium, let's take a closer look at why tools designed to give our children a reading advantage are not necessary.

Step Away from the Flashcards

I once had a library patron ask me for a book that listed important historical dates. When I asked her for what purpose, so I could better assist her, she explained that she wanted her daughter to get ahead in school by memorizing all the dates she will need to know, because, "I heard kid's brains are like sponges." Her daughter was 4.

Yes, children's brains are like sponges, able to suck up a ton of information. So shouldn't we be making sure that information is relevant? Dates are arbitrary to 4-year-olds; if you want proof, just ask them when their own birthday is. Letters and words on a flashcard are also random and disorganized unless we connect them to a bigger picture.

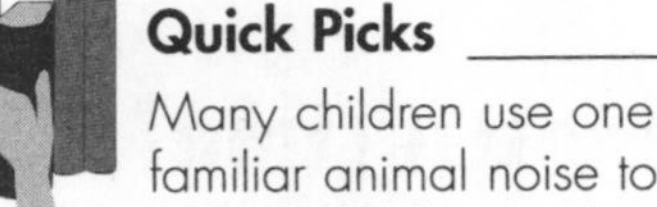

Quick Picks

Many children use one familiar animal noise to represents all animals while they learn to process the differences. Although it may be adorable that your toddler says "meow" when she sees a duck in her book, always model the correct sound, just as you would model the correct pronunciation of a word.

Children can memorize a deck of cards with various words, no doubt. But will that same child recognize those words in a different context? This is a basic component in comprehension: understanding that "dog" in *Go, Dog, Go* is the same "dog" in *Clifford the Big Red Dog.* Just like a picture of a cow in different books will cause your child to make the same "moo" sound, the same words appearing in different texts will be recognized.

Even if I could be convinced that flashcards could "teach" vocabulary (which I do not believe), the most important reading element would be missing: pleasure. Who is staying up late at night because they just have to know what happens on the next flashcard? When you have a literacy-rich home filled with age-appropriate, high-interest story books, there is no reason for flashcards. You will already be providing the essential oral and written repetition necessary to recognize words. And, best of all, a cozy lap.

Real Time Reading

As soon as you find out you will be welcoming a baby into your home, you are inundated with information regarding that child's future. Naturally, education becomes a top priority for most parents almost immediately. And I'm not just talking about college entrance exams; I'm talking about preschool entrance exams. Our hurry to hurdle our children to the head of the class has reached a fevered pitch. Many parents have convinced themselves that family reading routines and rituals are just not going to cut it. They want reading results, right now.

Well, the problem with results is that it takes a while before they are revealed. You will read to your children for a very long time before they read to you. But there is no reason, and no necessity, to panic over this process. Reading skills develop in their own time. As I explained, first we hear language, then we speak it, then we read it, then we write it. If your little learner is straying from your expectations, consider it a mere step in the process and adjust your expectations so that you may go with the flow a bit more easily. There are several uphill battles you will fight when raising your children; reading doesn't have to be one of them.

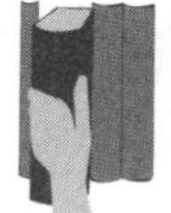

Quick Picks

Happy hands are dirty hands. Give your children lots of chances to get their hands into sand, water, flour, dirt, and mud. Squishing, squashing, molding, and mashing are cheap, easy ways to develop hand strength.

Reading Is Not a Spectator Sport

When children are engaged in an activity, they lose track of time. They become focused, intent, and engaged, usually because they are in control of the action: building and knocking down blocks, savoring a self-fed meal, rearranging their stuffed animals just so. When we read to our children, we can sometimes lose track of our audience's needs. We flip through the pages too quickly, anxious to get that last load of laundry folded. We hold the book in front of our eyes, making it difficult for our children to follow. We comment on what interests us, but forget to leave time for our toddlers to talk.

The following suggestions can help you encourage your child to take a more active role in your read-alouds. Sometimes that means sharing reading responsibilities, sometimes it means facilitating an experience with books, and sometimes it even means leaving your child alone to find her own way. In all instances, we strive to put the child first so that he may own the experience, instead of merely watching it.

Audience Participation

You can take the teacher out of the classroom, but you can't take the classroom out of the teacher. I am so used to "running the reading show" that I would choose two or three board books to read with my son before bedtime, sit him on the loveseat next to me, and then hold the books as I read them in the order I preferred. It wasn't long before my son was distracted, and discouraged, after half a book. And who could blame him? I had made all the choices. Whose experience was this anyway?

> **Quick Picks**
>
> Inspiration can come from unlikely sources. Even though you and your neighbor might have totally different approaches to raising children, she may have a trick up her sleeve you hadn't considered. Keep your eyes and ears open and you just might find the answer you were looking for.

Then my husband, a mortgage consultant who thinks all great literature should start with, "There once was a man from Nantucket," clued me into their routine. Dad sits on the couch and tells Michael to go get the books (from the book basket) that he wants to read. Sometimes he brings two, sometimes ten. Michael piles the books onto the couch, raises his arms to be lifted up, and then spends a few minutes spreading out his choices and looking them over. Michael flips through a book that looks good and then when he is ready, hands it to dad to be read. Whose reading routine would you rather be a part of?

This is a perfect example of overthinking read-alouds. Because of my background, I wanted to get it just right. Instead, I took over and alienated the one person I was trying the most to include. If your child shows signs that this reading routine isn't working, give her a chance to tell you what she wants. Give her a more active role in your rituals and you'll be likely to bring her around. There is great pleasure derived from having a purpose.

Book Nooks

Too much of a good thing is not a good thing. Giving your children your attention: good. Giving your children all of your attention, all of the time: not so good. Enjoying your own company is a wonderful asset, and is one that you have to give your children the time to develop on their own. As you are trying to figure out the best routine time to read with your child, you may end up coming on a bit strong. When your reader seems more restless than usual, give yourselves a little book breathing room while encouraging independent play.

We have mentioned book baskets numerous times already, but we haven't yet talked about putting your child in the basket, so to speak. You can create an inviting book nook that is kid-friendly by turning a play tent, sheet fort, or toy wagon into a reading retreat. We have an outdoor sun-shade tent for the summers, which doubles as a great little library in the winter months. Free from prying eyes, little readers can come and go as they please. More than just a reading corner, these purposeful play areas invite little ones to stop by for a relaxing read.

Success Story

If the library's story-time conflicts with your schedule, consider hosting a book playdate. Ask two or three other parents to bring their toddlers, and two books, to your home for playtime. Take turns reading each other's books and arrange to swap some of your tried-and-true titles for another family's favorites.

The sooner we start a regular reading routine with our children, the easier it will be; but that doesn't mean that our read-alouds will always go off without a hitch. Even the most enthusiastic readers can lose interest in a favorite family activity. Take a deep breath, take a step back and find your footing; detours don't have to mean disaster.

The Least You Need to Know

- Adjust your routine, not your values. This will help your reader to learn that books are an integral part of her day, regardless of the type of day it is.
- You cannot rush a reader, you can only go as fast as the learner wants to go. Try celebrating personal milestones instead of being distracted by expert advice.
- Don't super-size your solutions. Look to other sources—partners, neighbors, and your own children—for simple tips on getting back on track.

Chapter 9

Twenty Great Titles to Try Together

In This Chapter

- Putting principles into practice
- Do what you like, like what you do
- Stories to get you started

We have talked so much about what to do and how to do it, it is finally time to talk about what titles you should use to help accomplish your family reading goals. The books listed here offer something for everyone; whether you are more comfortable trying an award-winning expert's recommendation or want a book that has been proven to work with real kids, I have a suggestion for you.

This is not, however, a required reading list. Remember, there are no requirements in building a literacy-rich home, just recommendations. Pick and choose the topics that sound appealing to you and your children, and start with those. If you strike out, don't panic. These recommendations are not the one and only quintessential read-aloud titles (no such list exists), but they are a sampling of high-interest, family-friendly stories that are engaging, colorful, and rhythmically pleasing. They worked for others, and they may work for you.

Trying to narrow down the great list of read-alouds available is like trying to name your one favorite ride at Disney World. Not an easy task. In the interest of time and space, books that have been suggested elsewhere are not repeated in this chapter. So while I love Eric Carle and Sandra Boynton, I wanted to use different titles here. Luckily, you can find more recommendations at the index in the back of the book, where a compiled list of all of the titles we have talked about is available, along with even more titles to try together.

Keep at It

At the beginning of this book, I cautioned against trying to tackle all the ideas in this book at once. The same slow and steady process can also be applied to building your home library. You probably already have some, if not many, books at home. If you start comparing your stories to the titles listed here, only to find that there is no crossover, do not discard your collection, and do not go out and buy every book I mention!

Any of the hands-on ideas we talked about in the previous chapters can be used with any book you already own. Dramatic voice changes, taking turns holding the book, quiet corners, and animated actions can be applied to any book. Use this list for fill-in or supplemental materials if you already have an extensive collection, and make good use of your local library if you are just getting started.

The important thing is to go with the ebb and flow of your family's reactions. When something works, build on it; and when something flops, change direction. There are plenty of different ways to get where we want to go.

Bookworms Beware

If you have children who are different ages, be aware that there is both crossover and time-sensitive material to be covered. Save time and money by reading the sections that affect your family.

You're on Your Way

We have learned a little bit about language development, discussed in detail the benefits of reading aloud, and come up with several strategies for making reading routines and spontaneous storytimes more appealing and interactive to our children. I hope that you are becoming more and more excited about reading with your children and less intimidated about tackling this important experience with your children. If you find yourself getting anxious or overwhelmed, remember that our goal is not to teach our children to read, but to help our children become readers for life. Today, look at taking one small step in this direction and reward yourself for your efforts. Don't worry about the reading finish line; reading together is not a sprint, it is a marathon. And we are just warming up.

Apply the Pleasure Principle

The more we like what we are doing, the more we are going to want to do it. This applies to both you and your children. If you have a bad back and cannot sit on the floor for extended periods of time, don't set up a reading corner on the linoleum. Reading together should never be painful, neither physically or mentally. Choose a space that is warm and inviting, make sure all parties present are well fed and not cranky, and limit any distractions. Setting yourself up for success goes a long way in getting your reading routine off on the right foot.

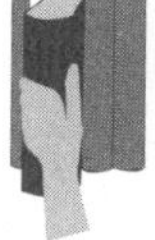

Quick Picks

Wherever you have books stashed—car, diaper bag, purse—always keep a small snack with it. A story and a snack can help get you through traffic jams and long lines without a meltdown (yours or theirs).

And if your routine seems to feel a bit forced or awkward at times, remember that there are plenty of opportunities throughout your day to sneak in a story or draw on your real-life reading materials. You are the expert. Trust your instincts, try some suggestions, and enjoy the process. A literacy-rich home is not built in a day, so you may as well have fun along the way.

A Look Back: Five Timeless Tales

The five titles that are recommended in this section are a sampling of great beginner books that many of us probably enjoyed when we were younger. I shy away from using the word "classic" because I think we have come to associate the term with mid-terms. I prefer "timeless"—a story that stretches across generations because it has tapped into some universal truth. When it comes to the diaper-wearing community, these truths are usually most poignantly felt by the reader of the story who connects to the book and wants to help facilitate that connection for the child.

Success Story

Some authors are just too good and too prolific to pin down to a single title. One such author is Dr. Seuss. From *Green Eggs and Ham* to *The Lorax,* his timeless tales are smart, sassy, and satisfying. A great place to start: the "Bright and Early Board Book" versions of many of his classics.

It is interesting to think about what characteristics make a tale timeless. With all of the new picture books on the market, and an increasing number of alternative entertainment methods available, stories with staying-power need more than a cute character and a catchy title. This does not mean that we have to read hefty books with dense narration; it simply means that we recognize some common denominator—be it humor, love, friendship, or problem-solving—that makes us feel as if someone else gets what we are going through. Board books like these are the ones that are kept in keepsake boxes and presented to future generations with hopes of continuing a much-loved read-aloud tradition.

The Little Mouse, The Red Ripe Strawberry, and the Big Hungry Bear, copyright © 1982 Don Wood, Audrey Wood

This clever tale of a mouse who must protect his precious strawberry from a hungry bear uses sparse texts and elaborate illustrations to convey its priceless humor. Any time a strawberry is disguised with glasses and a nose, you know you are in for a treat! The real message of sharing is subtle yet effective, making it a story that can be enjoyed over and over again.

Pat the Bunny, copyright © 1940 by Dorothy Kunhardt

Since it was first published in 1940, Amazon.com reports that *Pat the Bunny* has sold over six million copies. One of the first of its kind, this "touch-and-feel" board book invites little hands to explore the pages with tempting smells, things to move, and things to find. Simple, sweet, and soothing, this book begs to be held, making it a great gift to give to your restless reader.

The Snowy Day, copyright © 1962 Ezra Jack Keats

This book won the prestigious Caldecott Medal, but I chose to list it in the timeless section because the story is so simple, eloquent, and yet completely predictable, that you are just as likely to choose it for its familiarity as for its fame. One of the first picture books to have a black child as main character, Peter awakens in his city home to find his neighborhood has been blanketed in snow. Donning is red snowsuit, he heads outside to explore the magical powder. What he does, your kids will do, making it a story that helps connect reading to real-life enjoyment.

Pancakes for Breakfast, copyright © 1978 Tommy dePaola

This wordless picture book is not available as a board book, but could be a great first addition to your Special Shelf. Awakening one cold winter morning with thoughts of delicious pancakes, a kindly older woman sets out to make herself breakfast only to find it is not as easy as she thought. Humorous pictures invite even the most reluctant story teller to narrate the action. This book would make a great weekend morning read, which would have to be topped off with a pancake breakfast, of course.

Are You My Mother?, copyright © 1960 P. D. Eastman

Now available in board-book or cloth-book editions, this is one of the first books I ever remember reading as a child. When a young bird falls out of her nest, she goes in search of her mother, and instead finds cows, planes, and steam shovels, among other things, but no mother. When the two are finally united, it is a moment of pure joy for characters and readers. The repetitive text and simple illustrations help tackle separation anxiety in a gentle and reassuring manner, making it a lovely book to have on hand if your routine includes saying goodbye to your little ones each morning. It's comforting to know that mommies come back.

Hot Off the Press: Five New and Improved Tales

Over the past 10 years there has been a dramatic movement in the field of children's publishing. Picture books are more exciting than ever, with illustrations that can rival great works of art, both elaborate and minimalist, and weave stories with rhythm, rhyme, or repetition so pleasing to the ear, you forget that you are reading children's books.

Not only have there been great advances in the aesthetics, there has also been a shift in the spectrum that the actual stories can cover. From interracial families to nursing, children's books now feature a host of new storylines, while still remaining true to the subjects we love to see time and again, like goodnight kisses and counting fingers and toes. The selections recommended here are only a sampling of the great picture books that have recently become available, but they have already garnered an enthusiastic following.

Quick Picks

Great new titles are coming out all of the time. Sign up for newsletters at the major book chains like Barnes and Noble and Borders and enjoy new release updates and coupons sent right to your e-mail.

Time for Bed, copyright © 1997 Mem Fox

This is a well-read bedtime book in our house. Not only are the rhyming couplets simple and sweet, but the muted watercolor illustrations, depicting different animal parents bidding their babies goodnight, can help lull even the most unwilling snoozer to sleep. After we read this book from cover to cover, we go back and say goodnight to each of the animals in their own language: "Baa, Baa, goodnight sheep." This story can easily be worked into your bedtime routine, especially since the last page depicts a mother saying goodnight to her own child—the perfect exit strategy for you to emulate.

My First Taggies Book, copyright © 2003 by Kaori Wantanabe

There are currently two titles available in this series: *I Love You* and *Sweet Dreams*. Each super-soft cloth book has six sentences and three pages. But the warm pastel colors, super-simple format, and tagged edges make it a wonderful book to keep in the diaper bag or attach to your stroller. These books make great gifts to give to new parents, as they can be among the first books a baby learns to call her own.

Where Is Baby's Belly Button?, copyright © 2000 Karen Katz

This lift-the-flap book is a great interactive choice for toddlers and is also published in Spanish. Each page asks, "Where is baby's (body part)?" and inviting illustrations encourage little hands to look for the answer. When sitting still just doesn't seem to be working, stories like these can be a much-needed reprieve for both parent and child. Of course, you will most love helping your baby find his own nose and toes, making this book a great look-and-learn tool.

We Have a Baby, copyright © 1999 Cathryn Falwell

There are several books on the market that deal with bringing home a new baby, but this story has a few unique characteristics: it is not about sibling rivalry, but sibling love; the multiracial family is not defined as one culture, but could be any culture; and co-sleeping and breastfeeding are embraced as part of the family's practices. A paperback picture book, this choice could be another welcome addition to your special shelf, especially as your due date approaches.

Where's Spot? (Little Spot Board Books), copyright © 2003 Eric Hill

You absolutely cannot go wrong with any of the Spot books. This one features a lift-the-flap search for Spot, but all of the titles in this beloved series are beautifully executed. The illustrations are always crisp and clear, and the text is printed in a bold, black font, making it easy to follow along. If you feel more comfortable with books that have focused vocabulary, this series would make a great addition to your collection.

Playground Picks: Five Mom-Approved Titles

When it comes to knowing what actually works, I always try to go to the source. When the subject is great books that work with babies, other mothers are an invaluable resource. Beyond the award-winning lists and expert-approved titles are the recommendations that come from the trenches. When soliciting playground picks, I was most excited to find titles that are a bit off the beaten path.

While there could be crossover between what you find on a list like this and what you find selling out at the bookstore, these stories are suggested because they are really working with real kids.

Goodnight Gorilla, copyright © 1996 Peggy Rathman

A zookeeper is busy making his evening rounds and does not realize that the mischievous gorilla has borrowed his keys and freed the other animals, until a hilarious "lights out" moment at home in bed reveals the presence of his zoo friends. Readers will relate to the zoo animals all having stuffed animal toys in their cages to keep them company and their resistance to go to bed. A funny story to use whenever you must say goodnight.

Success Story

Want to get a hold of new books without having to buy them? Try a playgroup book swap. Write your child's name on the inside covers of his book and trade it with a friend's. You can enjoy a rotating inventory while seeing what is working for other moms.

I Love You as Much, copyright © 1998 Laura Krauss Melmed, Henri Sorensen

This soothing lullaby may feel similar to *Time for Bed*, but *I Love You as Much* highlights the love shared between a mother and child, regardless of the time of day. While the book ends with a goodnight, it really could be enjoyed anytime of day when you need to take it down a notch. The singsong rhythm set against muted watercolor illustrations begs to be read slowly and softly. This book would do well in the bedroom to help induce sleep, or in a high-traffic area, like the kitchen, where it can help make more peaceful transitions between activities.

Chicka, Chicka Boom Boom, copyright © 1989 Bill Martin, Jr., John Archambault

This could arguably be one of the funniest books around right now. When 26 adventurous lower-case letters all boldly make their way up the coconut tree, chaos soon ensues and they all come tumbling down. The board-book version ends here, but the original publication includes help from the capital (parental) letters. This simple story has great sound-effects, making it a joy to read aloud. Plus, you get the added benefit of reciting the alphabet in a whole new engaging way.

Owl Babies, copyright © 1992 Martin Waddell

This beautifully illustrated book features three baby owl siblings who awaken to find their mother has left the nest. Worried that something bad has happened, the oldest owl tries to console his siblings until mom returns safe and sound. As this book takes place during the night, it looks and feels different from other animal-themed board books. It is a nice story for reassuring children of all ages that just because a parent is gone, doesn't mean that she won't come back; this could be a nice book to use before heading off to work.

Breastmilk Makes My Tummy Yummy, copyright © 1999 Cecilia Moen

This book is included for a very specific reason: it shows realistic, unabashed nursing scenes. The pictures and the rhyming verse are good, but what sold me was having a board book that your nursing child could look at independently and relate her own experience to. Many nursing families have shared that they appreciate seeing breastfeeding depicted as a natural, not embarrassing, event and were impressed that the illustrations included older nursing toddlers.

Award Winners: Five Critically Acclaimed Books

According the American Library Association, "The Caldecott Medal was named in honor of nineteenth-century English illustrator Randolph Caldecott. It is awarded annually by the Association for Library Service to Children, a division of the American Library Association, to the artist of the most distinguished American picture book for children." Since 1938, artists have received the recognition they deserve for helping to make the world of children's literature more exciting and engaging through beautifully crafted illustrations.

Bookworms Beware

Remember, the emphasis of the Caldecott Medal is on illustrations, not content. Make sure you pre-read any medal winners for their read-aloud appeal before adding them to your collection.

Recipients of this coveted award may be recognized as either medal winners or honor books. While medal books are considered the category's winner, honor books are just as prestigious. The Caldecott is the Oscar of children's books. The books listed here are not only pleasing to the eye, but also a treat for your ears, making them wonderful additions to your read-aloud routine.

Ten, Nine, Eight, copyright © 1983 Molly Bang

This honored book has a couple of key components that make it an adorable, not overdone, read. First, the lullaby-like verse counts down to bedtime, which is reminiscent of *Goodnight Moon*, without being repetitive. A young African American girl is being tucked into bed by her adoring father, a character combination that can be harder to find. The illustrations are warm and inviting, and the text, all 70 odd words of it, is warm and inviting, just like her bed. This story could be a nice choice for daddy's bedtime reading routine. Spanish edition available.

Freight Train, copyright © 1978 Donald Crews

This is one of the most beautifully illustrated picture books I have ever seen. I remember using this book for a train-themed toddler storytime and the kids were captivated. The bold colors of this train give each individual car its rightful place, and when the train moves fast, the colors blend together to illustrate speed. A perfect read-aloud choice as your child will love choosing his favorite-colored car, making train sounds, and following the tracks to the end of the book. Spanish edition available.

"More, More, More," Said the Baby: Three Love Stories, copyright © 1996 Vera B. Williams

The sub-title, *Three Love Stories*, gives you an excellent idea of what this book is about. Three very similar tales are told about babies and their caregivers, who all love each other dearly and differently. The text should be read a few times through before being introduced to your audience, so that you can best emphasize the fun and joy of each little love story. Each pair depicts multiracial or minority families, doing what all families all over the world want to do: love their children.

The Red Book, copyright © 2004 Barbara Lehman, Caldecott Honor Book

This wordless book within a book invites audiences to travel within a magical red storybook found by a little girl with a vivid imagination. There are many layers to this book, and young listeners may miss many of the subtle nuances, but that only means that this story can be enjoyed for many more years to come. A perfect example of how smart and sophisticated picture books have become.

In the Small, Small Pond, copyright © 1998 Denise Fleming

Short, succinct rhymes chronicle the discovery of a pond and all its inhabitants from a frog's point of view, as seen by an Asian child. There is such playful language in this book that you and your children will love imitating the sounds of a pond while receiving a basic introduction to its ecological functions.

Consider these recommendations a blueprint for building your literacy-rich home. These suggestions can be used to help set the foundation for your family, but it is your personal touches that make your reading routines your own. Decorate your read-aloud nursery with the stories and strategies that work best for you and your little audience.

The Least You Need to Know

- Reading together can be a joyful journey when you search out titles and topics that are entertaining and engaging for all participants.
- Recommendations come in all shapes and sizes; just keep in mind that what works for others might not work for your child and that is perfectly fine. There are plenty of titles to choose from.
- Family literacy happens one story at a time; try being fully engaged in your reading routine without fretting over what comes next.

Part 3

I Think I Can, I Think I Can: Encouraging Emergent Readers

If your emergent reader has one mantra you are sure to hear over and over again, it's "I want to do it by myself!" These self proclaimed big kids have no interest in being treated like babies and will often, painstakingly, make you wait while they negotiate a zipper, put the toys back the "right" way and get themselves ready for bed.

In the same vein, children who are learning to read can often become frustrated with not being able to do so fast enough. They will pretend to read instead of ask for help, say they don't like a book when really it is just too challenging or insist that they are reading the words, even though it is clear they are making up an imaginary story as they turn the pages. For parents whose patience runs thin, this can be a trying time.

In this part, we'll take a look at how we can encourage our emergent readers to become active participants in the reading process with age appropriate materials and engaging activities that are fun, not frustrating … for anyone.

Chapter 10

Little Learners and Written Language

In This Chapter

- Big changes for little learners
- What to expect when you're expecting a reader
- Words, words, words, and some pictures

Your little learner is quickly becoming an independent force to be reckoned with. Preschoolers through first-grade-aged children will learn everything from how to dress themselves, to pedaling a tricycle, to reading and writing their own name, to "decoding" (figuring out) new words. With an increasingly dependent memory, children will recite nursery rhymes, ask "why" (at least 100 times a day), count, follow simple directions, and be eligible to take on more responsibilities, including "working" for an allowance. With such milestones being met, it makes sense to take a look at your reading routine and see what can be done to encourage even more cognitive connections.

While one word used to represent an entire sentence, soon your preschooler will begin using complete sentences to convey meaning, and then grow into a primary-school speaker who can ask questions, bargain, rationalize, and remember every single promise you have ever made (especially when it involves his upcoming birthday.) This is a great time to begin using more complex language in conversation and reading books that combine high-frequency words—the 100-or-so words we use all the time—and introduce new vocabulary terms. Continuing to foster an environment that is rich in conversation and reading can help promote your child's language fluency.

One of the most exciting developmental milestones is your child's writing ability. In addition to having access to numerous books, you will want to have tons of paper, pens, pencils, markers, and paints around. Our interest is not in *teaching* writing, but in helping our children make the connection between reading and writing by giving them lots of opportunities to draw, scribble, and doodle. Part of building a literacy-rich home includes writing; and like reading, there are interesting, effective strategies we can employ to take advantage of this blossoming skill without turning our book nooks into penmanship traps.

Pre-School Readers

We could accurately dub the pre-school age the "Age of Awareness." Parents of these attentive adventurers know that if you hide something behind your back, your child will turn you around to see where it went. When you run the bath signaling the start of your bedtime routine, they will run into the other room and pull out their toys. No longer are our mobile children at the mercy of our direction; they can explore more, retain more, and recall more than ever before. While these newly developed abilities can be exasperating—especially at bedtime—they can be embraced when it comes to reading.

There are three different points of reading awareness that pre-school readers will begin to focus on more acutely. This awareness is a precursor for independent reading and demonstrates a real certainty for how written language works.

- **Print awareness** The awareness that we read words, we look at pictures. Different sounds make up different words that combine to make different sentences, which convey different meanings.
- **Alphabet awareness** The awareness that letters have their own unique shapes and sounds. Letters are individual, have individual sounds, and combine to make up words.
- **Phonemic awareness** The awareness that words are made up of small, separate sounds. Recognizing that the letters of a word can be separated out to make individual sounds; then these sounds can be combined to make a specific word.

Keep in mind, awareness of concepts does not mean mastery, and few preschoolers demonstrate all three points simultaneously and accurately each time you read together. Most likely, your child will pick out favorite letters, mimic favorite sounds, and recognize high-frequency words. It is not necessary to start drilling her on her "awareness" levels; your read-aloud routines are already doing everything that needs to be done.

"No More Baby Books!"

With this more focused awareness comes the appreciation of favorite books and titles that are no longer of interest. While a much-beloved book may still make its regularly scheduled appearance, your maturing listening audience can greatly benefit from the introduction of new materials.

Success Story

Children will often adopt the language of their favorite characters and insist on "huffing and puffing" their bedroom door down. Encourage these active imaginations and be proud that what you are doing really is having an effect.

Children are beginning to appreciate that books sound different from conversation. There is a flow, a rhythm that is specific to the written word. Simply put, books just sound better. Give your child a pleasant earful by incorporating poetry into your read-alouds.

In addition to the sounds of books, try something that looks a little different, too. Your library may have oversized picture books available to use while you visit the children's room. These big books look and feel life-like, making the stories seem to come alive. If you haven't done so already, try adding titles that have photographs instead of illustrations, focus on high-interest nonfiction subjects (like dinosaurs or ocean life), or depict characters from different time periods, nations, and cultures. By doing this you can help your young readers to learn that books are not only entertaining, but can be relied upon to teach them new and exciting things in an entertaining format.

Concept Books

You will probably be pleasantly surprised to know that you already have several concept books on hand; you have just been calling them by more familiar names. Concept books are titles that focus on a single theme, be it the alphabet, colors, shapes, or sizes. They are intended to focus the reader onto a certain category that is meaningful to development. You may be wondering why your alphabet or colors book is now receiving so much attention. After all, haven't these already been read? Yes, they have, but now we can reread them in a new way.

Pre-schoolers are beginning to understand that words represent real things. "Big" really means something; it is no longer just a word. When we combine reading concept books with hands-on experiences, we further help to make the connection between reading and real life. Having pre-read your family's selection of concept books, see what materials you have on hand to promote a deeper understanding of the focused themes. For example, having a "big" kickball and a "small" tennis ball next to each other gives your reader a chance to hear, see, and touch the differences between big and small. Bringing literature to life in this simple manner can make the reading experience more engaging, which is always more fun. As is our intention, we always want our activities to reconnect us to the pleasure principle.

Quick Picks

Whenever you can, use specific, varied vocabulary to narrate your day. There are differences between walking, strolling, hiking, and running. Use the words that best suit the situations and introduce new vocabulary while it is happening.

Action and Adventure

When looking to add new books to your child's basket, you may become a little nostalgic for the stories of their babyhood. Most of the books we choose for newborns and babies depict families, especially parent and child, enjoying the daily activities that we recognize from our own routine. Most of all, the stories rely heavily on love, hugs, and kisses—the emotions and actions that define our relationship. And while I am not advocating you get rid of these heartwarming tales, I do suggest changing up the characters a bit.

Pre-schoolers love their parents, but they are also starting to love their friends. People their size who are not too tired to play, have imaginations as wild as their own, and appreciate the dedication it takes to build, knock down, and rebuild a block tower all afternoon. Books that can capture children interacting with other children, solving their own problems, and forging into uncharted territory—be it outer space or grandma's house—can awaken your reader to a whole new world of action and adventure. Adults aren't bad, and neither are the books that they star in; but children can and should be heard.

But you do not have to feel like you are left out of the fun. Your own adventures can make for great family story books. We have a mini-photo album entitled "The Adventures of Mommy and Michael" that shows us driving in our car, trick-or-treating, playing at the park, and shopping for treasures. A quick line of text written along the bottom of the page lends itself to a title, and together we point out what we see and talk about what we did. Never underestimate how much fun your preschoolers are having with you. In fact, I'm betting you could write a book about it!

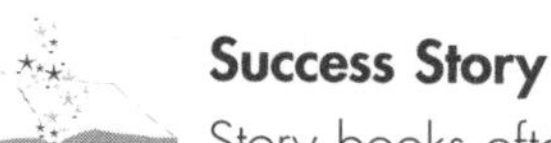

Success Story

Story books often use animal characters to represent children. These talking animals often have the same challenges and triumphs as real-life children, making their stories just as valuable.

"Finally, Dialogue," He Said.

A new and exciting format for you to look forward to reading aloud involves dialogue. No longer are you limited to super-simple sentences and third-person narration. Now, you can look for stories where a couple of characters speak directly to each other, helping your child to appreciate a key ingredient in all great literature: character development. We learn a great deal more about a character's motivations, expectations, and personality when we receive that information firsthand. The more time you spend in conversations with your child, the better he will be able to understand how conversations work in a book. Model how people in real life take turns talking, and the lesson will carry on to the page.

This is also an excellent forum for discussing those hard-to-handle topics like selfishness, tattling, and being mean. You can read the stories together and talk about how one character said something hurtful, and how another character reacted because of it. Instead of having to berate your own child for her misbehavior, you can use the characters as tools to point out inappropriate and appropriate behavior. You may also help your child to find answers to her own problems by practicing a storybook character's solution.

Primary School Readers

Independence is the name of the game for your kindergartner or first-grade child. Not only is she fully capable of matching her pink shirt with her purple skirt and red shoes, she also wants to show you how she can read and write all by herself and does not need your help, thank you very much (except, well, maybe every once and awhile). Children at this age want to do everything on their own, but need to know that you are only an arm's length away if they need help. Usually, they want your help to be specific and brief so they can go back to doing the whole thing on their own. You may find yourself walking a fine line between go-to guy and invisible parent. But don't worry, you still have plenty to offer your little learner.

During this time, your child will probably be able to recognize all the letters of the alphabet, both uppercase and lowercase, and know the different sounds each letter makes. Expect most children to learn consonant sounds first, because they are more consistent than the ever-changing sounds of vowels. He may want to write his own stories, and you can encourage him to read his masterpiece. While he will probably correctly spell the 100-or-so common words he has come to readily recognize, you may not do justice to the three or four misspelled words scattered across the page.

It can be extremely exciting for you to see your child blossoming into an emergent reader, and extremely frustrating for them. By the end of first grade, most children can recognize their own reading and writing mistakes. If they feel they are making too many mistakes, or are embarrassed when they struggle, they could quickly withdraw from an activity they once loved. As parents, we can encourage our kids to celebrate their accomplishments, have patience with their own process, and take on new age-appropriate reading and writing challenges to keep them motivated.

Bookworms Beware

If your child seems to be struggling with reading all of the sudden, don't panic. One of the most common reasons for reading frustrations is the need for glasses. Most schools conduct yearly eye exams; but if you suspect a problem, then make an eye doctor appointment on your own before contacting a reading tutor.

Big-Kid Picture Book

Just as newborns learned how language works by first hearing it and then practicing it, little learners master reading by hearing it modeled enthusiastically and correctly and then trying it themselves. There are so many wonderful picture books that this age group can enjoy—stories that inspire, delight, and educate. By continuing to look for great read-alouds, you can continue to model good reading practices.

Beautifully crafted picture books are also a joy to share with an "older" reader, who is more likely to appreciate the illustrations. Children are naturally creative and many will enjoy illustrating their own books, imitating the artwork they see in a published book, or redesigning the cover to better suit their artistic vision.

Quick Picks

If your busy schedules make it impossible to set aside daily reading time, make a "Reading Date" once a week and stick to it. Dim the lights, ditch the distractions, and dive into a great story together. Reading "quickies" get the job done, but a date is something to be savored.

Reading at school is not the same as reading at home with a parent or caregiver. Even in the most comfortable classroom, some intimacy is bound to be lost when you must share the experience with two dozen other listeners. Your children have not outgrown their need to cuddle up next to you for some one-on-one time. Choose titles that can help you reconnect with your big kid and learn more about what is happening inside their head.

Easy Readers

Easy readers, also referred to as "beginner books," use controlled, rhythmic patterns and picture clues as a means to present high-frequency words for mastery. But by no means are these books boring; their choice of vocabulary is just specific and purposeful. Concentrating on the 100-or-so most frequently used words, these books may come complete with an introductory page filled with words you will see in the book. Easy readers are often shelved separately in the children's room, making them easy to spot and giving your little learner a specific area to choose from. They can be a powerful tool for building reader confidence and competence.

These emergent readers will not have the ebb and flow of an experienced reader, and at times their lack of abilities may seem alarming. I mean, here you are, huffing and puffing and blowing your audience away with animated tales of heroes and villains, and your child rewards you by read-ing-a-sent-ence-that-sounds-like-this. The only way to move from the machine-gun-sounding reading to a more natural flow is through good modeling and plenty of practice. Encourage your children to read aloud a little bit each day. Pick a well-worn story whose test is predictable and repetitive, don't rush in to rescue, and keep smiling, no matter how painful it sounds. If your child feels safe and secure, she will be more likely to keep at it.

Quick Picks

Here's a fast way to evaluate if the book your child is holding is the right reading level. Have her read one page aloud while you (silently) keep track of the words she misses. If there are five or more words that are unfamiliar, consider the book too challenging for independent reading and add it to your read-aloud list, or wait until she can more confidently handle it on her own.

Purposeful Play

There is a whole world of purposeful play that takes place both before children enter school and as they move throughout the primary grades. As children mature, we tend to stop referring to play as play, and instead dub it "extracurricular activities" or "organized sports." But the fact remains true for any age: play gets our creative juices flowing, often helping us to see things from a fresh perspective. Whether you are preparing for a big presentation at the office or worried about an upcoming exam, getting out of your seat and onto your feet can help you to think more clearly, making obstacles seem like puzzles instead of problems.

When it comes to reading or writing, play is a valuable asset. These ideas require little preparation and are not intended as "continuing education" classes or supplemental exercises, but are offered as another means to have fun with books and language. I truly believe that as we keep the focus of reading on pleasure, our children will continue to pursue books with a passion. Here are a few family-friendly games to try together. Game on.

Index Card Intelligence

Encourage your children to *journal* about their day. Help your child write "morning," "afternoon," and "evening" on three separate index cards. Place them in front of your child, left to right. Instruct him to draw a picture of a favorite, or not-so-favorite, activity that happened during that time. If your child struggles with these time concepts (many do!) try writing "breakfast," "lunch," and "dinner" instead, and focus their attentions to that part of the day. Share these new memories over dinner. You've just reinforced an important aspect of reading comprehension, sequencing, using kid-friendly reading and writing materials.

Using one card per letter, write out your child's name. Start by showing her what her name looks like. Then ask her to see what other words can be made by rearranging these letters. If her name is super-short, add middle and last names. Or add your name (yes, mom and dad, you still have a first name). This is a great game for siblings with different reading skills to play, as the letter combinations become more advanced with practice. You've just helped emphasize that letters represent individual sounds, which, when combined differently, make new words.

I Spy a Sound

Truth be told, it's much easier to learn rhymes by hearing them, rather than by silently reading them. Hearing rhymes helps isolate sounds and increase vocabulary. In addition to the great poetry books you have already tried, and the countless nursery rhymes you have sung together, you can practice rhyming patterns throughout your day. With the help of these simple games, model as many different rhyming examples as you can.

Bookworms Beware

When games start to feel like hard work, it's time to back off a bit. Reading and writing games should have the same sense of camaraderie as board games and cards. Don't focus on the lesson, focus on the fun.

- While making dinner, pick out a specific item in your kitchen, like a spoon. Do not tell your child your choice, but give rhyming clues until he guesses the item. You could say, "It rhymes with *noon*, *moon*, and *balloon*." After your child correctly guesses, give him a chance to pick an item and offer you clues.
- While driving in the car, take turns finishing each other's silly rhyming sentences. Use your changing environment to come up with varying sentences. For example, you could say, "I'm stopping at this *light* …," and your child could finish with, "Let's not have a *fight* …." Always be sure to emphasize the word you want to rhyme and don't worry too much about the sentence making sense. If your child was to answer, "… alligators bite," she would still be practicing her rhyming skills, the goal of your game!

Guided Reading

The premise of guided reading, also called shared reading, will probably sound a lot like read-alouds, since it involves reading an engaging storybook together. But guided reading emphasizes the way language works on a page. Instead of just reading a story through and then looking back over the pictures, children can be encouraged to look for particular details in the text. Guided reading activities work best with small groups, making it an ideal practice for parent and child.

Using repetitious books that have simple rhythms and rhymes, you and your child can look for recognizable words, such as I, am, or is; find all the words that are capitalized; name all the different types of punctuation you see. Readers at this age see that there are spaces between words and sentences, and that punctuation and capitalization are used to separate thoughts. Taking note of all the parts of a sentence and locating familiar words can bring a new dimension to your read-alouds.

You can also look for books that your child will enjoy reading independently. After a few modeled readings by you, your little learner may be able to tackle the text on her own. Let her hold the book, turn the pages, and read as much as she can. If she gets stuck on a word, wait until you are asked for help and offer clues before giving her the entire word. Instead of saying, "You know that word," try, "Where have we seen that word before," or "Do you know any of the letters? What sounds do they make?" Guided reading is not about testing your child, but about encouraging her to start using the tools she has to figure out the answer. If trouble persists, pronounce the word without fuss or fanfare and move on. No one likes to feel stupid or embarrassed. Be encouraging, yes; but also empathetic—she is just learning.

Instead of just dragging a finger along the sentences, pick up hand and point at individual words—like the bouncing ball idea.

You Read to Me, I'll Read to You

This section was inspired by a parent-child interaction I became accustomed to seeing when I was a librarian. Zach, Gianna, and their mother would choose a few books from the shelves and find a comfortable place to sit. Zach would take great pride in reading stories like, *The Foot Book* by Dr. Seuss, a story with kid-friendly repetition, funny pictures, and high-frequency words. If he became stuck, his mom was there to help him along; but he did the bulk of the reading in his own. His younger sister beamed at her big brother who was able to read on his own. When he finished, mom would read a more "advanced" story aloud to both children. Not to be left out, Gianna would choose an "eye spy" book and often be the first one to find the hidden pictures. Everyone in the family contributed to choosing materials, everyone took turns being in charge of his or her book, and everyone enjoyed the experience. This family is onto something.

As your children learn to read more proficiently, you may be tempted to turn the read-aloud routine over to them, thinking that the more they actually do the reading, the better readers they will become. While this kind of thinking is on the right path, it isn't quite the whole picture. Modeling for your emergent reader is just as important as reading to your nonreader. Children need to hear the ebb and flow of language, see the relaxed manner in which you move from sentence to sentence and page to page, and hear the tone and inflection of your voice so that they can become stronger readers. Plus, as we will discuss at the end of this chapter, you always want to be "reading up," giving your children a taste of more complicated story lines, fresh language, and new subjects. When you practice the "You read to me, I'll read to you" idea, you get the best of all worlds.

Success Story

Many parents are quick to dismiss a child's reading ability as mere memorization. But memorization is a key component of reading. The 100-or-so high-frequency sight words are learned by seeing them over and over again; in essence, they are memorized. Use "memorized" books to build reader confidence, and work on articulation, timing, and pronunciation, and your reader will be well on her way to comprehending what she has memorized.

Cover to Cover

I love all parts of a book: I love covers that entice me to pick them up, I love reading the synopsis of a story on the inside cover, checking to see who the book is dedicated to, and learning about the authors and illustrators at the end of the book. But I must admit, this information tends to go by the wayside in my rush "to get to the good stuff."

But a published book is more than just a great story, it is someone's job, a company's product, a dream realized. Walk your emergent reader through all the parts of a book and see how much there is to learn without even coming near the first sentence.

- Front Cover: Title, Author, and Illustrator. Talk about each person's job and what to expect from the title and cover art.
- Synopsis: Lengthier storybooks will have a brief summary of what awaits the reader. If applicable, use this preview to make predictions about what might happen and how the story may end.
- Copyright Page: While there is a lot of cataloguing jargon here, there is also the very important phrase, "All rights reserved." Talk about what it means to have a copyright and how it protects authors and illustrators from having their work stolen. Don't be surprised if your first grader requests a copyright be placed on his bicycle!
- Dedications or Acknowledgments: This is such a personal glimpse into the lives of the creators. I especially love when there are just initials listed and I can guess the names of the people and their relationships. Talk to your child about who they would dedicate their work to.
- About the Authors: It is great when authors and illustrators write about where they live, their inspirations, and other books they have published. If your child likes the book you are holding, this page could be an excellent resource for making your next library selection.

There is no denying that we read the book for the story; but when we take time to look at the rest of the book, we are privy to so much more reading magic.

Multiple Special Shelves

At this point in time, your child may begin to really understand the sacredness of the Special Shelf. The treasures stored here are reserved for one-on-one time with mom or dad, safe from sibling hands, and are not eligible for sharing. Look over the shelf together and add new meaningful items and remove dated or less significant pieces. The more active your child becomes in designing and maintaining the Special Shelf, the more significant the shelf will become.

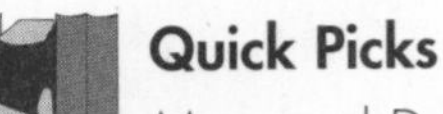

Quick Picks

Mom and Dad should have separate (but equal) Special Shelves. Individuality is what makes your family's dynamic so unique and it can be celebrated with a simple shelf.

If it hasn't happened already, be prepared: your child will ask where your Special Shelf is. I would strongly encourage you to erect your own Special Shelf in your bedroom—even if it is in the closet due to lack of space or aesthetics. Remember, you are not only a parent, you also are an individual with likes, interests, hobbies, and your own unique items. Display your treasures, too.

The "Good" Books

Alongside your son's latest karate plaque and your daughter's class picture, use the Special Shelf for the "good books." These are stories whose reading level is too advanced for your child to enjoy independently, but whose themes reflect their personal interests: a beautiful photography book about horses, a riveting mystery in 12 chapters, a beloved poetry book. These books are designed to be shared together and take on a certain air of prestige, being as how they are reserved for particular reading routines. While these books do not have to be expensive or flashy, they should be handled with extra attention: no jelly-stained finger marks on the cover, no dog-eared pages, no crayon creations. The Special Shelf is a great way to foster a sense of respect for the precious gems in your child's life. And at the end of the day, is there anything better than having your child ask you to read him a good book?

Raise That Reading Level

As much as you want your child to take an active role in the care of the Special Shelf, I would encourage you to take the lead on one or two titles. Having children who want to read themselves is wonderful, but for the time being, this will greatly limit your selections. To round out your read-alouds, we always want to make sure we are "reading up" to them.

A great way to "read up" is by choosing a chapter book that is one or two reading levels ahead of their current stage. For example, a kindergartner may really enjoy hearing E.B. White's *Charlotte's Web*, although she is not able to read an entire sentence on her own. Children's auditory comprehension is much more advanced than our reading comprehension. Don't miss out on great titles because you think they are too advanced; chances are, if you try a page or two at a time you could introduce your little learner to a whole new world of storytelling, while revisiting some old friends of your own.

Your little learner is a reading and writing wonder to behold. From concepts to early comprehension skills, your children are well on their way to becoming a literary masterpiece of their own. Using the activities and ideas suggested in this chapter, you can help continue to foster an environment rich with reading and writing.

The Least You Need to Know

- Writing complements reading; it doesn't replace it. Focus on enjoying stories instead of insisting on writing assignments.
- Make reading a "hands-on" experience that happens in real time. Look for opportunities throughout your day to read aloud signs, directions, and points of interest.
- Read aloud even as your child begins to read independently; it will reinforce that successful readers are smooth, clear, energetic, and enthusiastic.

Chapter 11

Handling Sticky Situations

In This Chapter

- Read-alouds get serious
- Reading toward a solution
- Ideal stories for your less-than-ideal situation

I was once told, "The bigger the kid, the bigger the problems." When we think about the challenges that face our little learners, it sure can feel that way. Once your child starts school and you are no longer at his side to help playdates run more smoothly and make sure that they're all using their manners and sharing, things can get really messy. Making friends and socializing is one of the biggest components of childhood, and one of the more complicated. Add to this the possible stresses of going through a divorce, burying a pet, looking different, or living differently from everyone else, and you've got the makings of major mess on your hands.

In several of the following book recommendations, adults do play a major role, which may seem contradictory to my earlier advice that the best books for this age group are adult-free. But when problems are too big for children to solve on their own, we want to encourage them to seek help from a trusted adult. The adults in these books don't swoop in with magic cure-alls, but they do step in with valuable suggestions. Ultimately, the children handle the sticky situation; but there is nothing wrong with a parent cheering for them from behind. As parents, we want to do everything we can to give our children a joyful life, and we can be quick to rush in and clean up a mess; but sometimes sticky situations are best handled when we turn the cleaning tools over to our children.

This approach does not mean that we send them out unarmed, but it does advocate seeing things from their perspective, engaging in an active and honest dialogue, and empowering our children to take action. But when trouble strikes and everyone is affected, it can be hard to see clearly. Luckily, storybooks are available to help us shed some light into a dark corner. This chapter reads a little more serious than previous chapters because the topics are more serious. Instead of offering advice on how to improve reading readiness or be creative in your reading routine, I focus on book recommendations that have insightful advice, solutions, and storylines for sticky situations. All of the books are intended as read-alouds and all promote positive interaction and conversation. How you work these books into your reading routine is up to you; but as the titles are meant to spark conversation, it may be best to make sure you give yourselves ample time to talk about the story and complete the associated activities.

Playground Politics

So there you are, discreetly wiping at your eyes as your little bundle of sunshine joyfully makes her way to her coat hook, carefully slides her new backpack off her shoulders, and proudly puts on her name tag for her first day of school. You manage a brave face, kiss her goodbye, and try to make it to the parking lot before collapsing in a puddle of sentimental tears. After pacing the floor all day, anxious to hear about the new friends she has made, you return to school to retrieve your little learner. But instead of being greeted with tales of new friends and fun activities, you are met with tears. Hers, this time. The other kids wouldn't let her on the slide, her snack was stupid, and she hates school.

Ah, the politics of the playground; and you thought you were the one who was having a rough day.

Life for a little kid is not always easy. Kids can be mean. Really mean. The kind of mean that can make an otherwise rational mother want to go over and pull that bratty girl's ponytails herself. But since that won't get us anywhere, except maybe forcibly removed from the premises, we need to come up with a better solution. This can be a particularly thorny subject if you struggle with making friends, feel uncomfortable in new situations, or were the victim of a playground bully. Fortunately, as with more growing pains, you are not the only ones dealing with these issues; there are some very talented authors and illustrators who know exactly what you are talking about. And they have been kind enough to write about it.

Making Friends

Hopefully, your child will start school or a new playgroup or karate with kids who are just as new as he is. Everyone will feel a little lost and insecure, but with the help of a warm caretaker, the ice will soon be broken and the fun will soon begin. Unfortunately, that is not always the case. Sometimes, due to a recent move, different interests, excessive shyness, or any other host of reasons, your child will feel like an outsider. But before you go and invite the entire class over for a backyard playdate, consider looking for tools to help your child better manage on his own.

Quick Picks

Many primary school teachers read books with these themes to their class, but if there is a story about making friends that really resonates with your child, send it to school to be shared. Whenever possible, teachers will look for ways to use a family favorite, especially one that is beneficial to everyone.

How to Be a Friend: A Guide to Making Friends and Keeping Them (Dino Life Guides for Families), copyright © 2001, Laurie Krasny Brown, Marc Brown

This book gives straightforward advice on how to make friends ("take turns") and how not to be a friend ("call them a name they don't like"). Young dinosaurs demonstrate the pleasure of being a friend and the negative consequences of being a bully. Simple and clear cut, this book spells out the do's and don'ts of friendship without glossing over the fact that some dinosaurs (read: some kids) are just not good friend material.

Join In and Play (Learning to Get Along), copyright © 2004 Cheri J. Meiners

Part of the well-received Learning to Get Along Series, this book depicts children making friends, which isn't always easy. It stresses being polite, waiting your turn, and seeking out someone with a similar disposition. The children come from all different cultures, helping to emphasize that making friends is a universal goal, and struggle. Each segment ends with several suggestions for how parents can help reinforce the ideas in each story. This can be especially helpful if you are feeling particularly helpless.

Bullies and Troublemakers

It used to be that every class had one bad kid; the kid that was always getting sent to the principal's office, the kid that everyone knew to stay away from. Now it seems that bullies are everywhere and a lot more children are getting in trouble. It can be difficult for your child to handle such intimidating individuals (or cliques), but this is a life lesson that just won't quit. Even as adults, we have to interact with strong personalities and questionable characters. Here are some titles that may help ease the difficulties.

Bookworms Beware

There has yet to be a book written that cures bullying. But acknowledging the problem and working toward a solution as a family can be a step in the right direction.

The Bully Blockers Club, copyright © 2004 Teresa Bateman, Jackie Urbanovic

The first day of school becomes a battle against the classroom bully for a young female raccoon. Despite trying the tried-and-true tactics like ignoring the bully or walking away, he will not stop harassing her. The raccoon decides to start a club with other harassed "children" and they all watch out for each other. This is a great example of children solving a problem on their own; while the teacher is supportive and helpful, it's the children who take control of the situation with an unconventional solution.

King of the Playground, copyright © 1994 Phyllis Reynolds Naylor, Nola Langnor Malone

Each day Sammy heads to the playground in hopes of enjoying himself, and each day his hopes are squashed by a bully. Fearful of the bully's threats, he shares his fears with his father who lovingly points out that these threats are unrealistic and that Sammy is not helpless. While this book does feature a father as a main character, the advice and counsel of the parent is encouraging, not suffocating; and it is wonderful to see the father-and-son dynamic at work (no mother in the book). Sammy finally gets up the courage to face the bully with wit and wisdom, not violence, and a resolution is reached.

That's Mean, copyright 2004 Francesco Pittau, Bernadette Gervais

This board book pulls no punches. A little boy is mean, and I mean, mean: making fun of blind people, kicking the cat, and scaring his little sister. What happens if you are mean? You end up all alone, of course. Some parents may think this book is a bit over the top, but having spent a lot of time on playgrounds, I can assure you, sadly, it is not. This could be a good tool for drawing your child out and having him talk about what mean things have been done to him, how it feels, and what can be done. A nice platform for talking about solutions together.

Last to Get Picked

No one gets out of school unscathed. And perhaps the children who wear the deepest scars are the ones who must line up in gym class, on the playground, or at the ball field and watch with horror as they are, once again, the last one chosen for the team. These are often the same children who are not invited to birthday parties and receive the least amount of Valentine's Day cards. While there is no way that you can allow your daughter who needs glasses to go without, or make your son grow faster, you may be able to help them see that they really aren't all that different. The most compassionate people I know are ones who learned to reach out to others because they had been singled out in the past. The following book is a great example of how to help that happen.

Don't Laugh at Me, copyright © 2002 by Steve Seskin, Allen Shamblin, and Glin Dibley

Told from the point of view of a boy with oversized glasses, a girl with braces, a boy in a wheelchair, and others, these ostracized children rally together to point out our similarities and the importance of including everyone, even the small boy on the playground who is the last to get picked. This book is part of the Operation Respect movement, a non-profit organization whose mission is, "To assure each child and youth a respectful, safe, and compassionate climate of learning where their academic, social, and emotional development can take place free of bullying, ridicule, and violence." Visit them at www.operationrespect.org to learn more about you can become a part of this compassionate community.

Sticking Up for Oneself

I don't think there is any more misleading nursery rhyme than "Sticks and stones may break my bones, but words will never hurt me." Giving children pat advice like, "ignore it" or "don't worry about it" when they are being harassed or tormented is unfair and useless. Words can and do hurt. We can help our children to see that they have choices and help them find the nerve to stick up for themselves without resorting to violence. This also means sticking up for others who are in trouble, and learning the difference between tattling and asking for help. Courage is contagious, and these books can help your child get caught up.

Stop Picking on Me (A First Look At Series), copyright © 2000 Pat Thomas, Lesley Harker

The author, a counselor and psychotherapist, uses simple and direct language to offer solutions that may help your child find the courage to stand up to the neighborhood or schoolyard bully. The illustrations of the little girl bullied in this book will break your heart, as her hurt when singled out by a bully is poignantly depicted. This is a great resource for talking about what is really going on—namely, the awful feelings a bully can make you feel and what you can do to protect yourself.

Say Something, copyright © 2004 Peggy Moss, Lea Lyon

A female narrator carefully explains that while she feels bad for the kids who are teased, she minds her own business and doesn't join in, either to hurt or help. This plan works until the bullies turn on her and no one comes to her aid. It is then that she realizes she must take action to protect herself and others. This story tackles the complicated question: is a bystander as guilty as a bully? Straight-forward advice and ideas for discussion are included at the back of the book.

Nobody Knew What to Do: A Story About Bullying, copyright © 2001 (Concept Books) Becky Ray McCain, Todd Leonardo

When Ray is picked on by the playground bully, other children want to help, but they are afraid of the consequences of confrontation and instead just hope that the problem goes away. Finally, one boy decides that Ray needs more help than wishful thinking and asks his teacher what to do. Sometimes a problem is too big for children to handle and they need to know that going to an adult is the courageous, not cowardly, thing to do. Learning how to stand up for others is just as important, and difficult, as learning to stand up for oneself.

Success Story

Be sure to explain the difference between "tattling" and "telling." Many children are reluctant to tell an adult that a friend is being harassed because they have been taught not to tattle and to mind their own business. "Tattling" is when you are trying to get someone into trouble; "telling" is when you are trying to get someone out of trouble.

When Things Go Wrong

"But, why?" may be one of the toughest questions any parent will have to answer. Children in this age group are not only developing reading and writing skills; they are also developing their rationale. Telling our kids we love them is so easy when compared to telling them why daddy has to live in another house or trying to explain why kitty is not coming back. Considering that it takes most people their entire adult lives to understand why marriages fall apart or come to terms with the death of a loved one, it is no wonder we can be dumbstruck when it comes to answering, "But, why?"

While we want to protect our kids from hurt, it is not always possible to do so. Luckily, there are some really great books to help us find the words when we are feeling lost. Life is not a storybook, and they can't solve problems, but they can help handle the hurt.

Death of a Loved One

If your young child is grieving, you are most likely grieving also, making talking about death and offering comfort even more challenging. But when we talk to our kids about dying and death, we find out what they know about the subject. and usually their ideas are frightening and guilt-ridden. We can help them see that death cannot be controlled, either by good actions or bad deed, and that grief and sorrow are healthy, natural parts of life.

It can be hard to help when we are grieving, and it can be difficult to try to talk about topics when we don't have all the answers. But when we "put on a brave face," we send the message that death is too big, too scary, and too upsetting to talk about. Now, more than ever, we can turn to our trusted treasures, our books, and begin the all-important dialogue of dealing with grief.

Success Story

Just because these are children's books doesn't mean that you can't benefit from the content. Whenever possible, complete the activities, in your own words and drawings, alongside your children. If you want your children to open up to you, start by opening up to them.

Help Me Say Goodbye: Activities for Helping Kids Cope When a Special Person Dies, copyright © 1999 Janis Silverman

This art therapy book is designed to be written in, offering age-appropriate activities for preparing for a loved one to die to dealing with the loss of that person. Each page offers a simple prompt that encourages the child to express, remember, and reflect on her emotions. This handbook is an excellent tool for children, and for the adults who love them, who don't know how to talk about what they are feeling. It is a tangible keepsake for remembering a loved one and can be turned to time and time again.

Saying Goodbye to a Pet (Saying Goodbye Series), copyright © 2005 Nicola Edwards

When I was a librarian we purchased this series for our Children's Room and it was very well received. The illustrations depict real families with real animals and the very real sadness that is felt when such a special member of the family dies. Simple text can help promote conversations, and there are several activities to commemorate a pet's life. Other titles in the series deal with the death of a grandparent, parent, and sibling.

I Miss You: A First Look at Death, copyright © 2001 Pat Thomas, Leslie Harker

This lovely book discusses death in plain and simple terms without religious overtones. It focuses on the circle of life, how all things grow, change, and die, and includes facts like "young people can die" and "death can happen suddenly." Grief is embraced as normal and healthy. A short glossary in the back defines key terms like "funeral" and "grief."

Differences and Diversity

By the time your child reaches schools, he will have noticed that boys and girls look different, from each other and from him. He will start to ask questions about why people look, sound, and live differently from him. If you are divorced, a same-sex couple, or a blended family, your child may have even more questions regarding differences, namely, their own. Today's picture books do not shy away from exploring differences and diversity; instead, they celebrate unique styles while commenting on universal truths. If you are looking to start a specific dialogue with your child about your family, be sure and preview books that cater to your situation, making sure that they fit your needs. The suggestions below are a good place to start.

If your family is made up of 2.5 children, a mother, father, dog, and cat, you may be wondering if you can just skip over this section. Maybe you live in an area where one ethnic group is strongly represented and most families look and live like you do, and you're unsure of why you would need to introduce such topics to your little learner. Well, simply put, even if diversity doesn't live on your block, it exists. One of the best ways to avoid prejudice and discrimination is to make your child aware that people of all colors, cultures, and creeds live, work, play, eat, sleep, and celebrate. These titles are a way to introduce diversity and differences in a kid-friendly manner and can be added to your read-aloud routine even if the subject is new. And isn't learning new things one of the best things about books, anyway?

Success Story

Divorce is not always friendly, but if you can, share books that you are reading with your child about divorce with your ex-spouse so that both parents are delivering the same message of loving comfort to the children.

The Family Book, copyright © 2003 Todd Parr

From single parents to adopted children to multiracial marriages, this book covers just about every type of family dynamic you can think of. Light and colorful, the illustrations use both human and animal characters to characterize each family's differences but to ultimately celebrate their similarities.

It's Not Your Fault, Koko Bear: A Read-Together Book for Parents and Young Children During Divorce, copyright © 1997 Vicki Lansky

This is a very specific read-aloud book that is written for the parent as much as for the child. While the story works to reassure the child that divorce is not her fault, the bottom of each page provides specific advice for how parents can help navigate their children during this difficult time.

Two Homes, copyright © 2003 Claire Masurel, Kady Macdonald Denton

In addition to the previously mentioned handbook about divorce is the picture book, *Two Homes*. This story focuses on a child having two actual homes, not living with one parent and visiting another. Instead of talking about the parents' situation or reasons for divorce, the story focuses on the effect it has on the child and his living situation. Simple and positive.

And Tango Makes Three (ALA Notable Children's Books Award), copyright © 2005 Peter Parnell, Justin Richardson

Based on the true story of two male penguins residing at NYC's Central Park Zoo who forge a relationship and build a nest together, this heartwarming story is an excellent introduction to same-sex families and what it means to be a parent. The penguins are given an egg to hatch and raise, and a family is born. All families can appreciate this loving and diverse family and use it as a jumping-off point for more personal, in-depth conversation if circumstances warrant.

Dangers and Disasters

When bad things happen in front of our children, we cannot pretend that they did not see it. If children are anything, it is observant. Whether it is a terrorist attack, a destructive hurricane, or an abusive situation at home, children need help processing what they have witnessed. There are no easy answers for why tragedy strikes, but ignoring a painfully real situation often turns children resentful, angry, and aggressive.

I wish we lived in a world where my son would never have to see buildings in Manhattan collapse or a city devastated by flood, but, unfortunately, he will probably witness some awful things in his life. If your children have witnessed the unthinkable, try not to let your own guilt or fear prevent you from helping them heal. Keeping the explanations short, simple, and honest, and using a book like the following recommendation can help open up a most important dialogue in your family.

A Terrible Thing Happened—A story for children who have witnessed violence or trauma, copyright © 2000 Margaret M. Holmes, Sasha J. Mudlaff, Cary Pillo

Without specifying the type of trauma witnessed, we read about Sherman Raccoon who cannot forget about the bad thing, becomes sick and nervous then angry and upset. Finally, with the help of his school counselor, he is able to talk about the tragedy and feels much better. Specific and extensive advice and additional resources are listed for parents.

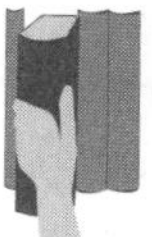

Quick Picks

Gone are the days when a family must suffer in silence. If tragedy has struck at home, reach out to your school's guidance counselor as a resource for additional kid-friendly titles that could help your family cope with catastrophe.

A Formula That Works

When trying to decide the best time to cross into uncharted water with your children, it's prudent to follow their lead whenever possible. Children tend to stare and point at things that are unfamiliar to them, and our reaction can often be to turn them away and say through gritted teeth, "Don't stare." Of course we want our children to have good manners, but let's not overlook a teachable moment, either. Recently my son saw an elderly gentleman in a wheelchair and was mesmorized by the big wheels. Catching his eye, the gentleman waved hello and we exchanged pleasantries while Michael touched the wheels. What nice times to talk about what wheelchairs do, and as an unexpected bonus, the gentleman had a great sense of humor and spun his chair around for us. Of course, every interaction isn't going to go this smoothly, but when the opportunity is there, we can take it.

The same is true for books. As soon as something starts weighing heavily on your child's mind, the subject becomes age appropriate; but that doesn't mean every available resource is fair game. Look for ways to effectively communicate using stories that are still kid-friendly: picture books featuring dinosaurs talking about divorce (good); a handbook written by a lawyer about how to burn the other guy in court (not good). Complicated titles are made more accessible when we choose materials that complement our audience.

I can't help but recall a story about the little girl who came home from school and asked her mother, "Where did I come from?" Wanting to have an open and honest conversation with her daughter, she sat down and explained about the birds and the bees. When she was done talking, her bewildered daughter looked at her mother, held up her homework, and said, "I have to write down what town I came from." In our effort to want to be open and honest, we can accidentally be *too* open and honest. Give simple, straight-forward answers, don't be afraid to ask for clarification by saying, "What do mean by that?" and remember that when it comes to sticky situations, everyone sometimes gets stuck.

Character Cues

The benefit of adding titles such as these to your reading routine before they are actually needed can help to put you and your child at a communication advantage should the challenge arise. Reading stories that feature blended families, bullies, or death can give your child an accurate basis of knowledge to draw on when she finds herself meeting a new multiracial family at the library, runs into a bully on the playground, or sees grandma crying because her friend died. Having already breached the topic in a safe and unaffected environment, like the kind of space that you have created in your book nooks, you will be able to draw on other character's situations and stories and relate that to what is presently happening in your child's experience.

On the other hand, when an unexpected tragedy happens, stories like these can help take the pressure off of the people who are experiencing the pain. It is often easier to start talking about how sad the boy in the story was, rather than try to find the words to express how sad you are feeling. Having a tool in your hand, like a book, gives you people to point at, words to use, and illustrations to relate to. Although we often feel alone in tough times, we are not; books can help bridge the gap between family members and get everyone talking about what each person is thinking about.

Success Story

It can be helpful to write out your child's plan for a peaceful resolution and read it aloud before heading out the door each morning. This reaffirming mantra is tangible evidence that a solution is in sight.

Empowering Your Child

My favorite thing about using picture books such as these to tackle tough subjects is the way that the children are always kept front and center. We are not told what they feel by an adult narrator; we see the situation develop through their own experience. Illustrations help to make the scenes more tangible as we watch children go from isolated to involved, powerless to proactive, fearful to friendly. While difficult to hear, it is important and useful for a child who is struggling with challenges to be able to read about other children's experiences and say, "That's how I feel."

Even when adults play an important role in the book, it is ultimately the child who must ask someone new to play, tell a bully to back off, and find her own way to say goodbye. As parents, we can offer advice and help spot a solution, but it is more important to facilitate than dictate. Books can be the happy medium that helps us help our children.

Reading with your young children is most often thought of as a light, amusing activity enjoyed by the participants; but when tough times come up, and they will, these trusted companions can be counted on in a new way. You have worked hard to make reading a source of calm and closeness in your home; during difficult times, use your read-alouds to find comfort during those uncomfortable moments.

The Least You Need to Know

- Read-alouds aren't just for entertainment, they are useful tools for addressing hard to handle topics like death, divorce, and bullying.
- Reading and real life go hand in hand, so look for content-appropriate materials when faced with a challenging scenario.
- Simple stories can help soothe complicated situations. Try to encourage your child to use examples from his stories to talk about personal problems and solutions.

Chapter 12

An Aggressive Campaign for Reluctant Readers

In This Chapter

- Reading at school vs. reading at home
- Motivating your little learner
- Planning family read-aloud events

What do you do with a kid who doesn't want to read? There is no easy answer to that question; but we don't have to close the book on reading just because our child is having a tough time getting it open. As parents, we want to try to engage and inspire our children instead of berating or bribing them. To do this, we'll want to take a look at the different reading techniques used at school and see how we can help level the playing field at home. Heck, instead of just leveling, we may need to get out the fertilizer, watering cans, and weed treatment, too.

The important thing to remember is that if you want reading to be valued in your family, you will have to dedicate valuable time to reading. This doesn't mean fancy designer reading programs or nightly reading marathons, but a couple of well-designed special events used in conjunction with spontaneous reading opportunities and a rejuvenated reading routine could help get your little learner back in the game.

If things are progressing nicely, this chapter still has something to offer. There is nothing wrong with wanting to make a good thing better. Use the ideas in this chapter as a way to keep things interesting. Encourage everyone to pitch in for planning and see where your special events take you. Since the ideas in this section are not bribes, or arbitrary rewards, they can be trusted to help further inspire your readers, not conspire against your hard work.

Skills, Drills, and Few Reading Thrills

I loved books as a little kid, and I love books now. But between then and now there were some rough reading spots. Having had grandparents who insisted that, "Reading is the single most important thing you will ever learn to do," I was always given plenty of time to be with books. But when I got to school, "reading" usually meant sitting at my desk and practicing phonics lessons. When we did read stories, they were dull, trite, and lacked colorful illustrations, if they had any pictures at all. Workbooks replaced picture books. We can definitely assume that the pleasure principle is in jeopardy when every reading activity begins with the word "work."

When your child enters school you will quickly learn which approach to "reading" the classroom takes. While the best approach to reading involves reading, "teaching reading" is a different animal altogether. School districts tend to favor either a phonics approach or a whole language approach, and a few talk candidly about the need for a balance between the two. Whatever system your school subscribes to, chances are, reading in school will be very different from the environment you have created at home. Unfortunately, this is when our once-voracious readers can start to become bored with books. Fortunately, there is plenty we can do to get them back in the stacks.

In this chapter, I will talk a little bit about the different approaches to teaching reading. As this is a book about raising a reader for life and creating literacy-rich homes, the pros are really not as important as the cons. The reason we want to look at the cons is not to dismiss or degrade different methods for teaching reading, but to make sure that we are not trying to fix a problem by emulating the problem. If your child resists her reading program at school, then complete the assigned work at home but don't insist on more of the same. Instead, look for ways to complement the curriculum with more engaging activities.

Let's look at several activities that can help bring that reluctant reader back into the fold.

Phonics Worksheets

I would never advocate the abolishment of phonics. On the contrary, I think learning phonics skills is critical to reading. The National Institute for Literacy states that phonics instruction teaches children the relationships between the letters of written language and the individual sounds of spoken language. If we want children to be able to decode new words, they need phonics. But I think putting a worksheet in front of a child and calling it reading misses the mark. Phonics in isolation is isolating. It needs a companion—a good book.

If your child is struggling with phonics worksheets, and is becoming turned off to reading, more phonics worksheets are not the answer. My son is in the "I hate broccoli" stage. But I know broccoli is good for him. Now, I could continue to give him plain broccoli (phonics practice) and have the same negative reaction we've had in the past (crying tantrums); or I can hide the broccoli in a casserole (storybook) and not have to hate mealtime. Sometimes the best way to make sure our kids are getting what they need is by making it easier to swallow.

Never has language tasted better than when it is served by the master, Dr. Seuss. *One Fish Two Fish Red Fish Blue Fish* contains some of the most ridiculous rhymes, and wonderful sound combinations, to ever grace the pages of children's literature. You can't go wrong with any of the Seuss books, but this one points out that "From here to there, funny things are everywhere." An important reminder if everyone is starting to take reading a bit too seriously. Read the book through together, then go back and reread all the rhyming words as you point out the letter combinations that rhyme. Try and think of more words that rhyme with these words and voilà! Instant phonics fun with no messy tantrums.

Whole Language

Remember how when you didn't know how to spell a word your parents would tell you to go look it up, and that didn't make any sense because you didn't know how to spell the word to look it up? That is the problem with relying exclusively on whole language. If you don't know the letters of a word or the sounds the letters can make, how can you figure out what word the letters are making?

Children who have no background in phonics come upon new words and stare at the page, stare at the teacher, and then stare at the floor. Embarrassed and longing for the excruciating silence to be over, this unequipped reader guesses at the word, sometimes using context clues or available illustrations, but usually it is just a blind guess. The rhythm of the sentence being lost and the story having been interrupted, it no longer feels like reading, it feels like water torture. Who wants to curl up with water torture?

Quick Picks

When it comes to phonics at home, remember K.I.S.S. (Keep It Short and Simple). Pointing out words and letter combinations that rhyme, for instance, is enough; you don't need to turn a read-aloud into a school lesson.

If your child is frustrated that she doesn't know the words and "can't read," modeling reading is still an excellent route to go, and the Dr. Seuss books can come in handy here, also. The *Start to Read!* books by Barbara Gregorich are specifically targeted for the emergent reader and come in three levels. You and your child can find high-interest, entertaining stories at a level that is comfortable, helping to make reading enjoyable again.

As suggested in the previous section, it isn't necessary to create school at home and explain to your son that you have chosen these books to work on his phonics skills. Introduce a new title as you would any other and read for the sake of reading. The more we keep reminding children, especially reluctant readers, how much work reading is, the more disinterested we'll end up making them.

Balancing the Books

When your child begins school, take a close look at what and how she is reading. In fact, I would encourage you to do a taste test of reading and tweak your reading routines to balance the flavors: too much phonics, mix in some stories. Not enough phonics, target your picture books. The premise of this book is not how to teach reading or how to hurry a reader along; it is about nurturing a reader for life. Think of reading with your children as a marathon, not a sprint, and offer a variety of support along the way. Keep inviting them back to the book nook. Replenish and update materials. Choose high-interest titles for your read-alouds. Most of all, don't panic. A challenging mile or two does not mean that you are out of the race.

Ideally, your school district will embrace both phonics and whole language. But even in the best of circumstances, it does not mean that reading will top the list of your little learner's favorite subjects at school. This may be your first experience with your child losing interest in something he once loved. Instead of pulling the plug on the TV or ordering him into his room until he comes out reading, you can try to facilitate more reading fun. Home is always where the heart is, and you can help remind him how much he loves reading.

Success Story

Is it bow (on a gift) or bow (before) an audience? We need phonics skills to recognize the letters that make up the words and whole language to know what the word says.

Self Motivation

One of the biggest culprits in hindering a child's love for reading is grades. Reading used to be enjoyed for the sake of reading; now there is pressure to read the right way. I've seen the same kind of thing happen with organized sports for the little kids. Instead of being aloud to run around chasing a ball with their friends, they have to sit and wait to be told how to play. Every child exposed to books will tell you she knows how to read; just like every kid who has ever chased a ball will tell you she knows how to play. But instead of encouraging that "Go get 'em" attitude, we kindly (or condescendingly) explain, "No, you don't really know how to," take the book, or the ball, out of her hands and insist on showing her the right (read: school) way. No wonder so many kids want to throw in the towel.

I'm not here to argue whether there is a right or wrong way to teach reading, as I am not concerned with teaching reading; but I am concerned with what grades do to reading enjoyment. While we don't usually give grades out at home, we can be too quick to bribe our kids with rewards that have nothing to do with reading. "Read for 30 minutes after dinner and get a hot-fudge sundae" really sounds strange when you compare it to, "Watch TV for 30 minutes and get a hot-fudge sundae." We know that reading is entertaining enough (like watching television); we don't need to sweeten the deal with arbitrary rewards. We can, however, find ways to remind our children that reading is its own reward.

"Five More Minutes, Please!"

What kid doesn't want to stay up later? As a child I was absolutely convinced that all the really good stuff in our house happened after I went to bed. Staying up late was an absolute thrill; but as my parents needed a break, I had to figure out a way to stay up later without bothering them. We compromised, and instead of having an "evening bedtime," I had an "evening bedroom time." With teeth brushed, water drank, and pajamas on, I had to be in my bedroom by a certain time, but I could stay up reading for an additional 15 minutes. And, truth be told, I stayed up longer than that and didn't tell my parents, who pretended not to notice. Everybody got what they wanted. What none of us probably realized at the time was how those sacred moments helped turn me into an enthusiastic reader.

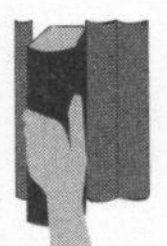

Quick Picks

Have an obscenely early riser? Invest in an outlet timer that the nightlight can be plugged into. That way, your child can read in bed in the morning without having to disturb the peace.

Of all the things you can put in your children's bedrooms, one of the most valuable is a reading lamp. Nightstand lamps work well, but so do funky lights that attach to head boards, or mini book lights that are sold specifically for late-night reading and available at most major book stores. No handheld computer games, no extra TV time, just books. This is a great time to let them read whatever it is they want. Consider this part of your reading-routine dessert. Counting calories when ordering dessert ruins the treat. Don't insist that your children read what you want; let them choose what they want. It doesn't matter whether it is a joke book, a comic book, or a wordless picture book; this reading is purely the icing on the cake—the extra-creamy, ultra-smooth, full-flavor kind of icing.

Quick Picks

Looking for a great stocking stuffer or grab-bag gift? Consider an "itty bitty" book light from Zelco. These lights attach to a book and illuminate the page without disturbing others. For your kids, they are just a great reading accessory that prolongs bedtime; for you, they are another way to promote reading in your home. Available at amazon.com.

The Late Show

Independent reading at night is one way to make reading its own reward, but if you are looking for something a little more family focused, try hosting your own late-night reading program. You don't need to wait until 11 P.M. to get the show started, but going past your regular bedtime routine will help to mark the occasion; for this reason, plan on a late show once a week or once a month, depending on your schedule. The idea is to promote fun, not fatigue.

The beauty of continuing your read-aloud routine with your growing children is the one-on-one time it provides. In a previous section we talked about the benefits of setting a "reading date," and this idea builds on that one. Mark the calendar and plan on enjoying a late show with one, not all, of your children. Choose a new book that this particular child would love. Remember, this is about them, not you, so if your son is obsessed with potty humor right now, reading from *Oh Yuck! The Encyclopedia of Everything Nasty* by Joy Masoff might be right up his alley. Disgusting titles aside, prepare two desserts, retreat to a hidden corner of the house, unwrap a new book, and read together. With minimal cost and preparation you will …

- Convince this child that he is your favorite (at least for tonight).
- Be privy to the secrets that are revealed during intimate moments like these.
- Create a heartwarming memory (for both of you).
- Make the ultimate connection between books and pleasure.

An idea like this works best in conjunction with daily reading, but can be a welcome reprieve (for both of you) from the regular routine. If one parent's schedule dictates late nights or early mornings, this once-in-a-blue-moon book bonanza can help family members reconnect with each other and a great story.

"Put It on My (Library) Card"

If you have not already done so, help your children get their own library cards. Some libraries have no age restrictions, while other towns prefer that children be at least 5 years old or capable of signing their own name. As soon as they are eligible, introduce them to the amazingly accessible world of the public library. The children's room of your library is bursting with new adventures, information, and entertainment. Making your child a part of this important community is an excellent way to promote the reading and pleasure connection.

Beyond great books, which these rooms are loaded with, you will most likely find puzzles, manipulative toys, right-size furniture, stuffed animals, posters and paintings, and, if you are very lucky, plants and animals. Children's Rooms are fun. They are designed to make children want to spend time there and return again. A weekly trip to the library can become as natural as your weekly trip to the grocery store. In both places, everyone will be happy to head home with a treat.

Success Story

In addition to his own library card, your child may enjoy his own library bag. Look for a plain-colored tote that can be personalized and decorated by your little learner and used to carry books back and forth to the library.

While it is probably a good idea for you to hold onto your child's library card until he is old enough to keep track of it, letting your child choose the book of his choice and teaching him to check it out are valuable skills. Of course, you can help him pick out books or grab a few recommended titles you'd like to try together, but no matter what, always leave room on his card for his own choice. You will take home hits and misses, but giving your child the opportunity to choose makes him a more active participant in his own reading routine; a nice change from the myriad of materials he must read in school. Given the choice, our preferences are always preferred.

Recondition Your Read-Alouds

As your child starts to learn to read more independently, you may be wondering if reading aloud to her is still worthwhile. It may also be harder to find time for reading together, because the older children get, the more activities they become involved in. Grabbing a quick dinner from a fast food restaurant and eating it in the car on the way from soccer practice to girl scouts is the norm, not the exception. Who can blame you for all being exhausted at the end of the day?

To compound the problem, kids can convince themselves that reading is just for school and not for pleasure. Reluctant readers especially can become bored with the same routine, and the idea of a read-aloud may be met with groans and moans instead of grins and giggles. By this point, children understand that books have a front cover, pages are turned after reading words left to right, and pictures illustrate what the words are saying. To capture the attention of our little learners, we'll want to get our creative juices flowing and take fresh perspective on our read-alouds. The following sections offer some manageable suggestions to do just that.

Living-Room Campout

Is it me, or does it seem that the summer months fly by while the winter months drag on? Children love to be outside, and fresh air does us all a world of good. But when temperatures drop and we are spending more and more time indoors, it can seem like the walls are closing in on us. Avoid seasonal suffocation and invite the outdoors inside with these easy-to-assemble storytime suggestions:

Quick Picks

Since you have out the flashlights, why not enjoy a starlit night? Shine a flashlight through a colander and watch the stars come out in your living room. Take turns making up stories about visiting outer space.

- No campsite is complete without a tent. Get out your camping gear, pull out a play tent, or use old sheets and furniture to set up your destination location.
- Have tasty trail treats on hand by mixing finger-friendly cereal like Cheerios with dried fruit, pretzels, and Goldfish crackers.
- If you have a fireplace, make sure and use it. If you don't, try building a homemade bonfire. Place flashlights at the bottom of a pasta pot and cover with crunched-up orange, red, and yellow tissue paper. Warm yourselves by the glow of these kid-friendly flames.

Having created a classic campground motif, it is time to enjoy your selected stories. There are a ton of great outdoor tales to read together. Take turns reading aloud to make the experience even more interactive. If your child is struggling with reading, let him choose the order of books to read, be in charge of turning the pages, or have a chance to narrate the pictures as he sees fit. Here are some titles to track together:

Bailey Goes Camping, copyright © 1997 Kevin Henkes

Too young to join his bunny siblings on a camping trip, Bailey's creative parents help him experience camping at home where he makes a homemade tent, fishes in the bathtub, and enjoys hotdogs and marshmallows to eat. This is an excellent book for parents to preview in anticipation of your own living-room campout. If you are feeling particularly enthused, you could enjoy the suggested activities in the story. While this book is targeted for a younger audience, the relevant theme is too irresistible to pass up.

Toasting Marshmallows: Camping Poems, copyright © 2001 Kristine O'Connell George, Kate Kiesler

Written from the point of view of a young girl on a camping trip with her family, these sensory-inspired poems capture the sights, sounds, and smells of the great outdoors. Beautiful acrylic paintings capture the essence of what the words are trying to convey. With selections that range from poignant to funny, there is something for everyone.

Pajama Party

I am never uncomfortable in my pajamas. Made of the softest cotton, loose, well worn and warm, my pajamas immediately put me at ease. Why not enjoy that comfort all evening long? I mentioned how staying up late makes a reading routine seem more special; well, the reverse can also be true. A few adjustments to the dinner hour can help you serve up a read-aloud supper club that everyone will enjoy:

- Call it an early night by inviting everyone to slip into something more comfortable before dinner. Pajamas, slippers, teddy bears, and security blankets are all welcomed attire.
- Arrange your throw pillows, couch cushions, and sleeping bags in the center of your family room and get prepared to love lounging around.
- Since very little sleeping is actually ever done at a slumber party, have some fun activities planned. Decorate plain white pillow cases with fabric markers or make use of those mysterious single socks by creating sock puppets.
- If you have invited teddy bears and dolls to your party, don't leave them out of the fun! Arrange comfy spaces for your special guests, play hide-and-go-seek with these stuffed friends, and invite them to sing along to party favorites like "Old McDonald" and "The Wheels on the Bus."
- Keep the meal simple and tasty with pizza and juice.

After you have all enjoyed dinner, it is time for some entertainment. Hand out flashlights, light candles, and arrange them out of reach, and party in your pajamas with these entertaining choices.

Ira Sleeps Over, copyright © 1975 Bernard Waber, Larry Robinson

When Ira is invited to sleep over at a friend's house he is thrilled at first, but becomes upset wondering if his friend will welcome, or make fun of, his bedtime companion, teddy bear. A lovely story about self-acceptance and compassion. The multiple characters lend themselves to voice changes, making this a great, animated read-aloud story.

Pajama Party: All Aboard Reading (Level 1), copyright © 1998 Joan Holub, Julie Durrell

This easy reader captures all the fun and excitement of planning and participating in an up-all-night pajama party. Complete with sharing secrets, pillow fights, and ghost stories, this female cast of characters tries their best to stay up all night, but of course, can't quite make it. Simple text and warm illustrations make it a welcome addition to your own festivities.

Christmas in July

If sweltering temperatures make you feel like you need a little Christmas, break out the holiday hoopla and revisit cold-weather classics. If the weather outside is already frightful, turn up the heat indoors and head for your beach blankets at the poolside playroom. While I look forward to enjoying holiday books and seasonal selections as they come up, it can be fun to break from tradition and recreate some fond memories with a little read-aloud calendar chaos.

Bookworms Beware

As you plan these special events, remember to focus your energies on the books. All the other activities are wonderful bonuses, but don't lose sight of the actual storytime.

The holidays are tailor-made for children. Lights, music, sweets, and treats all cater to kids. If you are feeling like you are in a seasonal slump, spice up your plans by presenting the unexpected reading presents.

- No need to drag your decorations out of the attic. Instead, designate a particular area, like a corner of the playroom, to party. Using construction paper, help your children cut out snowflake designs, weave colorful Kwanzaa mats, or color in paper menorahs.
- Food is a favorite part of any celebration. String popcorn, whip up a batch of potato pancakes, or bake a holiday dessert to help set the mood.
- Instead of blowing your budget on a second round of shopping in one year, rewrap favorite books that you may have not enjoyed together in awhile, including a holiday photo album.

Now that you are ready to get the party started, check out two of these holiday treats that make for great read-alouds.

The Polar Express, copyright © 1985 by Chris Van Allsburg

Does Santa really exist? Only if you really believe. There are dozens of Santa Claus books on the market, but this Caldecott Medal book leaves most of them back at the station. Hop on board and embrace the magical miracle that is revealed.

Pearl's Eight Days of Chanukah: With a Story and Activity for Each Night, copyright © 2003 Jane Breskin Zalben

Sharing your home with extended family members can put a strain on everyone's patience, but these sheep cousins come to realize, through simple text and fun hands-on activities, the best part of the season is being together. Ambitious families will enjoy replicating the activities at home.

Success Story

Because you are looking for titles in the "off season," you won't have to fight off the crowds. This would be a great time to take advantage of all the choices available and try a few new titles.

All in the Family

If it takes a village to raise a child, it takes a family to raise a reader. Building a literacy-rich home depends on all members of the family pitching in, be it some cherished one-on-one time or an activity-driven family event. As parents, we cannot solely rely on school reading; we must continue to motivate our little learners. This is especially true of reluctant readers who will soon find a way to fly under the reading radar if we do not keep a close eye on their book behavior.

Aside from worksheets and routines, children can become wary of reading if the material they are being presented doesn't fit. It's a good idea to give your read-alouds the "Goldilocks Treatment." We want to read material that is not too hard, not too easy, but just right. Some children may thrive on reading and become turned off by "babyish" books, while other kids become intimidated if there are not enough pictures or too much text for their taste. How do you know if what you're reading is just right?

Publishers have helped to decipher which books will most likely be well received by which age group by including reading levels on the back of their books. Some publishers use icons like RL4, for reading-level four, or target age groups with numbers 005–007 or 0507 for ages 5 to 7. Unfortunately, these levels are only guidelines, and many times your child will not conveniently fit into this mold. Instead of relying on reading levels, use them as a frame of reference, but trust your child's comfort level. Just like pajamas, when we are more comfortable, we are more relaxed, a key element in reaching your reluctant reader. Let's look at the two different ends of the spectrum.

Indulging Your Advanced Reader

When children act restless or disruptive, we can easily lose our patience, and our perspective. Not understanding what is wrong, we can inadvertently aggravate a situation by failing to see that a change is necessary. Reluctant readers are not necessarily poor readers; they can merely be bored readers. You may be surprised to learn that your child doesn't need more attention, she needs more action.

If you are computer savvy, having designed your own website, creating your own online Christmas cards, and downloading home videos, could you imagine how painful it would be to sit in a "Computers 101" class where the goal of the day was saving a Word document? Yet for children who have been read to their whole lives, understand how books work, and appreciate great illustrations, plot, and humor, reading "A is for Apple" is excruciating.

Bookworms Beware

Just because your child can read a book doesn't mean he should. Always preview unfamiliar titles to make sure the content is age-appropriate before giving it your okay.

Because we as parents have been the ones to introduce great books all along, if we stop doing that, our children will assume that they have already read all the good books and give up reading for pleasure. We have to keep showing our children what is next. If your little learner is dissatisfied with the titles recommended in this chapter, take a look at the next section and use some of those suggestions. Luckily, there will always be new authors to discover, new characters to meet, and new adventures to discover. Let's not let our kids convince themselves they have already read all the good stuff.

Nurturing Your Slow Reader

Unlike the advanced reader who tends to act out in frustration, the slow reader tries to fade into the background. Praying that she is not chosen to read aloud in class, embarrassed that everyone else seems to have cracked the reading code, this reluctant reader has come to relate books with feeling bad—the complete opposite experience we are hoping our children will have. This child will try to avoid reading at all costs and become agitated, often to the point of tears, if you broach the subject. But because we know ignoring this behavior will just exaggerate the problem, we want to find a way to gently reach out to this suffering little soul.

We can start by taking a similar but opposite approach to finding materials. Instead of calling attention to your child's low reading level, you may want to take a trip to the library and ask him to help you pick out books for a younger cousin, sibling, or neighbor. Assured that these "baby books" aren't for him, as he is a big kid, he can browse and choose titles that he once enjoyed. You can check out more books than you "need" on the pretext that when you get them home, you'll go through them together to pick out the "best ones."

Insisting that your child really is a "reading expert" can help to empower him in an area that now feels overwhelming. Reading through books that he enjoys, talking about favorite parts of the book, and reliving memories, can help to re-establish reading as a pleasant activity. It doesn't matter that these books are at a lower reading level; what matters is that reading is happening in your home without fears or tears.

Leading By Example

The "practice what you preach" mantra rings true when it comes to reading. We can become so focused on getting our children to read that we may lose sight of our own reading practices. In all of the activities mentioned in this chapter, there is room for you to bring along your favorite books. At any given time, I usually have one novel and two magazines to read. When planning for your family's special events, pencil in some independent reading time and reach for your reading material. Your children can look through the books you just read aloud, and you can sneak in a quick chapter or a quick article. We want to facilitate our children's reading habits, but we don't want to lose sight of our own in the meantime.

Remember, too, that reading in real time happens all of the time. We are just so accustomed to reading directions, recipes, and instructions, that we take this reading for granted. As you decide which activities from this chapter you would like to try, look for the built-in read-aloud opportunities to share with your children. Planning for the reverse holiday season? Consult your recipe book and read aloud. Putting together a tent in the living room? Read the instruction manual out loud. The more you look for real-time reading, the easier it will be to spot the opportunities.

If your child no longer enjoys reading, do not assume that this is a setback he will merely outgrow. In order to get good at something, we have to do it over and over again; children do not become enthusiastic readers unless they are reading enthusiastically. This means figuring out which types of stories our children like the most, providing meaningful reading experiences, carving out specific reading routines that complement spontaneous reading moments, and making reading a priority in our home. No easy task. But the ideas mentioned in this chapter are designed to help you help your child remember why reading is a pleasure, for everyone.

Bookworms Beware

When I talk about everyone in the family being an active reader, I do mean everyone. Both parents, all caretakers, and any siblings are encouraged to make time for reading. Keep all sorts of reading materials around the house so there is never an excuse not to read.

The Least You Need to Know

- School doesn't signal the end of read–alouds. At home, make sure you are making time for unassigned reading.
- Each family member can help a reluctant reader by modeling positive reading behavior through sharing favorite titles and topics with each other.
- Reading solutions are both entertaining and educational. Try combining reading with hands on activities like cooking, art, or exercise and move out of the sit still zone.

Chapter 13

Great Emergent-Reader Titles to Try Together

In This Chapter

- Reading aloud is as important as ever
- Smarter stories take center stage
- Repeat characters can mean repeat success

I love the recommendations that are found in this chapter. I think they hold a special place in my heart because many of these read-aloud titles are ones I used for storytime as a librarian and a teacher. There is something so gratifying about a sea of smiling eyes hanging on your every word, anxious for you to turn the page so that they can find out what happens next. We meet characters we want to cheer for, laugh out loud at the antics of some four-legged friends, and shed sentimental tears as the last page is revealed.

As our children mature, so do their books. We can look forward to read-alouds that make us think, "I love that book." Having this kind of reaction to a story is sure to rub off on our kids. Board books have been replaced by big-kid books—books that have real pages with real characters and real stories. This means that you are all in for a really good time!

Keep at It

Children never really outgrow read-alouds. There is no magic cutoff date signifying that entertaining picture books should be put away or easy readers best left to the school day. But all too often, when the backpacks appear, the read-alouds disappear. Convinced that school will take care of things, many parents stop reading aloud, thinking it is an activity to be shared until kids can read on their own. But as we have talked about, enthusiastically reading with our children is necessary if we want to raise enthusiastic readers. Besides raising competent readers, we also want to take advantage of the more complicated conversations read-alouds can provoke.

As I mentioned earlier, no one gets through childhood unscathed. Hurt feelings, disappointment, and less-than-ideal circumstances are inevitable. When our family is hurting, it can be particularly hard to find the right words, to be of comfort. Story books can help us help our children; with books on our side we can be a confidante and a comfort.

In addition to providing help, books for this target audience also feature more sophisticated humor, making them a joy to read. Moving beyond alphabets and lullabies, we meet characters who are wise, witty, cunning, and clever. Fortunately for us and our children, the books just keep getting better and better. Keep your read-aloud routines firm but flexible, and you'll end up enjoying the stories as much as they do.

Peaks and Valleys

As you and your family make the transition from home to school, you can expect to have mixed feelings about all the experiences your children are having. Whether you are kissing your daughter goodbye in the morning before she gets on the school bus or an active part of a homeschooling co-op, it is no longer just the two of you. Some days will be filled with wonder and splendor, while other days will be terrible, horrible, and no good. In the middle of all of this change, your regularly scheduled reading routine may suffer some. Don't panic; just like getting back into an exercise routine after a holiday lapse, you do have the ability to get your family back on the reading track.

Your child may love reading and beg for more books, or become cool and withdrawn at the mention of storytime. Chances are, most kids will fall somewhere in between the two. Just like introducing books to your newborn and toddler, who would one day sit for an extended amount of time and the next day squirm like a fish on a hook, reading with your little learner will ebb and flow. But by having plenty of reading materials within reach, planning the occasional family reading event, and making read-alouds cherished one-on-one experiences, you can enjoy more peaks than valleys and continue to build your literacy-rich home.

Bookworms Beware

Before you ask your children what they are reading, ask yourself what you are reading. Remember how important it is that you set a good reading example. If your own practice has slipped, take time to get yourself grounded in a good story.

Apply the Pleasure Principle

When we like what we do, we do more of it. Now that your child is approaching a more independent age and can communicate exactly what it is he likes and dislikes, we want to keep reading in the former column, not the latter. To do that, as always, we want to connect children to great books. Luckily, we have many selections to choose from.

The following recommendations are only a sampling of the many satisfying stories available on the shelves of your local library and bookstores. Depending on the strength of your reader and the particular book, you may want to take turns reading to each other, or give your child the responsibility of reading the title and finding the author and illustrator's names on the cover. Any time you can invite your child to read aloud with you is advantageous; but if the invitation is declined, don't belabor the point, just get to the good stuff. An invitation to read, like an invitation to a party, should signal the start of fun, not frustration.

A Look Back: Five Timeless Tales

No heartstring is safe from a pull when you revisit story books you enjoyed as a child, with your own child. Perhaps you have fond memories of curling up with your own parents, or maybe you remember reading these books over and over again in the privacy of your own room. Either way, anytime you open up a conversation with your child that begins with, "When I was your age," you should pack some tissues for your trip down memory lane. As endearing then as they are now, these stories have timeless kid appeal. If you can, find a picture of yourself from the time that you enjoyed one of these stories and fasten it to the inside cover of the book, next to a recent picture of your child. Not only does this make a lovely addition to your Special Shelf, but it could be the book that someday makes it into your grandchild's hands. Now, that's timeless.

Success Story

Take time to review the proper handling of books. Books are treasures and should be treated with respect and care. Check for clean hands, turn the pages carefully, and stack books neatly in baskets or line them up on shelves. Big-kid books mean big-kid book responsibilities.

Harold and the Purple Crayon, copyright © 1955 Crockett Johnson

How far can a child's imagination take him? Enjoying finding out with this simple but very clever story of a boy and his crayon. The character is irresistible in his footsy pajamas, and although he embraces his adventures, he still finds his way home.

Cloudy with a Chance of Meatballs, copyright © 1978 Judi Barrett, Ron Barrett

This delightfully humorous story about a town whose weather is absolutely delicious will have you and your children laughing out loud. But when too much of a good thing turns out to be bad, the townspeople must come up with a plan to save their homes. Pure fun.

Quick Picks

Timeless tales are often commemorated in special-edition publications and can make a beautiful gift for expectant parents. You know how fast time goes; it's never too soon to begin building a quality home library.

Alexander and the Terrible, Horrible, No Good, Very Bad Day, copyright © 1972 Judith Viorst, Ray Cruz

From the moment he wakes up. Alexander is having the worst possible day of his life and contemplates moving to Australia several times. Everyone has days when everything goes wrong, and parents and children alike will empathize and relate to poor Alexander's plight.

Nate the Great, copyright © 1977 Marjorie Weinman Sharmat, Marc Simont

Success Story

What could be more fun than your child starring in her own book? Check out www.iseeme.com for a complete list of personalized book ideas.

Nate the Great, neighborhood detective, is the boy you call when you want the job done—a job like finding a lost toy, picture, or goldfish. Best read in a dry, monotone voice to capture the seriousness of his work, Nate invites readers to help him solve mysteries; after a pancake breakfast, of course.

Velveteen Rabbit, copyright © 1922 Margery Williams

The story of a stuffed rabbit who anxiously waits to become real; possible only when the little boy he has been gifted to chooses to really, really love him. An excellent choice for children who adore their playthings, and a sentimental message for parents who know that these things will, all too soon, be outgrown.

Hot Off the Press: Five New and Improved Stories

And the hits just keep on coming! Just when I think that the talented authors and illustrators have written every picture book possible, I am delighted to find out I have again sold them short. Picture books continue to be more sophisticated, more beautiful, and more engaging than their predecessors. Adaptations of classic tales, original works and activity books all offer audiences a new and exciting reading experience. As an added bonus, parents can enjoy discovering these new gems right alongside their little learners, making each trip into the new-releases section of the library and bookstore an adventure in reading.

Success Story

Even if the actual text doesn't come with recipes, you may want to use food-related stories to inspire your own meals. Field stones can easily be collected and used in homemade soup, and the internet is full of culturally diverse, kid-friendly cuisine. Eating is always a welcome ending to reading.

Stone Soup, copyright © 2003 Jon Muth

A retelling of the classic French folktale, Muth's depiction follows three Buddhist monks into a village where everyone hoards their belongings and is skeptical of their neighbors. With breathtaking illustrations, this multicultural tale crosses all boarders and reminds readers that we have so much more when we share. A great read-aloud to use around a holiday feast.

Yoko, copyright © 1998 Rosemary Wells

When Yoko opens her lunchbox to enjoy the sushi her mother lovingly packed for her first day of school, some of the other children are appalled and poke fun. Yoko's teacher helps the class embrace new ideas, and foods, in one of the first Yoko stories by Wells. All of the Yoko titles eloquently intertwine ancestry and acceptance.

Lily's Purple Plastic Purse, copyright © 1996 Kevin Henkes

Lily loves everything about school, especially her teacher who is wonderfully funny and always gives out tasty treats; but when he takes away her purse, she is crushed and immediately changes her opinion. When he returns the purse, complete with a special note and treats, she must find a way to salvage their relationship. A heartwarming story about the special relationships children and teachers share.

Olivia, copyright © 2000 Ian Falconer

About an energetic, overly enthusiastic pig who must try on every outfit she owns and hates naps, but loves sandcastles and her cat. This picture book uses perfectly chosen black and white illustrations that are enhanced by red in all the right places. There is a little bit of mischievous, though endearing, Olivia in all of us and this simple read-aloud will inspire you to read her other adventures.

Play and Find Out Series, copyright © 1999 Janice Van Cleave

Now that your kids are at school, they will be learning new subjects. These books have easy-to-do home experiments to help your whole family better enjoy our wonderful world. Subject titles include *Bugs, Math, and the Human Body*. A nice alternative to a regular read-aloud routine, these experiments can get everyone up, moving, and learning with books.

Playground Picks: Five Mom-Approved Titles

It was interesting to find out that many parents recommended books that were part of a collection or whose characters appeared in multiple stories. I think one of the nicest things about tapping into a primary-level series is the consistency. You have a destination at the library and a sure-fire request when family members ask what they should buy for your children. Instead of having to say, "She likes books," you can confidently respond, "She loves the Magic School Bus," and send your in-laws off in search of the latest installment. This is also the time when we come to trust authors. If something has worked before, we want to believe it can work again. Fortunately, it usually does. These recommendations can get you started on your own patterned read-alouds.

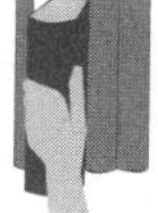

Quick Picks

Remember, all reading counts, so be sure to read out the list of items you need for an experiment, the order of the steps, and any safety precautions. Instead of reading silently, digesting the information, and paraphrasing for your kids, give them the chance to hear the actual written material for themselves.

If You Give a Mouse a Cookie, copyright © 1985 Laura Numeroff, Felicia Bond

Who knew that satisfying one request could lead to such a commotion? The antics of the mouse and the efforts of the young boy to keep up with a growing list of demands is told in a simple, circular pattern that ends where it starts. Predictable without being boring, Numeroff has used the same kid-friendly concept in *If You Give a Pig a Pancake* and *If You Give a Moose a Muffin*.

The Magic School Bus at the Waterworks, copyright © 1986 Joanna Cole

For over 20 years Mrs. Frizzle and her class have stumbled upon outrageous learning experiences thanks to their wacky science teacher and her trusty school bus. Having now covered everything from science fairs to dinosaurs to the human body, this bus, and these books, can take you and your children on entertaining explorations.

Arthur's Underwear (Arthur Adventure Series), copyright © 2001 Marc Brown

Is there anyone alive who has not feared ripping their pants in public and having their underwear show? Marc Brown's same cast of characters take part in this series that is neither too sweet nor too sour. Children can be mean, everyone can feel embarrassed, and readers will relate to the fears and humor. As usual, Arthur and his friends can be counted on to teach a valuable lesson without being preachy or heavy-handed.

Click, Clack, Moo: Cows That Type, copyright © 2000 Doreen Cronin, Betsy Lewin

Demanding better living conditions in the barn, the cows use a discarded typewriter to air their grievances to Farmer Brown. Before long, other farm animals get in on the action and stand up for their rights, like electric blankets. The pen, or in this case the typewriter, really does prove to be hilariously more mighty than the sword.

Bookworms Beware

The more your children read, the more they will know. If you have put off important family practices like recycling, now is the time to get your house in order. Include your children in your commitment to environmental awareness and use books to help you all learn how to do your part.

Recycle!: A Handbook for Kids, copyright © 1996 Gail Gibbons

An easy-to-follow introduction to the importance of recycling, how to make a difference in your own home, and things kids can do to help. With bright, bold illustrations and short, functional text, this read-aloud would do well in your kitchen book basket as a reminder of the importance of recycling.

Award Winners: Five Critically Acclaimed Books

Four out of the five recommendations found here are Caldecott recipients, honored for outstanding illustrations in a children's book. The fifth title is the winner of the Irma S. and James H. Black Honor for Excellence in Children's Literature. Presented by the Bank Street College of Education, "the Award goes to an outstanding book for young children—a book in which text and illustrations are inseparable, each enhancing and enlarging on the other to produce a singular whole." Each of the books has its own unique design and distinct feel, making them all honored choices.

Don't Let the Pigeon Drive the Bus, copyright © 2003 Mo Willems

This recently published Caldecott Honor book already has a faithful following. All the librarians I know use it for storytime because the children can't help but yell at the pigeon, "No!" despite his many pleas to drive the bus. Young audiences will relate to begging, whining, and bargaining to get their way, and parents will be pleased that no means no, for now.

Joseph Had a Little Overcoat, copyright © 1999 Simms Taback

Originally published in 1977, this new and improved version by the same author won the prestigious Caldecott Medal. In our disposable society, this Yiddish folktale turned picture book reminds us that something new can be made out of something old, and each has its important purpose. Die-cut pages give readers a glimpse of the treasure about to come, and repetitious, humorous text makes it a visual and lyrical treat.

A Tree Is Nice, copyright © 1956 Janice May Udry, Marc Simont

Trees offer us so many pleasantries: shade for picnics, sticks for forts, leaves for piling. This Caldecott Medal book has a uniquely long, slim shape, standing tall, like its subject matter, next to its counterparts. After reading together, you may want to leave time to plant a tree of your own, as the character does, to enjoy all the benefits of nurturing such a gift.

The Ugly Duckling, copyright © 1999 Hans Christian Anderson, Jerry Pickney

Pickney's adaptation of this immortal story garnered a Caldecott Honor and tells the tale of the little duck (read: child) who just didn't fit in. Looking different, he is ostracized until he blooms into a swan. All readers will identify with the duck's isolation and have the hope of one day recognizing themselves as beautiful.

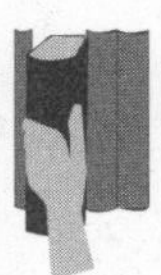

Quick Picks

Picture books with outstanding illustrations can inspire the inner artist in all of us. Consider reading books like these in a playroom book nook where blank paper and drawing materials are readily available.

The Dot, copyright © 2003 Peter H. Reynolds

Once a confident artist, musician, and poet, your little learner may begin to doubt his abilities, as does the character in this slight story. An encouraging teacher helps him get something down on that glaring blank paper and he rediscovers what an artist he truly is. Winner of the Irma S. and James H. Black Honor for Excellence in Children's Literature, this read-aloud is inspirational and moving.

The read-aloud selections found here all have staying power. Whether you choose to hook into a series and follow a cast of characters from adventure to adventure or opt to reread the same storybook over and over again because, like a good movie, you always spot something new; these books are worthy of your family's attention because your family will take pleasure in paying attention to these books.

The Least You Need to Know

- Reading pleasure is more important than reading pressure. Make sure you are choosing titles that work, instead of choosing titles that are work.
- Identifying with characters is an essential read-aloud element. This enables your child to make sense of the story while learning more about his own place in the world.
- Have read-aloud titles throughout the house and see where the stories take you.

Part 4

The Independent Reader: Leap Into Literature

Making the leap from dependent to independent reader is an exciting milestone for you and your child. No longer limited to having a parent decide what they can read, children are free to browse the bookcases themselves and make educated decisions based on book covers, reviews and recommendations.

In this part, we will look at ways to lighten the reading load, so to speak. Yes, we want to keep our reading routines going, but we may also want to take a look at more age appropriate ways to do that. I'll also offer some strategies for handling weightier issues like death, divorce, and disappointment. There are several kinds of books that can help make a tough topic more manageable. At home we can encourage independence and shared reading with a variety of books and activities that respect the individual but do not neglect the family's goals.

Chapter 14

Learn to Read, Read to Learn

In This Chapter

- A parent's changing read-aloud role
- Great genres for intermediate readers
- Embracing reading entertainment

The shift from learning to read to reading to learn usually happens around fourth grade. At this time, it is assumed that children know how books work, appreciate that a story has fundamental elements, and read with an understanding of a story, not just sentence by sentence. Reading assignments can be completed independently and books are seen as a reliable source of information and entertainment. So is your job as read-aloud companion accomplished? Hardly. In fact, we could argue that we are just getting to the really good stuff—the kind of reading materials that inspire great conversations and really foster closer relationships. There is a great deal of emphasis on bonding with baby, but I think we do ourselves, and our kids, a disservice when we assume we have crossed a read-aloud finish line once our children learn how to read.

True, as an independent reader your child has mastered basic reading skills. But these skills need to be fine-tuned through continued reading practice, best done by exposing them to different kinds of written material on a regular basis. Think of it this way: just because your son can hit a ball with a bat doesn't mean he is ready for the major leagues. Learning how to connect the ball and bat, or words and stories, is just the first step. There are still plenty of curve balls that you can help him practice for. As always, reading together is instrumental in making that happen.

Every Reader Is an Individual

One of the frustrations that I faced as a teacher was trying to balance "covering the curriculum" with meeting each individual's needs. This balance was harder to negotiate than I ever could have imagined. My sixth graders, all 100-plus of them, came from different elementary schools and had various backgrounds, both educational and cultural. I dare say no two were exactly alike. Yet there I stood with an armful of mandatory novels that each student was supposed to read and comprehend at roughly the same rate. Try as I did, assuming that reading levels, interests, and abilities were identical just didn't make sense to me.

Luckily, as parents we can address the individual reading peaks and valleys of our children. School assignments aside, we are not obligated to read particular materials or cover certain subjects in a mandatory order. We can bring the books that our families want to read into our home and continue to make it an environment where literature is appreciated and enjoyed. If you have concerns about reading levels or are skeptical that you are reading the "right stuff," I hope the following pages help assure you that when you and your children head to the library or bookstore in search of entertaining and engaging stories, your mission is not impossible.

When Reading Levels Don't Measure Up

There are dozens of professional systems used to calculate a book's reading level. Some count the amount of syllables per sentences, or the amount of sentences per page, or compare the amount of common vocabulary words against the number of "unusual" vocabulary words to determine difficulty. Some methods are intended only for nonfiction works, and all tend to fall short when dialogue is concerned. Plus, just because your child can read the words doesn't mean that she should. It's even more difficult to rate reading levels when you try to balance vocabulary selection with content. Is it any wonder that reading levels have most parents shaking their heads?

It is not unusual for your children's reading-test results to be all over the board. You may be told that they are high-level oral decoders (they can pronounce the words) but have below-level comprehension (they don't know what they mean). Not very helpful information when trying to pick out a book. I always advocate a reading test that is fast, easy, and reliable; so again, I'll mention the five-finger rule. Have your child read one page of a book out loud, and count the amount of times she struggles with a word or has to stop and ask what is happening because the context makes no sense. If it is five or more times on the same page, then the book is beyond her reading level. While this doesn't take into consideration age-appropriate topics (that is for you as the parent to monitor), it is a reliable method of choosing a new book for your independent reader. If your child is dying to read a book but can't yet do it on her own, read it to her or take turns reading together.

If your child is reading "below level," don't panic. Reading levels are extremely subjective and can be used as a snapshot of how your child was reading that particular day. Of course, talk to your child's teachers if you are concerned about a real reading problem. But the best thing that you can do for readers of any level is continue to read to them. Whether the issue is fluency, comprehension, vocabulary, or decoding, every problem can benefit from read-alouds. One size does not fit all when it comes to reading levels, and not even publishers can agree on the best methods to use. Use reading-level guides as just that, a guide, but don't let a level label sabotage your successful read-aloud home.

Bookworms Beware

If your child continues to favor "easy" books, don't mock his efforts. Use the familiar text to practice voice inflection and oral presentation. A smooth read with recognizable material is a valuable literature experience for your child.

I Know What I Like

In the beginning of this book I reminded you that you are an expert on your child. And as an expert you have done everything you can to choose books that are appealing and engaging to your audience. But you no longer have to go this road alone. The older our kids get, the better they will become at telling us what it is they want. While I'm sure you have seen plenty of proof of this around the holidays, the truth is, intermediate readers are starting to develop their own personal tastes in reading. For us as parents, this can mean being introduced to new genres and authors by our children.

Now that we know we don't have to be a slave to reading levels, we are free to pursue the interests and individual reading preferences of our intermediate readers. One of the most wonderful things about helping your child to pursue a passion on the pages of great books is that this interest lends itself to enthusiastic read-alouds where you are still needed. For example, after you check out every possible independent reader on airplanes or horses, you can find books on the same subject that are beyond your child's reading level, but not beyond her comprehension level. Miraculously, we can understand what is being read to us even if we can't read the words ourselves (think back to reading to your newborn). Take advantage of your children's interests, and perhaps learn something new yourself, by indulging them in as many books on airplanes, horses, skateboards, or princesses as you can find.

Independent Doesn't Mean Isolated

Let's not overlook your changing role in the read-aloud. Basically, you used to be in charge of the read-aloud—how much to read, when to read, how to read. Now the tides are turning and you are the participant while your child is the leader. Instead of being in charge of read-alouds, you can facilitate them.

Independent readers are most usually independent thinkers. No longer will the two of you finish a read-aloud routine with you explaining what the book was about and then turning out the light. Now your son will comment on why those characters deserve what they got and your daughter will point out flaws in the book's ending. From here on in, it is important than ever to structure your read-alouds with time for discussion. This is so important to the pleasure principle, and such a key part of connecting with our kids, that given the choice between reading more and talking less and reading less and talking more, I would choose the latter. While this may seem a strange recommendation coming out of a read-aloud handbook, I know how packed today's family schedule is and truly believe that reading with our maturing children is a springboard for not only meeting new characters, but for discussing what kind of character is important to develop.

Variety Is the Spice of Reading

I don't think I started reading nonfiction for pleasure until I was well into my 20s. My reading relationship was wrapped up in fiction. I looked for compelling characters who were describing real-life experiences, but I wasn't necessarily interested in reading about real life. Quite frankly, I had become convinced that nonfiction and biography were published solely for school book reports. Yes, I was reading all the time, but I was reading all the same things all the time.

There is nothing wrong with developing a preference for a particular writing style. After all, most of us enjoy seeing movies based on our favorite actors; it goes to reason that we would enjoy reading books about our favorite characters. But we don't want to miss out on something new just because we don't know it exists or we have preconceived notions about what it has to offer. Helping our children explore different types of reading materials, while appreciating that they already have beloved books, can be a nice way to keep your read-alouds moving forward favorably. We will take a look at how to help round out your home's reading selections. As always, our emphasis will be on great books to enjoy reading aloud together.

Success Story

If you tend to get tongue-tied around your kids and find it hard to get the book conversation going, try a game of "Best/Worst." Take turns commenting on the best and worst thing in the book and give reasons for your choices. Remember, there is no right or wrong answer, so relax and enjoy the commentary.

Fiction

Fiction is hardly ever a hard sell. Your children have probably already enjoyed singing pigs, jumping monkeys, and trips to outer space in their primary readers, so making the leap to even more interesting characters visiting even more exciting locations is a logical next step. If your kids love a good story, try looking for stories where the kids are doing great things. Children should be the main characters and direct the action. While adults are available to lend a helping hand or empathetic ear, the decisions and consequences should be the responsibility of the child stars.

There are several different ways to approach reading fiction novels with your children. While there are no pictures in most of these books, you still want the experience to be easy on the eyes. If the printing is squished on the page, the print small, or the pages yellowed, look for another version. Then consider your child's reading style. You could choose to each hold onto your own copy of the book and take turns reading selections or pages. If your child is struggling with reading, share one copy of the book and use a ruler to mark the line you are reading. You may also want to see if the title is available in an oversized printing to make reading along even easier. You can apply the same critical eye you used when electing beginner books to choosing intermediate read-alouds. At the end of this part (Chapter 17), there are several excellent titles to try together.

Quick Picks

If your kids think books with illustrations are better, encourage them to make up pictures for the text. Read a page together and use index cards to capture the story in color. Display the work on a corkboard near the Special Shelf.

Don't fret if your child still likes to hear a favorite picture book or seems to gravitate toward reading that relies heavily on illustrations. Many picture books are quite smart and stylish. What you will want to avoid is re-reading the same tired picture books because you don't know where to go next. A picture book diet can not exist on green eggs and ham alone. Since the name of our game, always, is reading enjoyment, I would highly recommend any picture book by Chris Van Allsburg, as he has an absolute knack for treating his young (and older) audiences with absolute respect and reverence while creating stories that are suspenseful, fun, and memorable.

Biography

In school, everyone did the same biography reports on the same men (Ben Franklin and Martin Luther King Jr.) and the same women (Mother Theresa and Eleanor Roosevelt). Even though I, too, did these reports, several times, I cannot remember a single thing I learned from those books; of course, I know a great deal about the wonderful contributions these important people made to our society, but unfortunately, the information was not learned from my rote book reports.

Today, however, biographies have been written from a fresh perspective, one that highlights an individual's accomplishments and encourages the reader to learn more about the events that shaped this person's life. Sandra McLeod Humphrey's *Dare to Dream!: 25 Extraordinary Lives* copyright © 2005 profiles individuals who all overcame obstacles to realize their dreams. Short and to the point, these four pages' sketches focus on the accomplishment of historical and contemporary figures. A book like this can whet a young reader's appetite to learn more about a prominent figure without shoving too much information down a kid's throat.

Quick Picks

If your children love a particular author, help them learn more about their life and projects by visiting their author sites. A great place to start is the publishing house's home site, listed on the copyright page of a book.

History and Herstory

Along the same lines of dry biographies comes even drier history. Sitting in history class as a kid, I always wondered where all the children were; sitting in history class as a young adult, I also began to wonder what happened to all of the women. One of the best ways to get kids interested in nonfiction is to make them a part of it. When I am reading a great story, fact or fiction, and I find myself nodding along, connecting with the character, I know that the story is really onto something.

You can share the following books with your children and watch in wonder as they begin to realize that someday people will be reading about what *their* lives were like.

We Were There, Too!: Young People in U.S. History, copyright © 2001 Philip Hoose

The author's research proves that children were not quietly sitting in the background waiting for adults to secure their future in America; instead, the more than two dozen children profiled in this book experienced poverty, notoriety, riches, fear, and courage. Children are at the center of each event highlighted by Hoose, making this a valuable and entertaining read.

The Little House on the Prairie, copyright © 1953 Laura Ingalls Wilder

If your reader favors novels and has a penchant for time travel, this collection is not to be missed. It is highly likely that your children will just not believe that this is how people really used to live. A great springboard for discussing your family dynamic and the important contribution each member makes to the household.

When kids reach middle school, they start to become vaguely aware that the world did not begin, nor will it end, with their life. Appreciating that we are part of something bigger and therefore have a responsibility to those who came before us and those who will come after us can be celebrated with the help of read-alouds. Philip Hoose gives us another great title to try with our children: *It's Our World, Too!* Share these moving stories of youthful activism with your own children and help them shape the story they themselves will leave behind.

Poetry

When we first talked about incorporating poetry into our read-alouds, we looked at the benefit of using this genre when we were short on time or had a few minutes to read together, but didn't want to get into a whole book. What worked then can still work now. Poetry is flexible and friendly. Its rich, descriptive language is pleasing to the ear and intended to be read aloud, making it a perfect addition to your read-aloud routine.

Poetry can be extremely difficult to write, but many children greatly enjoy the challenge and look forward to finding the perfect rhyme or metaphor to use in their original work. Incorporating your children's poetry into your read-aloud routines can be a wonderful way to encourage their blossoming writing and enjoy some new material together. Although a great deal of time may have passed since you have done so, consider writing a poem or two of your own to share with your children. Shake of the notion that all poetry has to rhyme, be a masterpiece, or express some universal truth about the human condition. A little ditty about the family cat, food shopping, or hitting a homerun will be met with heartfelt applause. You don't have to be perfect; you just have to be you.

The following titles are an inspirational place to start.

If I Were in Charge of the World and Other Worries: Poems for Children and Their Parents, copyright © 1981 Judith Viorst, Lynne Cherry

A lovely collection of poems that depict the horror and happiness of being an adolescent. Instead of relying on a lot of hidden meanings that the reader is supposed to figure out, the familiar vocabulary and clear, rhythmic word choices make the poems easy to enjoy and digest.

I Froze My Mother and Other Seriously Funny Family Poems, copyright © 2005 Ted Scheu and Peter Lourie

With brutal and hilarious honesty, Ted Scheu gives us a glimpse inside our own families, warts and all. Photographs of young children making silly faces complement this collection of "family secrets" that are neither sacred nor safe.

Quick Picks

Try hosting a poetry reading in your own home. Each member of the family can bring a favorite published poem to dinner, read an original work, or recommend a book of poems he or she has enjoyed. Since poems are often soft and sweet, celebrate this special occasion with a delicious dessert.

"Do These Really Count?"

We have touched on this question before, but as your children are now old enough to insist that they know what they want to read, we want to revisit what constitutes "real reading." In short: words on a page. So yes, series books and comic books both count as real reading. So why all the negative press?

Series books and comic books have earned an undeserved reputation for being predictable, monotonous, and vulgar. Of course, such examples do exist, but saying these entire collections are worthless is a gross overstatement. Series books and comic books give independent readers a collection to connect with, a target to look for when visiting the library or bookstore, and a huge sense of accomplishment as they knock off another installment from their favorite author. Most of all, this kind of reading bridges the gap between picture books and early readers to more complex novels. Let your child explore the possibilities of this lighter fare and before long, she'll develop more mature tastes.

Seriously Good Series Books

When I was a librarian, I saw plenty of parents rolling their eyes when their kids headed over to their favorite section of the children's room—the shelf that held their favorite series. What is so strange to me is the idea that rifling through a stack of books, pulling one out, and excitedly exclaiming, "I haven't read this one yet!" would ever be a bad thing. Yet parents would continually try to take the books out of the child's hand and drag them over to a new shelf. The problem with this approach? Dragging hardly ever denotes pleasure.

While you may see the ending of *The Babysitter's Club #2* or *Goosebumps #2002* coming a million miles away, your child obviously finds comfort in characters and plots he can depend on. Instead of turning his page turners into an argument, use these treasured favorites as a bridge to even better books. Personally, I like Junie B. Jones, *The Babysitter's Club* and *Goosebumps* (and I am a closet *Sweet Valley High* aficionado), but I appreciate how reading the same basic story again and again can leave parents feeling a bit unsatisfied. Your kids will outgrow these stories, just like they outgrew *Goodnight Gorilla*, and until then, you'll do your read-alouds a favor by going with the flow.

When you do see your reader growing bored with her own selections, try the "Since/Then" equation. "Since you like the *Goosebumps* series so much, then you'd probably like *The Harry Potter* series. It has a lot of mystery and magic in it, too. Should we give it a try?" I love when friends make recommendations based on what I already like, and I prefer to tackle new roads with somebody else whenever possible. Chances are, your kids are the same way. Volunteer to read new stories with them and get them comfortable with the new characters and new plot lines. Oftentimes the most encouraging thing we can have on a new journey is an experienced and enthusiastic tour guide. Here are two contemporary series to try together:

A Series of Unfortunate Events: The Bad Beginning, copyright © 1999 Lemony Snicket

These books are deliciously disastrous. Everything that can go wrong for the three Baudelaire orphans does, and then some. Thank goodness the children are able to rely on their industrious gifts for inventing, research, and biting, or they would be absolutely doomed. This is probably the smartest, and by far most satirical, series I have ever read.

Harry Potter and the Sorcerer's Stone (Book I), copyright © 1998 J. K. Rowling

Is there anyone on the planet who hasn't heard of this kid? Even if you hate the idea of magic, mayhem, and Muggles, you have to wonder what it is about these monstrous volumes that has millions of kids glued to their seats. My guess? It must be a really great story worth checking out.

Bookworms Beware

Seeing the movie is not the same thing as reading the book. Whenever possible, read the books first, and then watch the movie. Your kids will be surprised, and dismayed, about how much "good stuff" is missing.

Comic Books

I know respectable, grown men who have dynamic financial portfolios, well-manicured lawns framing their four-bedroom center-hall colonials, and take stunning family vacations each year; yet these guys are reduced to nervous 12-year-old kids on Christmas Eve if you dare mention the ultimate man of steel, Superman. Comic books are an integral part of childhood culture, hooking more kids into reading than any expensive manufactured reading program, yet the work has failed to receive its well-deserved kudos. But I am hard-pressed to find another genre whose writing is so succinct, witty, and wise as that found in comic books. Good versus evil delivered in compelling dialogue, accompanied by action illustrations. What could be the problem?

For those of you who have visions of male-dominated bloody comic books with grotesquely disproportionate women, I want to assure you that child-friendly formats are available. While many do incorporate mild violence, it is reminiscent of cartoon violence, not late-night movie violence. The magic and mysticism used helps the heroes fly, disappear, and rid the world of evil, not conjure up dangerous potions or poisons. If you are a stranger to this genre, try the following suggestions:

- "Teen Titans": Presented by DC Comics, these young superheroes are the sidekicks to such legends as Batman, Wonder Woman, and Aquaman. These characters can also be seen in their own cartoon series and are available on DVD.
- "The Incredibles": Based on the blockbuster movie, these comics retell the story of a family of superheroes who must hide their identities from the neighbors while trying to make the world a better place.
- "Spider Girl": Marvel Comics' longest-running comic featuring a female as a lead character, it tells the tale of Peter Parker's daughter, Spider Girl.

Bookworms Beware

When searching for comic books online or at the library, make sure to target "children's comic books." General comic books and graphic novels are intended for older audiences and have material and situations most parents would object to.

Raise the Reading-Aloud Bar

Most likely your read-aloud routine will be reserved for bedtime if your children are in school all day. If you home-school, you will have more opportunities throughout the afternoon to carve out read-aloud time; but either way, it is most probable that increasing commitments to sports and community activities will mean a daily, focused read-aloud routine will work best.

To make the most of this time, try to alternate reading materials. I have given you a few different subject areas to try to talk about shared reading and taking turns. When it is your turn to read, keep in mind that children can understand what is being read to them, even if they can't read it themselves. You do not have to worry about choosing a book that matches their reading level, because you are the one who is doing the reading. Knowing this, you can continue to introduce your children to what is next. "Reading up" to your kids, instead of down to them, can keep your intermediate reader interested in books that are just beyond their reach and encourage them to keep reading so that they may someday (soon) make these same books their own.

Home Library Additions

If your read-aloud routine seems to be continuously put on the back burner because of scheduling conflicts, take a look at ways that you can build readable moments into your day. I am not going to launch into a tirade about turning off the television, but you may want to try replacing some viewing time with some listening time. Books on tape and CD are not just for little listeners. Your library probably has a hefty collection of children's novels that are recorded and available to check out. This may seem like a tough sell, but I have seen the results of independent readers listening to books on tape and the results were amazing.

As a middle school teacher, I participated in an after-school homework club for students who struggled with time management, which is the politically correct way of saying they were not turning in their assignments. Many of these students I had in my own Language Arts class and I knew that they were struggling readers. When work was finished or we were at the end of a week and assignments had been turned in, I would offer to play a book on tape. Using the novel assigned in class, students would opt to lie on the floor and follow along with the professional readers. These kids, who often could not articulate what they had just read, were laughing in the right places, nodding along with the

> **Quick Picks**
> When looking for recorded books, it's important to know the difference between unabridged and abridged versions. Unabridged means that the book is read in its entirety, while abridged means that the work has been edited for recording.

dialogue, and all turning the page at the same time. Relaxed and calm, these children were enjoying a book that had eluded them for a long time.

Inspired by their reaction, I rearranged my schedule and tried the book on tape for my whole class with similar results. Even my best readers enjoyed hearing the characters come to life, complete with accents, dramatic pauses, and emotion. Out of curiosity, I kept track of which chapters we listened to on tape, which chapters we read in class, and which chapters were read independently and compared them to quiz scores. The highest scores came when the book had been read aloud.

While it is not a great idea to start handing out reading quizzes at home, it may be a good idea to add professional recordings to your collection. Need some downtime while getting dinner on the table? Pop in a CD. Rainy afternoon and everyone is bouncing off the walls? Light a fire and curl up with a reading expert. Read-alouds don't have to be your sole responsibility; you can utilize the materials available to make the experience more manageable for everyone.

Special Shelf Gets a Facelift

When you first set up the Special Shelf, it was designed to be predominantly off limits because you wanted to keep precious pages from being torn and lovely souvenirs from being squashed. But now it is time to invite your children to take a more active role in maintaining their Special Shelf.

By now, your kids have a collection of their most prized possessions. Pictures, awards, birthday cards, or projects that are near and dear to their heart. Giving their choices a rightful and respectable place on this shelf further solidifies its meaning. But don't forget the original purpose of holding books that are to be shared with someone special.

If your regular reading routine is right on schedule, you can choose a week's worth of titles to keep on the shelf for this cherished time. Anticipation and expectation are a wonderful part of any experience. If you are looking for new materials to add to your permanent collection, it is a great idea to encourage your child to ask for a new book when a holiday rolls around. To keep things fresh and exciting the rest of the year, head over to a new section of the library—something in the adult section may seem appealing—and check out a beautiful book of classic artwork or contemporary photography. Picking out titles to try together and keeping them on the Special Shelf is a valuable reminder that reading is valued in your home.

Pace Yourself: The Beauty of Bookmarks

Just because you want to read more doesn't mean you always have the time to do so. While reading materials for this age group do tend to lend themselves to shorter chapters, making for a natural break, sometimes you just can't manage that and you have to call it an early night. Part of becoming a reader for life is book etiquette, and so it is always a good idea to model how to save your spot.

Bookmarks are more than decorated and laminated cardstock; they are a promise of great things to come and a reminder of how much you have already accomplished. For independent readers, the idea of reading an entire novel may seem like a daunting task. A bookmark assures children that we will go at their pace, enjoy the process, and pick up where we left off; what a pleasant reading promise to make.

Once our children can learn to read, we may be inclined to put our reading routines on permanent hiatus, thinking that our job is done. But if we continue to make time for read-alouds, respecting our independent reader's pace and preferences, we will find that this shared time is not only worthwhile, it is wonderful.

Quick Picks

When you are traveling, consider purchasing a souvenir bookmark along with a local author's work. Collecting bookmarks is an inexpensive memento of a vacation and an important reminder that reading is all around us.

The Least You Need to Know

- Independent readers can still benefit from read-alouds. By reading above your child's independent ability you can continue to model reading rhythm while introducing more complex language and story structure.
- All reading counts. Make sure you don't overlook lighter fare like comics as it could be the material that turns your reader around.
- Intermediate readers are active read-aloud participants. They can recall what has happened, make predictions about what to expect and breath their own life into the story as they read.

Chapter 15

Books for Bumpy Roads

In This Chapter

- Staying the read-aloud course
- Satisfying stories for unsavory situations
- Mature themes promote mature discussions

Your independent reader, in an effort to become a more independent person, may begin to look for approval outside the home. Friends, media, and pop culture will become increasingly more influential, making your job as a parent more challenging. While we are not interested in raising perfect children, because it is impossible, we do want our kids to be well adjusted, well mannered, and care about the well-being of others. How can we make sure our calming voice of reason is heard when so many other influences are yelling so loudly?

Books are not the cure-all for what ails the pop-culture mindset, but they can certainly help. Today's media is fast and flashy and doesn't usually give us enough time to digest or reflect on what we are seeing or hearing. Reading together affords us that time. Quiet, settled, and available at our own pace, we can read and discuss issues as they arise, look back at what has happened, and make predictions about what is to come.

Reading gives us insight into character's motivations. With media, what you see is what you get; and usually what you are seeing is a well-orchestrated package. With books, we are afforded a "backstage pass" to character's lives, we have the insight of a narrator, and we can focus on one message at a time. Your reading routine may have its obstacles, but as always, it has its options.

Managing Media

Remember when your kids thought the only thing interesting on television was cartoons and they needed you to remind them when their favorite programs were on? Remember how computers were for games, and music CDs featured beluga whales? Now it's more likely that your child is heading to the computer to check her instant messages or download music onto her iPod before heading over to the television to check out what is on MTV. Our independent thinkers are also independent doers; instead of this making our lives easier, it often makes parenting even more difficult.

We want our children to pursue their interests, develop their personalities, and enjoy exploring new territory; but unfortunately, with new exploration comes new problems. With so many other entertaining distractions available for your kids to enjoy, it can be difficult to lure them away from the sights and sounds of modern media, especially when these devices offer instant gratification and ask for very little in return. But because pulling the plug entirely may not be realistic, we can look for ways and means to offer exciting alternatives.

Family Values vs. Pop Culture

In your family, saying please, cleaning up after yourself, and waiting your turn are not options, they are mandatory skills. In pop culture, however, pushing your way to the top, making no apologies for aggressive behavior, and saying whatever happens to come to mind is the norm. We are encouraged to buy more, save less, and make our presence known, no matter how unsavory our attitudes might be.

It is sad to note that the icons of our times, be they celebutantes or singers, often turn their noses up and thumbs down on quiet, one-on-one time. If it is not glamorous, loud, and frenzied, it is billed as boring. In the face of such attitudes, it can be harder and harder to make a case for books.

Yet being engaged, reflective, and creative is hardly ever boring, especially when you have the right tools to help you get started. If your kids are starting to roll your eyes at you every time you suggest they unplug, try getting them involved in some fabulous fun of their own. The paparazzi may not be knocking on your door, but that doesn't mean your kids can't be the (well-behaved) stars of the show.

Quick Picks

It seems like the super-star treatment usually means never having to wait for anything; but looking forward to something can be part of the fun. If the library doesn't have what you need, reserve the title and wait your turn. Then, remind your children to return their books on time, so the next person in line can use it.

Crafts for All Seasons, copyright © 2000 Kathy Ross

Your kids will be able to use ordinary household supplies to create their own craft collection. Fully illustrated pages with a spiral-bound format make this book even more user-friendly.

Family Fun Homemade Holidays, copyright © 2002 Deanna Cook

I have read Family Fun magazine for the past few years and I'm always impressed with their craft ideas. In the winter months when it can be even harder to come up with media-free activities, a holiday book like this can keeps hands and minds busy.

Sitcoms, Websites, and Song Lyrics

When I was growing up, one of my favorite television shows was Little House on the Prairie. Yes, I know the books are better; but I adored Half Pint, hated Nellie Olsen, and cried at every Christmas special. One of the appealing things about the show for children and parents were the clear-cut characters: Willie Olsen had to stand in the corner when he was bad. Nellie Olsen was selfish and didn't have any real friends. On today's sitcoms however, the bad kid's antics are often applauded, and being popular can be considered more important than being kind.

This kind of shift has even made its way into our clothing with preteen graphic tee shirts that read, "Your boyfriend wants me" and the like. I have even seen baby rompers that exclaim, "Diva in Training." Now, I do not live in a bubble nor am I suggesting that all television is bad. But I do think that our kids receive a tremendous amount of incomplete messages: song lyrics and videos that encourage promiscuous behavior without mentioning the consequences, and websites that invite participants to invent a persona who collects cyber friends without the responsibility of a relationship. We are trying to raise them one way, while everything that is deemed "cool" is clearly advocating a different approach. What can we do?

We can limit, without having to eliminate, outside influences in our own home. A reading routine can work like a television-viewing routine. Your kids know what time their favorite show comes on, and they can also know what time to turn to their favorite book. Turn down the distractions in your house by having reader-friendly time. This can be in the morning, afternoon, or evening, but it all involves the same thing. TVs, computers, and even music off. Reading materials available, and, truth be told, a little something to sweeten the deal. An after-school snack can complement storytime, as can a decadent dessert. Yes, some may say it's manipulative; I consider it good advertising.

Bookworms Beware

Your child is just beginning to trust his own tastes and develop his own preferences. Be patient with the process. It can be frustrating that sophisticated book choices don't happen overnight; but if we squash our kid's choices, they may not happen at all.

Titles That Can Engage and Enrage

I am a true believer in Murphy's Law; if a parent hates it, a kid will love it. Let's say you are lucky enough to have a child who climbs into bed anxiously awaiting her read-aloud routine, her treasured time with you. She is comfortably propped up with pillows, the nightstand light is on, and she smiles as you curl up next to her. She hands you her new favorite book, *Walter the Farting Dog*, and you shake your head in disbelief. You knew this was too good to be true.

At one time or another, your kids will find books that are not your taste, to put it mildly. And they will *love* these books. They will beg for you to read them, beg for you to make the sound effects, and be lost in a laughing fit as they anticipate the climatic, and all-too-disgusting, ending. Why oh why do they love these books?

Like it or not, farting is funny. So are poop, burping, and snot. Also (frustratingly) hilarious are other kids getting in trouble, talking back, and getting away with bad behavior. Before you host your own private book burning on the BBQ, remember that your child is doing exactly what we hoped he would: loving books. So you may have to read some less-than-savory tales. But if your threshold for grosser-than-gross jokes has reached its limits, there will be more family-friendly titles we can try to introduce along the way.

Bathroom Humor and Bad Manners

I would love to reassure you that your children are going to outgrow "potty mouth" as they develop more complex senses of humor, but my husband, one of the most intelligent and articulate adults I know, still cracks up when he "clears the room." But he has learned, as will your kids, that certain body parts are private and other people can become embarrassed or upset by potty remarks. If you are looking to put a lid on toilet humor, try substituting a more family-friendly title for your child's favorite potty pages.

The *Captain Underpants* series by Dav Pilkney has won the hearts of many young readers, but it tends to make some parents a bit crazy. For the record, I am a huge fan of any book that has boys running to the shelves to find the next issue, but if you wish your child's hero would wear more than tighty whities, try the recently released series from Kirk Scroggs, *Wiley and Grampa's Creature Features.* These fully illustrated, easy-to-read books offer plenty of zombies, monsters, and adventuresome bedlam, and everyone is

Success Story

Are you all in favor of things that go plop, plop, fizz, fizz? Then check out *Oh Yikes: History's Grossest Moments,* copyright 2006 by Joy Masoff, which celebrates all the wonderfully disgusting things humans are capable of.

fully dressed. Plus, I love how the multi-generational pairing of grandparents and grandson is rambunctious, not routine.

If your children loved Junie B. Jones but you are tired of correcting her grammar and reprimanding her manners, try the *Sammy Keyes* series by Wendelin Van Draanan. Sammy is a young detective who is secretly living in her grandmother's adult community because her mother has run off to become a Hollywood movie star. She gets into her fair share of trouble, but it is her resourceful nature and quick wit that make her such a memorable character, and this series so satisfying.

When the Bad Guys Win

As your children move through grade school they will learn the horrible truth about what humankind is capable of. Up until now, they have probably been insulated from such topics as slavery and the Holocaust, but these are very real parts of our history. It is impossible to explain, and even more difficult to justify or rationalize, why horrible things happen to innocent people. Part of the frustration of parenting can be not having the right answers for tough topics like these. But just because you cannot wrap the conversation up with a neat bow doesn't mean you can't handle difficult conversations. Due to the sensitive nature of certain subjects, you will have to judge what your child is ready for, and when. But if he should come home asking about upsetting issues, it is always better to keep the dialogue open and honest, even when you don't have all of the answers. Reading aloud and leaving time for discussion can make tough topics more manageable for your children.

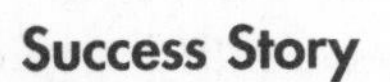

Success Story

Since *The Diary of Anne Frank* is read in just about every school, your child is bound to come home with it. When he does, get your own copy and read (or reread) along. The book is that important.

It can be helpful to use simpler formats for dealing with difficult themes. Patricia Polacco's *The Butterfly* is a brilliantly executed example of that idea. A full-color illustrated picture book, Polacco's work depicts a non-Jewish family who hides a Jewish family during WWII. A bond is formed between the daughters of the two families. Even in the face of such doom, there were those who tried to do what they could.

I was only recently introduced to *Follow the Drinking Gourd* by Jeanette Winter, and I think it is an excellent introduction to the underground railroad and the courage and bravery it must have taken to escape from slavery. Slaves were taught the folksong that gave directions to freedom using the night sky. Again, using simple text and bold illustrations can make a difficult dialogue more accessible.

When Things Go Wrong

While it can be difficult not to have the answers to our children's questions, it can be even more painful when they stop asking questions. "But, why?" is replaced by stony silence. "Do you want to talk about anything?" is answered with silent shrugs. Confused and hurt, our children become withdrawn and quiet. We know they are hurting, but we don't know what to do, especially because we are also hurting. How agonizing it is to see our kids suffering; how helpless we can feel. But as usual, we are not alone.

Age-appropriate books are available for us to read with our children. It is a good time to mention that if you have children of different ages, you should be quite selective about who reads which types of books. Divorce, death, and disappointment mean different things to different age groups, and it would be wise not to lump individual needs together, as you risk talking down to older children and talking above younger children. When it comes to sensitive subjects like these, your undivided attention can be instrumental in the healing process.

Divorce

Divorce can be particularly upsetting for children at this age because they tend to take on responsibility for the failed relationship. Old enough to know that something hasn't been right for awhile, children may think that if they had done something different their parents would have stayed together. Using the following titles together can help you both articulate what you are feeling, and provide a time to talk candidly and privately about upsetting emotions.

Since divorce is a common challenge for children, it is no surprise that authors have created both nonfiction and fiction books that deal with this complex family issue. I encourage you to consider using both types of books in your home and, if the relationship is amicable, share your chosen title with your former partner so that the conversation may continue when your child spends time with her other parent.

My Parents are Divorced, Too: A Book for Kids by Kids, copyright © 2006 by Melanie Ford

This candid book is written by kids, making the tone and verbiage familiar and friendly. Instead of adults telling kids how they feel, children are expressing themselves. A good tool for parents who can now use specific examples from the text to begin a conversation with their own child.

For Better, For Worse: A Guide to Surviving Divorce for Pre-teens and Their Family, copyright © 2001 Janet Bode

This book is divided into two sections, with the first being a brutally honest depiction of divorce from different kids' points of views. Using divorce as an excuse to get out of trouble and hating that a parent is having sex with someone new are among the candid conversations covered. The second half of the book is targeted toward parents and offers suggestions for talking with your children. Due to the honest content, it is best that you preview this book before sharing it with your child.

Quick Picks

If you like *Dear Mr. Henshaw* and *It's Not the End of the World*, commit Beverly Cleary and Judy Blume's names to memory. These two dynamic authors are responsible for a slew of excellent coming-of-age stories that are ideal to share with your children.

Dear Mr. Henshaw, copyright © 1984 Beverly Cleary

This Newberry medal book is told in letters written from a sixth-grade boy to an author. His school assignment reveals his angst over his parent's divorce, being in a new school, and trying to fit in with his new life. A moving and meaningful read for both parent and child.

It's Not the End of the World, copyright © 1986 Judy Blume

When sixth-grade Karen's parents divorce, she is devastated and at first believes that she can get them back together. By the end of the book, and through her own experience, Karen realizes that the divorce is real and her family will be forever changed. In true Judy Blume style, the character's voice remains honest and vulnerable, hopeful and heartbreaking, making this a great title to share together.

Death

Similar to their reaction over a divorce, children can feel responsible and helpless when a loved one dies. Not knowing how to articulate their feelings and fearing that they will upset everyone by talking about it, grieving children often retreat into their own heads. Alone and unsupervised with their own thoughts, they are likely to put on a stoic face and say everything is fine unless they are drawn out. But this is usually easier said than done. An excellent tool for helping to bridge the gap between solitude and mourning is *Fire in My Heart, Ice in My Veins: A Journal for Teenagers Experiencing Loss* by Enid Samuel Traisman. While the title implies the work is for teenagers, this keepsake journal is excellent for using with grade-school children. Simple text prompts the reader to remember and reflect on a past relationship and can help encourage important conversations.

Quick Picks

Journaling can be a great way for children to express themselves without feeling pressured to say things the right way. Purchase a small, welcoming journal for your child and encourage him to write in it before or after you read together. Be available to listen if he wants to share, but respect his privacy if he would rather keep things to himself.

Even if your child has not experienced the death of a family member or a pet, she is becoming well aware that people do die, sometimes slowly, sometimes unexpectedly. Media is chock full of death and destruction, and with television characters barely giving corpses a second look or more than a moment's consideration, it can be difficult to assess what her feelings on the subject are. You do not have to wait for a painful personal experience before talking about death; in fact, discussing the subject while you are not both grieving could actually make you more comfortable. The following fiction titles all handle death from a different perspective, and all three are worthy of your family's time.

Olive's Ocean, copyright © 2004 by Kevin Henke

This Newberry Medal book is eloquently written, and begs to be read in an almost hushed voice. Readers follow 12-year-old Martha on a family summer vacation where she becomes increasingly aware of her life and its meaning after finding out that a classmate who died considered her a close friend, even though they never spoke.

Wringer, copyright © 1998 Jerry Spinelli

A 9-year-old boy dreads his upcoming birthday because it means he will be expected to become a "wringer," responsible for strangling pigeons at his town's annual bird shoot. An incredibly interesting story about death, peer pressure, and coming into one's own, it should come as no surprise that this book won a Newberry Honor.

Tuck Everlasting, copyright © 1975 Natalie Babbit

It is hard to discuss death without coming to the question, "Why can't everyone just live forever?" In this fairy-tale-like book, such a question is posed to a young girl who must decide if immortality is indeed such a good thing. This one will have you all talking for hours.

Disappointment

My girlfriend's son recently found out that she is not perfect. Usually one of the most organized people I know, she overscheduled her day and completely forgot that her son's award ceremony was that afternoon. He was devastated that she forgot about him. She was crushed and is convinced that irreparable damage has been done. I'm pretty sure that this wasn't the first, or last time, that she will disappoint her son and even though it feels like the end of the world, everyone will survive (though probably not forget).

For our children, there was a time when everyone played by the rules, Mom and Dad had all the answers, and life seemed simple enough. But sooner or later, kids find out they have parents who mess up and friends who betray them. Instead of everyone believing that being unique is a good thing, differences feel detrimental. Caught between wanting to be independent young adults and still wanting their parents to fix all of their problems, children struggle to make sense of challenging circumstances. Knowing that they are not alone in their experiences and feelings can help smooth, though never solve, some rough spots.

Chicken Soup for the Preteen Soul, is part of the hugely successful series that profiles short stories, anecdotes, and memoirs that are designed to comfort and inspire. This edition is no different, and young contributors have included their age, making their stories even more riveting to your reader. The shorter lengths and concise writing make the chapters manageable, and the topics invite meaningful and moving conversation.

Success Story

If your child loves the *Chicken Soup* stories, then check out their website at www.chickensoup.com where you can read guidelines for submitting your own story for an upcoming book.

If your daughter is finding that being herself is increasingly more complicated, try *Define "Normal"* by Julie Anne Peters. A familiar tale of two middle-school girls, one "perfect" and one "trouble," who find a way to help each other and become friends, this book reads more realistically than others of its kind and does not rely on a heavy-handed "can't we all just get along?" theme.

For boys who are struggling with fitting in, Jack Gantos' *Joey Pigza Swallowed the Key* is a fast-paced look at a troubled boy with A.D.D. Even if your son does not have this disorder, he may well relate to Joey's desire, but inability, to do well and just be like the other kids.

A Formula That Fits

Reading aloud with your intermediate reader will delve into new stories and situations, but many of the techniques we have already talked about are still applicable. Regardless of age or reading ability, your reading routine will benefit from the three C's:

- **Consistency** Sticking to a regular time and having regular rituals, such as certain lighting, a particular blanket, or a certain book order can help signify the beginning of this special time. Removing any distractions and focusing on the event at hand can help you both shift gears from your busy day into a much more relaxed and receptive mode.

- **Comfort** Settle in for your read-aloud time. Slip off your shoes, put your feet up, and relax; don't rush. Children can pick up on your body language. If you are checking your watch and perched at the edge of a chair just going through the motions, they'll know it. Get comfortable and you will make them more comfortable.
- **Companionship** Best friends, best teachers, and best coaches are wonderful people in your child's life, but no one else is Mom or Dad. Setting aside time to focus on one child is a priceless gift for your son or daughter, and you.

Perhaps you have been doing this all along and know exactly what works and what doesn't work. Maybe you are trying to get a new read-aloud routine going in your house. Either way, trust your instincts, watch your child's cues, and make this time your own.

Shared Reading

As your independent reader becomes more adept at reading aloud, invite him to take a more active role in your routine. You may want to have two copies of a favorite novel on the Special Shelf so you can each hold a book in a comfortable position. This way, you can take turns reading out loud. Even if your child wants to read that day's page, chapter, or book on his own, always try and leave time for you to read, too. Modeling inflection, pace, and enthusiasms are all important techniques that will continue to improve with your efforts. Besides, relaxing and hearing a story is a pleasant way for your child to feel cared for.

Success Story

For a change of pace, read the same book together quietly and then talk about what has happened in the story. Children can often read more quickly and comprehend more accurately when they read to themselves, and this can be a nice change from your regular routine.

Shared reading also means shared emotions. As characters confront moral and ethical issues, stories become more complicated and situations become more complex, it is important to take time and digest what has been read. If possible, save the reflections until you have finished reading for the evening so that your child can become more engrossed in the story.

If you find it hard to start talking, keep small journals and pencils nearby to jot down your reactions and then take turns reading what you have written. This can be very helpful for tougher topics that illicit a strong emotional reaction. Don't try to hide your emotions from your child, whatever they may be. Parents cry, just as they laugh, get angry, and feel afraid. The more open you are with your children, the more likely they will share their feelings with you.

Identify, Don't Compare

If you are finishing this chapter and have a solid marriage, healthy family, and well-adjusted children, you don't need to dismiss the suggestions. Instead of looking for ways that these books are different from your circumstances, look at the message of the story and see what feelings you can connect with.

For example, feelings of loss don't just happen in death and divorce. If a long-time friend suddenly cuts off contact, or a family rift keeps you from spending holidays together, you can feel angry, abandoned, and fearful. If everyone makes it on the team but your child, it can be a huge disappointment. Details may differ, but the feelings can be the same. Great literature, like the titles suggested here, are great because they tap into universal sentiments. Each suggested title is likely to have something you can identify with, making it a valuable book to share together.

When the going gets tough, the tough get going to the book shelf. Sometimes you'll be reaching for an alternative to the media masses, and sometimes you'll be looking for a novel that reads like a handbook. Either way, reading together can help reinforce the values that we want to instill in our children and open up a safe and satisfying discussion for why those values are important.

The Least You Need to Know

- Children never outgrow needing your undivided attention. Books are still a wonderful way to make time for important conversations.

- Tough topics can be made more manageable with relevant read-alouds.
- If it works, don't break it. There is no expiration date on your family's personal reading routine; continue enjoying the experience as long as it is enjoyable.

Chapter 16

When Booklovers Get Bored

In This Chapter

- For whom the school bell tolls
- Time limits and limitations
- Making yourself and reading materials available

As parents, we must decide whether we are going to treat recreational reading as a hobby or a value. The difference is subtle, but meaningful. A hobby is something you enjoy in your free time. When everything else is done—homework, laundry, bills, or shopping—you reward yourself with a much-deserved reprieve from your to-do list by turning toward a hobby. Unfortunately when you ask most people what they enjoy in their free time, their answer is all too often, "What free time?" Weekends used to be reserved for such enjoyment, but now even those precious days are jeopardized by cell phones that keep us on call constantly, game schedules that have us running all over town, and huge homes that demand competitive upkeep. If we accept that hobbies are negotiable, a fringe benefit that can be dismissed in the line of duty, then we are much more likely to forgo our reading routines and chalk it up to, "What free time?"

A value, on the other hand, is an integral part of your routine. It is part of your list of things to do. In addition to housekeeping, working, and shopping, we can add weekend worship and family visits or much broader practices like vegetarianism, manners, and recycling. Values are not something we hope to get around to; they are a natural part of our daily lives. When discussing our values, the idea that "I could take it or leave it" would seem preposterous. We make time for our values regardless of the circumstances. When we treat reading as a value, instead of hobby, we recognize the distinction between preference and practice and are more likely to continue our reading routines.

Once you decide which side of the fence you sit on, you'll be faced with how to manage that decision. If reading is to be a value in your family, then homework, extracurricular activities, outside influences, and interest levels will all need to be taken into account. Your independent learner has a lot on his plate, and we want to continue to make reading as appetizing as apple pie. Luckily, I can suggest reading materials and complementary activities to help you discover a few new tricks up your sleeve.

Recreational Reading: An Endangered Idea

Once upon a time, in a land not so far away, your children looked at books as an endless source of entertainment. Dramatic monologues from Dad, monster faces from Mom, and shared sound-effects made books burst with energy. Discussions focused on what might happen next, favorite parts of the story, and finding letters and new words in a spontaneous eye-spy activity. So why then, when kids start bringing home assigned reading, is that joy so often lost? How can we keep all reading material from suddenly becoming suspect?

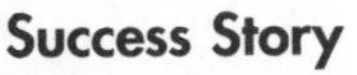

Success Story

If you have just joined us in this section and are worried that you do not have the right reading foundation, relax. The ideas recommended here can be taken piecemeal, helping you get your family on the right literacy track. It is never too late to bring a reader around.

If your once-enthused reader is suddenly backing away from the bookshelves, you'll want to figure out what is going on before they go screaming from the stacks. Usually, the problem, which are most commonly time constraints, can be managed with a creative perspective. But this is the age when we as parents may really need to roll up our sleeves and flex our literacy muscles. We have done so much good work to create a literacy-rich home that we do not want our efforts to go unrealized. First we'll take a look at a common culprit of book boredom and then talk about ways to lead our straying bookworms back to the pages before they can crawl away completely.

The Hassle of Homework

The National Parent Teacher Organization has recommended 10 minutes of homework per grade level, but whether or not that recommendation is followed is completely up to teachers and individual school districts. There has been a tremendous movement to "raise our schools' standards" and often this means piling on the take-home paperwork. If your child is spending more and more time in front of textbooks, organizing projects, and studying for exams, that leaves much less time for other activities like reading for pleasure. After all, when they're fried from so much "school reading," who can blame them for lumping all literature into "work"?

If we want our kids to read for fun, we must keep reading fun. As you read together, stay away from "school words" like "main character" and "plot," and focus on talking about the story instead of making a discussion feel like a quiz. Choose materials that have a great deal of humor like picture books or comic books that rely heavily on visual enjoyment and can be finished in one sitting. Homework reading can tend to go on and on, but starting and finishing a shorter book can help give your child a sense of pleasant satisfaction. Never use reading as a punishment, but extend reading routines, either together or independently, as a reward. Last but not least, put your child in charge of the reading selections. All day long she must read and write about subjects in which she has little say; with your help, this reading time can be her own.

Over-Scheduled, Over-Stimulated

Proponents of homework argue that the time it takes to accomplish assignments would be more manageable if children were not being chauffeured to and from extracurricular activities all afternoon. It is not unusual for children to have more than one club, lesson, or practice in a single evening, meaning any downtime has virtually disappeared. With children up and going from first thing in the morning until they collapse in bed at night, it can be increasingly difficult to help them unwind and relax. Again, "zoning out" in front of the TV or computer seems a welcome reprieve, for kids and parents, from all of the activity. But when we consider how stimulating media can be with its constant flurry of pictures, quick images, and oppressive volume, we may want to reconsider what "downtime" really means.

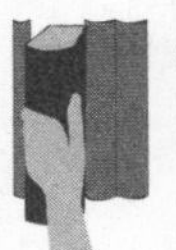

Quick Picks

Running from place to place, you are bound to have a few minutes to kill in the car. Keep a joke book within reach and get your sense of humor back while you wait for (another) practice to start. *500 Hilarious Jokes for Kids* by Jeff Rovin is good clean fun.

Reading is by far one of the most relaxing activities available to us. We have talked a great deal about the importance of setting the stage for reading to make it more conducive for comfort. We can add particular books to our collection to help ease the transition from chaos to calm. At the beginning of this book we looked at lullabies to read in our sing-song voices, making the time together even more tranquil. While our kids have outgrown *Guess How Much I Love You*, there are peaceful pages still available for our enjoyment.

Carolyn Kennedy has put together an anthology of exquisite, well-diversified poems in the book *A Family of Poems: My Favorite Poetry for Children*. Now, I am not usually a fan of celebrity books. I think actors should stick to acting, singers to singing, and paparazzi should stay off the pages of picture books. But Kennedy's choices show a real commitment to the range and scope of children. No choice is too complicated or simplistic. But the real charm of this book is Jon Muth's watercolor illustrations. Full-page, muted tones set off each selection, making this read a pleasure to hear and see. Beautiful words on beautiful pages; what a beautiful way to unwind.

Fill In the Blanks

No matter what grade your children are in, it is important to know what they are reading. Not only so you can help them with their school work and see what kind of topics and discussions are being had by this age group, but also because you will want to know what is missing. No curriculum is 100 percent complete. For that to even have a chance of working, it would need to cater to each individual student's interests and specific reading level. But as parents, we can reach out to our reluctant readers by keeping our home libraries stacked with revolving inventory that engages our children without demanding anything but enjoyment in return.

Quick Picks

Remember *Mad Libs*? Remember how much fun it was to put random words into nonsensical order and then read the whole thing out loud. This is a fill-in-the-blank activity worthy introducing your children to. Check out http://us.penguingroup.com/static/packages/us/yreaders/madlibs to join in the fun.

As we'll see, fill in the blanks and multiple choices can signify suffering, not satisfaction, in the schools. At home, we can continue to look for ways and means of widening the gap between boredom and books. In the comfort of our reading routines we can all enjoy a much-needed reprieve from assignments and get reacquainted with pages of pleasure.

Definitions, Details, and Doldrums

I am sorry to say, as a teacher I was completely guilty of running many a reading class like this: look up all the vocabulary words in the chapter, read the assigned chapter (don't read ahead), come to class, and take a quiz focused on miscellaneous details that have little to do with the actual story and more to do with me needing to make sure you are actually reading, rinse and repeat. Thank goodness, there were many other wonderful reading activities, but when lessons start to replace literature, and details like "What color shirt was the man wearing" take precedence over open-ended discussions like "How many of you have felt overwhelmed by circumstances beyond your control?" is it any wonder that our once-riveted audience now regards reading as an activity with "right answers"?

I truly believe that the most successful stories ever written achieve such status because they remind us of ourselves. Whether it's overcoming fear, finding great love, or saying goodbye, great literature is an extension of ourselves. When we reduce that to looking up key terms and recalling inconsequential details, we sacrifice a story's meaning and momentum. I don't have a solution for test-taking that is brief enough to fit in this chapter (or this book, for that matter) but since we are concerned with raising readers for life in our homes, we can round out reading approaches.

Because your children are bombarded with a slew of influences, some good, some bad, many questionable, it is not always so easy to come up with a one-size-fits-all answer for ethical and moral issues. In fact, it can be even harder to find the words to prompt important conversations you want to have. One title that can help get you both talking is Gregory Stock's *The Kids Book of Questions: Revised for the New Century*. While the short text and pictureless pages may make this a better choice for a "reading date" or to carry with you when a readable moment makes itself available, the rich questions are thought-provoking and inspired. You will want to preview the pages, as some topics are tougher than others; for example, "Are you afraid there will be a nuclear war?" may not be an age-appropriate for your children yet, but "Do you think boys or girls have it easier?" might be right on the money.

Success Story

If you want even more insight into communicating with your children, try *How to Talk So Kids Will Listen and Listen So Kids Will Talk* by Adele Faber and Elaine Mazlish. It is loaded with practical tips for connecting with your kids.

A Mere Means to an End

The idea of reading having "right answers" is taken to the nth degree when we look at test-taking. After distributing multiple quizzes to students, we expect them to study the book for a final exam. No longer are our kids reading for enjoyment; they are reading because they have to if they want to do well on the test. The reader's reaction in no longer enough; we must insist upon standardized measurement. If there are any words that work in direct opposition to the pleasure principle, they are "have to" and "test."

In your own home, remember to emphasize the process, not the end product. Bookmarks are a great tool for this, but so is the right to abandon the book altogether. With so many great books to be read, why waste time on the ones that aren't great? Built into the reading-for-pleasure model is the notion that if it is not pleasurable, you can give yourself permission to change directions. The best way to do this: put the book down. Students cannot pick and choose which books will be part of the curriculum, but they can, and should, be encouraged to pick and choose books that appeal to them. As soon as we say, "Finish that book before you get another," we again turn books into plain broccoli. Keep up with weekly or bi-monthly library trips, update magazine subscriptions, and look for sales at your local bookstore so there are always plenty of reading materials on hand. That way, when your child puts a book down, he'll only be an arm's length away from picking up a new one.

Back to Basics

As I've mentioned before, if it is working, don't break it. Perhaps you and your daughter had enjoyed a lovely evening reading ritual, but you assumed that she was getting too big for bedtime cuddling and it gradually went by the wayside. Maybe your son forgot to mention he would like you to renew his beloved Your Big Backyard subscription and, with little fanfare, it has long since expired. If you now find yourself with kids who are reluctant to read, try revisiting techniques that worked in the past. They may need to be updated, but the premise that worked once could work again. A couple of oversized throw pillows in the corner could be an inviting space for you and your daughter to read in the evenings before she gets ready for bed, while a new subscription to National Geographic for Kids would entice your son away from the video games. True, as our children grow, their needs change, but that doesn't mean their needs go away. Look for new ways to recycle reading rituals that worked and you may be surprised to learn that you knew what to do all along.

Model and Mentor

When it comes to our kids, there is no denying that "monkey see, monkey do." Because you don't want your home to turn into a jungle, you make your bed, pick up after yourself, and use your manners, expecting the same from your children. The same goes for reading. If you want your kids to read when they grow up, then they must be surrounded by grown-ups who read.

Every time we model a behavior, we are in essence mentoring our children about what is important to us. The most successful way to do this is in its natural time. Instead of sitting your son or daughter down and having a lengthy discussion about the benefits of reading, show them the benefits of reading every day. Using teachable moments, instead of contrived conversations, often yields a much more successful and meaningful lesson. Here are some simple suggestions to help keep the lessons light and easy:

- Be prepared—Keep a running list of great titles you want to read.
- Try new things—Browse the aisles of bookstores and libraries and pick up something unexpected that catches your eye.
- Hit the road—Use literature to plan trips, both near and far.
- Take 5—It is not enough to value your kid's reading routine; you must value your own. Each day, try to spend 5 minutes reading what you enjoy in front of your children.
- Raise your voice—Remember to read recipes, cereal boxes, directions, and mail out loud. All reading counts.

Bookworms Beware

When faced with a huge task, such as a long novel, children will draw on their experience to tackle a problem. If you articulate a one-step-at-a-time approach to cleaning, working, or exercising, then your kids will be more likely to approach a new novel one page at a time, making the book more manageable.

Have Books, Will Travel

I grew up on Long Island, NY, and was convinced that my town was the beginning and end of the world. As a kid, and even as a young adult, I traveled to very few places and spent a great deal of my time inside. Imagine my surprise the first time my husband drove us halfway across the country to Wyoming. I had absolutely no idea our country was so beautiful, so different, and yet so familiar. I came home from that trip, and subsequent travels, with a fresh perspective.

Be a tourist in a new town, or hit the trail to discover unknown treasures in your own backyard. Reading does not have to only happen in the comfort of your own home. If you want to stretch your imagination, and your legs, look into some of these books without boundaries.

- *The Scrambled States of America* by Laurie Keller is smart and funny, two absolutely necessary qualities when trying to inspire a reluctant reader. In perfect personification, Kansas rallies the other states to realize that they need a change. All head off in different hilarious directions, but of course, things just don't feel right, so they return home in time for bed. This all-ages picture book is a sure-fire way to get a great geography conversation off the ground and inspire your kids to plan a trip to a new destination.
- *The Jumbo Book of Outdoor Art* by Irene Luxbacher is a great field guide for the budding artist. Fully illustrated projects are explained in a step-by-step format and supplies are relatively easy to come by. This on-location book is useful everywhere from the forest to the beach and can give all participants focused, hands-on reading activity to enjoy creating together.

Success Story

While on your way to your destination, take advantage of a captured audience with the *Trip-Tracker: Travel Journal and Gamebook* published by Rand McNally. Songs, games, stickers, and memory pages are all part of this spiral-bound package intended to entertain and delight.

- *Crinkleroot's Guide to Walking in Wild Places* and *Field Trips: Bug Hunting, Animal Tracking, Bird Watching, Shore Watching*, both by Jim Arnosky, are friendly introductions to the great outdoors. Common-sense approaches to admiring, not disturbing, nature are highlighted and budding naturalists will be inspired to take notice of the natural world in a whole new way.

Whether you have the means to pack up the car or pack up your backpack, the important thing is to get out there. Exploring the environment does not have to be expensive or excruciating. Comfortable shoes and a sack lunch are often the only equipment you need to take a local day trip.

Think Outside the Book

It was only a matter of time before our talk turned to books that have been made into movies. I love books (obviously) and I also love movies, but not always the same ones. One of the problems with books made into movies is that I am no longer the one doing the casting and choosing the location; that has been done for me. And I have seen very few movies that didn't make me want to say out loud, "I can't believe they left out the part with …." But what movies can do is complement your reading routine. Call me a stickler for details here, but I really think there is a right way to use movies to promote reading.

First, the movie should not be the reward for reading; reading is its own reward. But because I think reading the book first is more valuable than seeing the movie first, what's a family to do? Make the reading as big as a deal as the movie. The chosen title should immediately be promoted to Special Shelf status. Don't read it every night, but try building suspense by turning to it every other day, and talk it up on your "off" days. Whenever possible, bring the book to life with relevant recipes or desserts. Titles like *Charlie and the Chocolate Factory* by Roald Dahl make this incredibly easy, but you can also serve ruby-red Jello in glass dishes when reading *The Wizard of Oz* by L. Frank Baum. When we make "book night" as much fun as "movie night" we are incorporating media into our family's entertainment, instead of relying on it.

Here's a list of great read-aloud books that you may want to watch after you read; but remember, because many studios take a great deal of "poetic license," preview the movie to make sure it is age and content appropriate.

- *Peter Pan* by J. M. Barrie
- *The Secret Garden* by Frances Hodgson Burnett
- *Alice's Adventures in Wonderland* by Lewis Carroll

- *Old Yeller* by Fred Gipson
- *Holes* by Louis Sachar
- *Black Beauty* by Anna Sewell
- *The Hundred and One Dalmatians* by Dodie Smith
- *Heidi* by Johanna Spyri
- *Shrek* by William Steig
- *Mary Poppins* by P. L. Travers
- *Swiss Family Robinson* by Johann Wyss

If you have a struggling reader, consider watching the movie first and then reading the book. Knowing the plot may make the book easier for your child. Remember, you know your kid better than I, so use your expert judgment.

High-Interest, High-Impact

If you can take but only one read-aloud suggestion from this book, take this one: the more we like something, the more we will want to do it. When our kids go to school, they are not going to like everything they have to do; and they're not going to be crazy about all of their responsibilities at home, either. But because we do not want reading to be a mere means to an end, just a stop along the way to better things, we want to continue to find books that keep our kids engaged. Simply put, the better we know our kids, the better we will know what kinds of books may interest them. A reading routine is a win-win situation for cracking this sometimes-complicated code.

Reading together gives us time with our children to find out what they like. When we know what they like, we can read books to complement these tastes. When our kids like our choices, they will want to read more with us. And the circle continues. Yes, your children are old enough to pick out their own books. Just like I am old enough to pick out my own birthday presents. But is there anything better than someone giving you exactly what you want? It is very validating to know that we are seen and heard. When we bring reading materials into the home because the subject is important to them, we are giving a great gift: recognition.

Conspicuous Materials

I love the holiday season. One of my favorite things is having our outdoor lights on a timer so that when I come home after dark, I am greeted by an illuminated home. No one is forcing me to enjoy the holidays; the lights are on for me to choose to enjoy or ignore. But who would want to ignore something so warm and welcoming?

The same approach can be used with reading materials. If your child is reluctant to read, piling the books on his bed might be a bit much. But, finding a great library book on skateboarding, sports, or antique cars and leaving it on the kitchen table might encourage him to pick it up and ask, "What's this?" Instead of jumping all over him with a desperate plea to "Please for the love of god get back to reading so you can go to a good college and get a good job and be a successful husband and father who will name your firstborn after me," you can simply say, "I saw that and thought you might like it." Then go back to doing whatever you were doing. Maybe this will work the first time, maybe the tenth time; but by offering a new book instead of demanding that it be read, you make reading his choice. WE are much more likely to enjoy doing the things we want to do, rather than the things we have to do.

Collections and Hobbies

Having a collection or hobby can help to make your child an expert on a particular subject. From stamps to crocheting to fish tanks, there is no shortage of books available for those who want to dive head first into a subject.

There are several nice features about a child, or adult, having a collection or hobby. First, to be an expert on a subject, you must know it inside and out, which takes dedication. I am all for people trying new things, but having a focused activity promotes patience and persistence, two valuable qualities. Next, it gives everyone something to be excited about. Holidays, vacations, and day trips all have more meaning when everyone has her eye on a common objective. Lastly, it makes that person much more interesting. It is such a treat to hear someone speak eloquently and enthusiastically about a subject I know very little about. When that information comes from children, it is even more special.

Helping your children to build a collection of their own or hone a hobby truly is a gift that keeps on giving. If you are looking for ideas, here are two popular choices:

Coin Collecting for Kids, copyright © 2000 by Steve Otfinoski, Jack Grahamm

An introductory, spiral-bound book to introduce your children to U.S. coin collecting. This book is a long-term project that can be enjoyed, put away, and returned to at a later time.

Success Story

These may not seem to be your typical read-aloud books, but they are great tools for getting your kids interested in further research, which, thankfully, almost always involves more reading.

Magic for Kids, copyright © 1999 by Kay Presto

This book teaches 25 magic tricks to children and gives useful tips for showmanship and having fun. The author treats the reader as a professional, making children more likely to take their new hobby more seriously.

Suggest, Don't Smother

There is hardly anything I hate more than being smothered. I need my personal space. I need time to look around, make a choice, sit with it for awhile, and then possibly change my mind. This approach is not limited to books. I hardly ever want help in the stores, detest phone solicitors, and try not to check e-mail after 8 P.M. I need a lot of breathing room to feel comfortable. If we constantly hover over our kids saying, "Do you like it, do you like it, do you like it?" they are bound to grow agitated. Who wouldn't?

When trying to reach out to reluctant readers, remember that less is often more. Yes, if reading is going to be a value in your home, you have to make time for it. But 20 enjoyable minutes sure beats an hour of hostility. Manage your media, make reading materials available, and then consider yourself "on call." Your kids are likely to come around, but they can't move if you are standing on top of them.

If you are wondering what can be done to increase read-alouds in classrooms, limit short-answer test-taking, and increase recreational reading for all students, then I'm sorry to say, there are no easy answers. Like it or not, teachers are responsible for covering a specific amount of material in a short amount of time. The system is not perfect, but hardly any system I know of is. But knowing that reading in school may not be as warm and fuzzy as it is at home can inspire you to keep your reading routine a valued top priority. Your child is just beginning to come into her own. Enjoy getting to know your amazing child one book at a time.

The Least You Need to Know

- A literacy-rich home is built on values. Continue making recreational reading a priority in your home.
- Reading is not restricted to a quieted, seated position, you can use books to explore different environments, be it your front yard or the frontier.
- Invitations are always more welcome than requirements. Make reading materials and quiet spaces attractive to your family and you're apt to find less reading reluctance.

Chapter 17

Great Independent Reader Titles to Try Together

In This Chapter

- Reading together is a family commitment
- Read-alouds through changing tides
- Super read-aloud selections to share

It is worth repeating that there is no right way to read with your children. Some days your son may want to read the entire page by himself, while other days he just wants to sit back and listen. Your daughter may love reading picture books out loud to a younger sibling, but prefer to have you read novels aloud to her. And of course, what was preferred yesterday may have little bearing on what is requested tomorrow.

Independent readers are independent thinkers, but no child wants to be isolated. Although it may be increasingly difficult for you and your child to carve out one-on-one time, it is a gift more important than any package he will ever find wrapped with a bow. The books we have talked about in this chapter and the selections that are to follow represent some of the best tools you have for connecting with your kids. Use these tools today to build bridges to a brighter tomorrow.

Keep at It

It can become all too easy to put off our reading routines until our timing is better, only to find that we have completely run out of time. A skipped session becomes a missed week, which turns into a forgotten practice. Reading together takes dedication, but the payoff is well worth the effort. If we want children who trust us with their secrets, come to us with their questions, and get a daily dose of our value system, we have to be available to administer it.

If you are struggling to find time to read, take a step back and consider your schedule. Would having dinner earlier help? How about moving bedtime back so both parents are home for the evening routine? Are you trying "reading dates"? Do you spend a tremendous amount of time in your car, but you haven't yet moved quick reads into the backseat? Reading as a family works best when the whole family can contribute to its success. Ask your kids and spouse for ideas of how to build this valuable book time back into your routine and don't be afraid to try new approaches; you may find just the habit-forming solution you were looking for.

Highs and Lows

As parents, we are definitely up against some stiff competition. From movies to music, our kids have plenty of means of distraction. Turning down the volume in your house may be met with the occasional uproar, but you are entitled to manage media. That's one of the benefits of being the one in charge.

When your reading routine hits a low and it seems that no connection is being made between your children and books, or your children and you, look for ways to jumpstart your book time. It could be as easy as updating the Special Shelf with new items, or it may need a bit more planning, like a book-and-movie family festival. Whatever the case, be assured that there is no family I know of that has continuous smooth sailing; everyone wants to head back to shore when the tide gets rough. But weathering the reading storm and navigating through challenging waters is bound to bring you out on the other side.

Apply the Pleasure Principle

The books recommended in this try-together section are all great stories. There are several books that rely heavily on humor, some that feature action adventure, and a few that are based on actual events. Choosing books for this section was particularly difficult because, truth be told, I have so many favorites. All of the books here bring me great pleasure, often for different reasons; but I love reading, and rereading, each.

I have definitely read some terrific titles in school, but because I associated that reading with tests, something was lost. Usually pleasure. I encourage you to read whatever books your children bring home from school and talk about the story, but keep recreational reading alive and well in your house. Don't let "assigned" reading interrupt your routine. Children of all reading levels need the opportunity to choose books based solely on their own interests, free from the expectation of quizzes or exams. When you look forward to reading a random choice you've made with your kids, the enthusiasm will rub off on them, making it a most pleasant experience for the two of you.

A Look Back: Five Timeless Tales

The selections here are considered timeless for a number of different reasons. First, even if you have not read the books, you have probably heard of them all; so they are definitely leaving a lasting impression on the collective conscious. Next they push the imagination envelope to new heights, making each the kind that you and your children will end up promoting because it will be so top of mind for both of you. Last, it can be enjoyed again and again, offering something new each time. Books that both adults and children respond to prove that literature has no limits. A few of these boundless books are recommended here:

Charlie and the Chocolate Factory, copyright © 1964 Roald Dahl

Lucky enough to find the last golden ticket, Charlie Bucket joins his fellow winners who all happen to be spoiled-rotten kids. Travel inside the mysterious Chocolate Factory gates where bad manners are not tolerated. Your "time out" corner will look like camp by comparison after this most delicious journey.

Wind in the Willows, copyright © 1908 Kenneth Grahame

Four animal citizens with very different personalities share adventure and camaraderie in an often-humorous and always-beautiful book. The language is rich with description, making readers feel part of nature's community. Originally intended as bedtime stories for Grahame's son, this book is sure to become an evening favorite in your home.

Chronicles of Narnia, copyright © 1949 C. S. Lewis

Meaningful and thoughtful for readers of all ages. Seven volumes chronicle the travels of four children who travel to a world beyond their wildest imaginations and yours. These books can be read in chronological order or enjoyed in their originally published order, depending on your preference for surprise or time.

Success Story

Many series books are now sold in collections. If you are on your second book in a series and you have a devoted young fan, consider purchasing all the volumes at once. It is quite a visual victory for a reader to see that she has read "every single one."

Anne of Green Gables, copyright © 1908 L. M. Montgomery

Anne (with an "e") Shirley is a feisty red-head orphan who wins over the reluctant hearts of her foster parents despite her knack for speaking her mind (loudly) at precisely the wrong moment. A feminist before the word existed, this book will have you cheering for such an independent spirit and a simpler time.

Harriet the Spy, copyright © 1964 Louise Fitzhugh

Armed with a notebook and a fierce attitude, Harriet is a self-proclaimed spy who takes great pleasure in her honest profiles of everyone she meets; but she becomes outed by friends when her notebook is discovered and read. Not preachy or pedestrian, Fitzhugh draws a character that we want to reprimand and empathize with, often in the same chapter. This is a story all about the "gray" area of truth.

Hot Off the Press: Five New and Improved Stories

And the hits just keep on coming. Just when you thought you had read every good story available, a new wave of books makes its way into the shelves and send us all back to the stacks. I love when authors treat their young audiences as sophisticated thinkers without bombarding them with inappropriate themes. Smart doesn't mean shocking. The thought-provoking titles listed here run the spectrum from animated dolls destined for adventure to evil super-geniuses hell-bent on revenge; truly, there is something for every reader in your household to behold.

Doll People, copyright © 2003 by Ann Matthews Martin, Laura Godwin, illustrator Brian Selznick

Toys that come to life is not a new story line, but antique china dolls who befriend modern plastic dolls and unite to solve a mysterious 40-year-old secret is at once captivating and entertaining. Subtle illustrations are peppered throughout this chapter book, making it feel and look very manageable, while still telling an involved story.

The Girls, copyright © 2002 Amy Goldman Koss

This fast-paced read immediately captures the fear and despair of being alienated from a tight-knit middle-school clique. Parents will find their stomachs turn just thinking about the power and pain of gossip. Each chapter is told from a different character's point of view, making for great conversation with your child who is most likely destined to play one of these parts.

Quick Picks

If you love a new title and want to read more of the same, try the super-easy site, What Should I Read Next. Type in a title and author, and the site will generate a reading list of recommendations. Visit at www.whatshouldireadnext.com.

Artemis Fowl, copyright © 2003 Eoin Colfer

This is about a 12-year-old criminal mastermind who is committed to restoring his family's fortune at any cost, even if it means kidnapping a fairy and holding her ransom. Oh, and did I mention he is a super-genius? Packed with folklore, action, and adventure, this scheming story is not all sugar and spice, but it sure does pack a mystical punch.

Al Capone Does My Shirts, copyright © 2004 Gennifer Choldenko

Set on Alcatraz Island during 1935, 12-year-old Moose Flannigan has his hands full watching over his severely autistic sister, trying to fit in at his new (strange) home, and trying to get out of the trouble the warden's daughter always seems to talk him into. This coming-of-age story is what great historical fiction is all about.

City of Ember, copyright © 2004 Jeanne Duprau

When dwindling supplies threaten their already-precarious existence, two young unlikely heroes must rise to the occasion and save their city, which is dependent on electricity and knows nothing of the sun. Readers will be on the edge of their seats, but not feel rushed, to see if the Shining City will be found.

Playground Picks: Five Mom-Approved Titles

As always, if you want to know what books kids will sit still for, go ask Mom. I love getting recommendations from other parents because it means that reading routines are really working. Each family has its own personalized style, but families who read aloud together all agree the book has got to work from the word go. Unlike adults who will give a new book a chance, kids want to hook in with a story immediately. These selections start strong and finish strong, making them an easy sell for even tough customers.

The Phantom Tollbooth, copyright © 1961 Norton Juster

How many times has a parents heard, "I'm bored"? Nothing about the tollbooth travels are boring for Milo, who puts this mysterious package together for lack of anything less boring to do. A clever, animated tale that works on many levels, making it a great ride for both parents and children. You'll be sure to agree that play on words has never been so much fun.

Magic Tree House Series, copyright © 1992 Mary Pope Osborne

Some of you may think that this series belongs in the previous chapter, and if you want to read it with your little learners, go for it. For the reluctant reader, these entertaining stories that combine fact and fiction as told by sibling adventurers have just the right blend of predictability and magic at just the right size. Many parents swear that these books alone got their kids back on the reading track.

Frindle, copyright © 1996 Andrew Clements

If your child is full of great ideas, he will love relating to fifth-grader Nick Allen who haphazardly decides to rename his pen "frindle" in an effort to instigate his dictionary-loving teacher into a battle of wits. The battle ensues, enough public opinion to create media frenzy. *Frindle* is a laugh-out-loud original.

Island of the Blue Dolphins, © copyright 1960 Scott O'Dell

This book won the Newberry Medal in 1961, and the Children's Literature Association named it one of the 10 best books in children's literature over the past 200 years. But awards aside, this adventure, based on a true story, of a girl who sustains herself physically and spiritually for 18 years alone on an island, is what makes this book unforgettable.

The Kid Who Only Hit Homers, copyright © 1972 Matt Christopher

This is one of many titles in the Matt Christopher Sports Classics series. This series shares a common thread: boys who want to excel in sports must overcome a personal obstacle on the way to victory. Set against an action-packed playing field, children live and learn about themselves while competing in a variety of sports. Boys love these books.

Success Story

Matt Christopher is usually pegged as a boy's author, but if your daughter is a sport's fan, try *Spike It,* which features the trials and tribulations of new sisters in a blended family set against the backdrop of a competitive volleyball team.

Award Winners: Five Critically Acclaimed Books

Books that receive awards are always a good place to start if you feel more comfortable with an expert recommendation. After all, with so many books published each year, there must be a reason that only a select few make it to the top of the heap. And there is. Like timeless tales, the books listed here do what only great stories can do: leave the reader saying, "That's exactly how I feel." The details may differ, but these books hit a nerve with their relatable characters, sense of timing, and emotional overtones. These stories seem to lift off the pages and come into our homes; what a great way to introduce our children to new characters.

Charlotte's Web, copyright © 1974 E. B. White

This Newberry medal book is absolutely timeless. The characters are multi-dimensional, yet approachable; lovely, yet faulted. This eloquent story of friendship, life, and death will be treasured by all readers for years to come.

From the Mixed-Up Files of Mrs. Basil E. Frankweiler, copyright © 1967 E. L. Konisburg

Who knew that the Metropolitan Museum of Art was filled with such mystery and intrigue? When Claudia and her brother James run away to the museum to teach their parents a lesson, we go along for the adventure. This 1967 Newberry Medal winner is smart and sassy and will have you and your kids plotting your own escape.

Hoot, copyright © 2004 Carl Hiaasin

Being the new kid in town is never easy, but quirky friends and over-the-top escapades can make the transition much easier. Determined to beat back big business, our hero and his eclectic new friends scheme to save the jeopardized miniature owls. Funny and poignant, this inspired book won the 2003 Newberry Honor.

Holes, copyright © 2000 Louis Sachar

Stanley Yelnats and his family are plagued by bad luck, so it comes as little surprise that he is blamed for a crime he did not commit. He is sent to pay his debt to society at Camp Green Lake, which is no fun in the sun at all. But the plot thickens as the holes are dug and soon Stanley figures out that the inmates are digging for buried treasure. A captivating story of camaraderie and perseverance that won the 1999 Newberry medal.

Esperenza Rising, copyright © 2002 Pam Munoz Ryan

The American Library Association co-sponsors The Pura Belpré Award, "established in 1996, is presented to a Latino/Latina writer and illustrator whose work best portrays, affirms, and celebrates the Latino cultural experience in an outstanding work of literature for children and youth." Esperenza Rising was awarded the medal in 2002 and it is no surprise why. A young, wealthy girl loses the life she knows and is forced to become a migrant worker in 1930s California after her father is killed by bandits. Based on the author's family history, this book is tailor-made for discussions about class and privilege.

The read-aloud books listed here are not intended to be finished in one sitting. There is no reason to rush. Take time to digest and discuss the pages you have enjoyed, and then mark your place and pick up where you left off next time. Reading is one of the few activities that affords us instant gratification over an extended amount of time. Enjoy.

Success Story

Louis Sachar has an excellent series of books that started with *Wayside School Is Falling Down*. If your child likes the novel *Holes*, she may enjoy reading about this zany school and its colorful cast of characters.

The Least You Need to Know

- Reading routines can be modified to meet your family's needs. Solicit your family's help and make a commitment to keep recreational reading at the top of your priority list.
- Literature at this level can be enjoyed by all ages. Enjoy rereading past favorites and being introduced to new authors with your children's help.
- Reading aloud always keeps you in good company.

Part 5

Tweens, Teens, and the Reading Scene: Young Adult Audiences

In this last part, we will take a look at reading with tweens and teens. This section is geared toward an attitude, more than a specific age group. Children who fall into this category are often walking the fine line between wanting to be taken care of and wanting total control over their own lives. To complicate matters, their preferred side of the fence tends to change on a daily basis, making it hard to determine if you are talking to someone who is asking for advice or someone who is asking to be left alone.

Reading together takes on a whole new meaning for this generation, and it is here that we look to help our kids make a personal shift from required readers to readers for life. A focused, hands-on parent such as yourself, armed with a variety of excellent reading resources and some informative ideas, can help make the transition from adolescent to young adult to adult a little bit smoother for everyone in the family. And what a time that will be.

Chapter 18

A Whole New World

In This Chapter

- Titles that can help motivate a reader for life
- Making reading together inviting, not "icky"
- Guiding tweens through tough topics

Tween readers can be difficult to pin down. Not quite teenagers, but no longer little kids, this diverse group of blossoming individuals is the new "it" demographic, with clothing designers, movie producers, and computer software programmers looking to target these influential spenders. When it comes to literature, however, the bookstores have not quite caught up with the changing needs of these young, young adults. When looking for content-appropriate stories, the children's section may seem like a natural choice, but for the more advanced reader, a title from the teen section may be more appealing. With no clear-cut division for the pre-teen/early teen who wants a sophisticated story without mature themes, parents can find themselves walking a fine line. Luckily, there are several strategies that can keep you and your kids from tripping over troublesome titles.

It is still so important to be reading with your children on a regular basis. Not only because it will bring the two of you closer together, but also because it is important to know what your son or daughter considers "age-appropriate" material. With more and more influences coming onto your home via television and computers, conversations you were hoping to avoid until senior high school may be more advantageous to have now. Reading together can be another important way we help navigate our children through unchartered territories.

Pages of Pleasure—Winning Selections

Here is another confession: some of my favorite books are young-adult novels. I don't mean I have some favorite YA titles that I like to recommend to kids and the adults who love them. I mean, my personal favorites just happen to be targeted for a much different demographic, one that does not have mortgage payments and a healthy appreciation for anti-wrinkle night cream. Great young-adult literature tackles identity, love, friendship, self-awareness, self-loathing, and a host of other topics seen daily on afternoon talk shows. But because these books are packaged with bright-pink covers and narrated by characters who are itching to get behind the wheel of a car just as soon as they're old enough to do so, adults disregard the genre. I think that a lot more parents would opt to stick with a tween (and teen) reading routine if they knew what a treat these books were.

Keeping reading a value in your home is still important. But, (dare I say it?) I think it might actually be easier to do with this age group than all the others, for purely selfish reasons. The older my son gets, the more I enjoy him. Yes, I loved him as a newborn, but I really do prefer him now that he is starting to develop his own personality. Granted, there are days I long to have the agreeable bundle of gurgling goo back in my arms, but overall, it just keeps getting better. I was fortunate enough to have taught preschool and middle school, and given my druthers, I would pick middle-schoolers any day of the week. You may be finding that your children are increasingly more interesting—challenging, of course, but really exciting people who you like to spend time with. The question, really, is no longer "Should I read with my children?" but "What can I read next with my children?" My hope is that you will give YA books their fair share of your attention. You may be surprised how much you enjoy yourself.

Magic-Bullet Books

There is no other word for it but magic. When your daughter comes to you with tears in her eyes because her favorite character has just discovered the secret her family has been keeping, or you hear your son cheering out loud as he discovers, right along with the main character, that he has won the coveted award, it is pure magic.

Having done everything we can to expose our children to a variety of exciting books, expert authors, and new subjects, there is nothing as satisfying as seeing our kids become independent recreational readers. This does not happen overnight, obviously, and one great experience does not a reader for life make; but, during your child's formative years it is highly likely that given enough opportunity they will transition from passive to active readers.

Magic-bullet books refer to the individual book that takes them there. For myself, after reading S. E. Hinton's *The Outsiders*, there was no going back to picture books, series books, or predictable books. This was, for me, the book that launched a love of reading. I cannot explain the exact reason that this happened, only to say, it was the right book at the right time. There is no way we can map out how to put a magic-bullet book in your child's hands; the variables are too great. But if we keep filling hands with books and heads with stories, we greatly improve their shot.

Quick Picks

If you have not yet found your Magic-Bullet Book, there is no time like the present. Hopefully you are learning to love reading right along with your children. There is no right book, no age-appropriate choice to wait for; by just being open to a variety of books, you are likely to find one that changes you from a "have-to-read" parent to a "have-to-read-because-I-love-to-read" parent.

Once your child discovers a book that he just cannot live without, keep the excitement going. Just because the book has ended doesn't mean the experience has to. Use a search engine to look for blogs, articles, or further reading suggestions related to this title. Websites like www.scholastic.com even have a book lover's club to help parents and child get the most out of one of their published books. Called Flashlight Readers, this online "members only" club is free and very kid-friendly. The purpose of the club is to encourage, "beginners through advanced-level readers explore quality books and communicate with favorite authors. We [Flashlight Readers] feature books at the third- to eighth-grade level; each title offers enrichment opportunities such as community-building games, activities, author interaction, slideshows, and more, while seamlessly building essential reading and writing skills. Parent support is provided with every featured book to help you help your child get the most out of each reading experience." Cool graphics, author links, and scheduled online chats, and rewards for completing fun activities, are some of the things you'll find. An interactive site like this can help you take a book, and your child, to the next level of reading enjoyment.

Sustained Silent Reading

If you are excited about the prospect of your child finding that magic-bullet book, and you are on board with reading some great YA novels of your own, the next step is to think about your home's reading arrangement. By now, book baskets have probably been put to other uses, book nooks are cluttered with sports gear, and family-fun reading nights are as welcomed as new socks on Christmas morning. While I am a true advocate for reading aloud with tweens, I know that we are entering the age of "ick" where curling up in bed with a parent before bedtime could be considered, as one of my former students so eloquently put it, "just plain sick." Setting up a sustained silent-reading routine in your home may well be the welcome mat your kids have been hoping for.

Bookworms Beware

Most schools have a sustained silent reading, SSR, reading workshop, or D.E.A.R. (Drop Everything And Read) program. Find out what your child's teacher calls this time and come up with a different name for your routine. This idea is not supposed to be school in disguise. It is a part of your family literacy, not an extension of the classroom.

There are three parts of sustained silent reading (often called SSR or some other catchy acronym in school) that you'll want to coordinate:

- **Sustained** Just as your baby's reading routine worked because it was routine, set a date and time for reading. Don't muscle your schedule or assume that more is better. Fifteen minutes in the den before dinner or 20 minutes on the living room floor before bed are great places to start. If you cannot find a regular daily time, look at your week's schedule. If there are still no opportunities, I hope you will reconsider adjusting some of your commitments; everyone needs downtime, even you.
- **Silent** Unplugging can be very difficult in the beginning. We are so used to noise and multi-tasking that slow and steady silence can be intimidating. If you must have some background noise, use it as a transition to silence. Two minutes of soft music that fades out could be all you need to move from chaos to comfort.

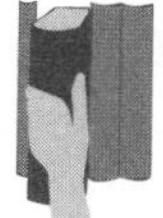

Quick Picks

I used to play music for my students while they read, thinking it would help them relax and concentrate. One day, a student asked me to turn off the music because it was so distracting. Point taken. It's called sustained silent reading for a reason.

- **Reading** This is a time for reading. Not writing, homework, bills, or e-mail. Reading. And everyone should be reading whatever she wants. If your child loves her school novel (hooray!) and wants to read that for enjoyment, you may make an exception to the recommendation; but ideally, I think this time should be school-free recreational reading.

In addition to having the above, make sure to have a slew of different reading materials on hand. No one wants to come to the reading party empty-handed. Keep reading resources within reach to avoid wasting time and hearing excuses. Finally, include yourself in this time. This is practice-what-you-preach time. Laundry, phone calls, and taking out the garbage can wait. You may not be lying next to each other anymore, but that doesn't mean that you can't read together.

Coming of (Uncomfortable) Age

If you have not done so already, be prepared (if that is even remotely possible) for the first time your sheer presence makes your tween embarrassed to be alive. There you'll be, going about your day as usual, unaware that you have just committed some unthinkable act of humiliation, like saying hello to your kid's friends. You'll both get in the car and your now-permanently damaged child will burst into tears and cry, "How could you?" She'll sulk the entire way home. You'll begin to fantasize about dropping her off at college.

The unpredictable tween years are certainly full of surprises, for them and you. But while many children will insist that they do not need your help ever again (except maybe later), the truth is, clichés and all, they still need you. And this means reading together. Yes, tweens needs personal space and some independence, but they also need some clear-cut boundaries. Sharing books can help define these boundaries.

Reading aloud at this age needs a little fine-tuning to avoid the "ick" factor, but this is not the time to abandon all efforts. The titles that are recommended in this subject should not be tackled alone. Chock full of weighty topics, these nonfiction and fiction books are best discovered together. Do you both have to sit on the edge of the bed and read a story together word for word? Well, if that works for you, go for it. Some kids still love to be read to. But you could also buy duplicate copies of novels and reference books to read independently, and then plan a one-on-one evening of dessert and talking, with the books in front of you. The important thing is to follow up; whether that happens on a daily basis as you read together or later that week on your way to soccer practice is up to you. Find a reading (and discussing) routine that is low on "ick" and high on interaction.

Nothing but the Truth

When I was a middle-school teacher, I could not believe how advanced my students were; and I am not talking about reading levels. Just about every one of my female students wore make-up and designer clothes and all of the boys returned from winter vacation having received the same holiday present: hormones. Always on the lookout for note passing, I intercepted my fair share of tightly folded communications that included last night's instant messenger wrap-up, plans for an upcoming weekend when parents would be out of town and who was doing what with whom. If I didn't know any better, I would guess these notes were written by high schoolers. They weren't. My students were eleven. And all were from respectable, middle- to upper-middle-class families.

This anecdote is not intended to frighten you (although I bet it does) but confirm your suspicions: yes, they know, and are curious about, sex, violence, puberty, drugs, and dating. If, as parents, we don't talk to our kids about these subjects, they will be left with the ramblings of other equally clueless students, pop media, and a vivid imagination. But because the idea of sitting down with your adolescent and coming up with a way to work the word "ejaculate" into a sentence may send you screaming from the room, here are some titles to help relieve the pressure:

The Middle School Survival Guide: How to Survive from the Day Elementary School Ends Until the Second High School Begins by Arlene Erlbach, illustrator Helen Flook

A frank look at starting middle school, the author uses straight-forward language and makes no apologies (why should she?) for talking frankly about sex. There are quotes and advice from children peppered throughout the book, which ranges from serious to humorous, but the tone is always smart and sophisticated.

Too Old for This, Too Young for That!: Your Survival Guide for the Middle-School Years by Harriet S. Mosatache, Karen Unger

With chapters that cover changing bodies, changing feelings, and changing family dynamics, this book uses straight-forward language to talk about a variety of subjects. Also featured are several margin notes that recommend websites and additional reading.

Reading these books together can help take the focus off of either one of you and put it on the material in the book. Of course, some topics would make us feel vulnerable even if we were standing behind a suit or armor; but that still doesn't mean we're better off pretending these things don't exist.

Success Story

If reading this chapter is making you queasy, you may want to try *The Rollercoaster Years* by Charlene C. Gianetti and Margaret Sagarese. This practical handbook is authoritative without being too heavy, and easy to read without being condescending. A how-to guide for helping you and your family make the transition from adolescence to young adult.

The Discomfort Zone

If nonfiction books on growing up are just too much for one parent to handle, or if your child turns six shades of red when you open to the page entitled "Your Changing Body," there is a softer approach. YA fiction can provide just the right amount of reality to help get a conversation going, but because these novels are free from full-color illustrations, both parent and child may be more comfortable with the content. Sex isn't the only topic that can make you both blush, though. Drugs, violence, cliques, fitting in, and moving apart are all uncomfortable realities that can leave us reaching for the remote instead of reaching for our reading.

Reading books whose characters make choices that conflict with your family's values doesn't mean that you are condoning these actions—no more than wearing a seatbelt should be seen as a reason to drive recklessly. What these characters can do is provide scenarios to talk about. Instead of using yourself, your child, or his friends as examples, you can talk about the decisions the characters made and your reactions to them. Not feeling attacked or preached to, your children may be more likely to speak candidly. When the conversation does get more personal, as we would hope for, you will have had some "practice" talking about tougher themes.

Sisterhood of the Traveling Pants by Ann Brashares

Four high school friends set out in different directions one summer but stay connected through a pair of jeans that happens to fit each one of them perfectly. Friendship, loyalty, emerging sexuality, and acceptance are among the themes the four girls wrestle with. This is a story that will ring true for you and your daughters.

That Was Then, This is Now by S. E. Hinton

The same author of *The Outsiders*, Hinton takes on the complex relationship of two boys who were as close as brothers, in this novel that was way ahead of its time. When the road begins to divide and each must choose a separate path, the results are violent, dangerous, and moving. It is rare to see YA fiction focus on male relationships, but this book works exquisitely.

Gateway Reading

By this point in your child's reading life, it is safe to say that we are standing at the threshold of some really exciting reading. YA literature, whether enjoyed by tweens or teens, is filled with stimulating and inspirational stories. The good news is, there are tons of great reading materials to choose from. The less-than-good news is, it takes awhile to find the great ones.

What you read as a child may not be found in favor by your own child. I must admit, if my son finishes my magic-bullet book, *The Outsiders*, with no more than a shrug of the shoulders, I will be disappointed. But his magic-bullet books and his reading experience can be his own. I have already had mine. Until the day when our children discover that they want to read on their own, and can confidently march into a library or bookstore and look up what they want, we can continue to help point them in the right direction.

These last two sections are really the gateway to independent reading. Learning to see a series through and finding an author to call one's own are important steps on the road to being a recreational reader for life. In your literacy-rich home, continue to find new ways to explore interesting series and authors, whether looking up author links online or purchasing the limited-edition note cards that complement the series. Supporting our tweens' reading choices and reading right along with them is a pleasant way to bridge our children to books forever.

Seriously Good Series Books

We touched on this topic in the last chapter and it is relevant here as well: series books are a comforting means of enjoying reading for young adults. Luckily, the books that are written for this age group tend to have greater character development and more interesting storylines than their predecessors, meaning, you are not going to feel like you are having dèjá vu all over again. Here are two series to try that you may not have yet found:

The Agony of Alice by Phyllis Reynolds Naylor

With well over 20 books in this series, girls will love to see how Alice grows from a precocious middle schooler to a thoughtful and introspective high schooler, dealing with her mother's death, puberty, boys, and friends along the way. This is a "real life" look at growing up, and the older Alice gets, the more complicated the books' themes become.

Alex Rider Adventures by Anthony Horowitz

A 14-year-old secret agent who is the world's premier spy enjoys a complicated lifestyle in these always-fast-paced, technically enhanced stories of mystery and intrigue. This James Bond in the making is sure to captivate young audiences.

Voices for a Generation

Every generation plays favorites. Be it music, celebrities, or authors, even those who give no credence to pop culture usually know the names of icons who left a distinguishable mark on the collective conscious. It is human nature to want something or someone to speak for you, to find the words that you cannot find. There are no hard-and-fast rules for determining how and why icons come to be, but there is no denying that when you see, hear, or read it, you know. In elementary school, my girlfriends and I passed around a copy of Judy Blume's *Are You There, God? It's Me, Margaret* with the same level of covertness one might use when crossing over enemy lines. Judy Blume's books took on almost a cult status; she really seemed to get it, whatever "it" was.

Quick Picks

A great website for your daughter is www.agirlsworld.com where all of the content is written by teen girls. Advice, columns, and reviews are among the things that you'll find at this bright and friendly site. Submissions welcome.

Just as my friends and I had found our "voice" in Judy Blume, your children will look for stories that speak to them and for them. Hooking in with an author is an excellent way to help your children really find their own reading niche. Reading the same author is the "grown up" equivalent of reading a series. Favorite authors are an acquired taste. If you and your children haven't sampled any books that made you go looking for seconds, this list of great authors may help develop your literary palette:

For Girls	For Boys
Amy Goldman Koss	Jerry Spinelli
Sharon Creech	Gary Paulsen
Meg Cabot	Loius Sachar
Karen Cushman	Jack Gantos

Of course there will be crossover between the two lists and their purpose is not to divide, but to conquer. At this age, boys and girls experiences are very different, and it can be helpful to hook in with a gender-friendly author who appreciates those distinctions.

Getting to know your tween reader can be as difficult as trying to pin one singular definition of what a tween is. Luckily, tweens, like the books that they are drawn to, have exciting, multi-faceted characteristics that can lend themselves to interesting discussions. As always, we find that connecting through books can help make every stage, and any age, more manageable.

Quick Picks

In my experience, girls will read books about boys more than boys will read books about girls, but that doesn't mean the opposite couldn't be true for your son. Keeping a variety or materials around can help book "crossover" and may encourage your kids to read outside their comfort zone.

The Least You Need to Know

- Young Adult literature comes of age along with your tween.
- Tweens need to be seen, heard, and read with so that they feel visible and empowered. Avoiding uncomfortable situations will not make them go away.
- When the going gets tough, the tough can head to the bookshelves. Try to remember this when your child trades in tantrums for tattoos.

Chapter 19

Rated "M" for Maturing Taste

In This Chapter

- Common grounds, uncommon reactions
- Giving gifts unconditionally
- Redecorating your home library

When will you know your tween has officially become a teen? Probably about the same time you realize that you have officially become your parents. Comments that you used to roll your eyes about now roll off your tongue with the efficiency of a well-wound clock. "Turn off the light," "Pick up your shoes," "Set the table," "Finish your homework," and "Get off the phone/computer/X-Box" are among your list of most popular directions. And who can blame you? Our parents told us these same things in hopes of raising us to be responsible, contributing members of society and now we are (gasp) passing along the favor. These messages are useful, but not all that meaningful. It is much easier to lecture about curfew than it is to talk about commitment, and much easier to give advice to our kids than to listen to them.

Teenagers are a walking contradiction. Part adult and part child, they fight for their independence, but are not ready to give up their security. They are counting the days until they leave for college, but are likely to pack to their teddy bears in their suitcases. What is a parent to do? As has been true from the beginning of this book, reading together can help strengthen a parent and child's relationship. Your teenager may seem to be more and more of a mystery, a hard person to talk to, an even harder person to hear; but with books on your side, you can learn to read in between the lines.

Teens and Adult Novels

I love the expression, "Be careful what you wish for" and find it always appropriate when talking about teens. We want to raise passionate, strong children who have a lust for life and want to become an active part in their destiny. We want to raise readers for life who turn to books for entertainment, counsel, and comfort. But we did not expect that this would mean living with a stubborn spirit who insists that Stephen King and Candace Bushnell are her new favorite authors. When our kids prefer adult novels over young-adult novels, we can feel like we are condoning rated-R movies for our underage audience. And in a way, we are. But just like watching a movie together gives us the opportunity to talk about our favorite and least favorite parts, so does reading together.

Reading skills having been learned; the trick now is finding books that are age- and content-appropriate, while still being interesting and engaging. For parents of teenagers, the tides may be turning; instead of your children being the ones who are reluctant about new material, parents may find themselves wishing they could avoid dicey subjects. Fortunately, it is possible to talk about tough topics without having tantrums (yours or theirs). As was suggested in the last chapter, using books as a neutral home base gives readers, both parents and children, a safe place to start.

"I Don't Want Her Reading About *That!*"

As you read the title for this section, there is no doubt in my mind that your thought immediately went to whatever your "*That*" hot topic is.

For some parents, any titillating sex scene is off limits for their teen, while others object to drug experimentation, homosexuality, challenging authority, having affairs, violence, or a host of other undesirables. The exact same thing that makes a novel interesting to an adult ("I can't believe he told his wife the baby died at child birth, when really it just had down syndrome," *The Memory Keeper's Daughter* by Kim Edwards) can be the exact same elements that we want to shield our kids from.

Interestingly enough, the proverbial cat may already be out of the bag. While you may not want your son to read about "That," it is highly likely that he has already seen most of these things in mainstream media. Video games, websites, magazines, and television make no qualms about attracting our kids to sex, drugs, and violence. Among their friends, they have seen, if not experienced, loss, fear, lust, resentment, and betrayal. Instead of thinking about protecting our kids from such undesirables or trying to paint a rose-colored world for them, we may be better off bringing these subjects home in more manageable means.

Success Story

Barnes and Noble has caught on to the teen market, categorizing Teen bestsellers by subject titles. If you are looking for titles that aren't young adult (too young) and not yet adult (too old), you may find their recommendations to be just right. Try www.barnesnadnoble.com.

YA and Teen novels are not the soft-on-the-inside read that leave everyone embraced in group hug on the final page. Stark, dark, and often right on the mark, you may be surprised at how much you get out of an adolescent's story. In the same way that an adult can appreciate an excellent YA novel for its universal themes, a teen can appreciate an adult novel for its stirring story line and familiar feel. Both teen and adult novels can have more explicit, mature themes, but these elements are hardly ever the crux of the story. Even foul language and violence are more often used to establish a character rather than incite a following. What these books can do is give us an opportunity to discover and discuss the choices people make, the consequences of those decisions, and our own reactions to a particular set of circumstances.

We have spent, and will continue to spend, a lot of time talking about the potential problems mainstream media can cause; but to always associate what is popular with what is troublesome is not an accurate picture. When trying to bridge the divide between adults and teens for our purposes, it can be helpful to see what everybody else is reading. The New York Times Bestseller List is an easily accessible resource to keep you current on great stories. Here are a few titles that will give you plenty to talk about:

Politically Correct Bedtime Stories: Modern Tales for Our Life and Times by James Finn Garner

A dozen classic bedtime stories are retold as not to offend anyone, anywhere at anytime; an excellent conversation-starter for our politically correct society. Short and smart.

Different Seasons by Stephen King

Four novellas written by a masterful storyteller, each with its own thought-provoking purpose. Readers may recognize two stories that were developed into the critically acclaimed movies *Stand by Me* and *The Shawshank Redemption.* It is Stephen King we are talking about, so expect sex, violence, and horror peppered throughout the text; but I bet you forget those details as you are caught up in the stories.

Running with Scissors: A Memoir by Augusten Burrows

At once hilarious and disturbing, this is not your typical coming-of-age memoir. To say the author grew up in a dysfunctional household would be a huge understatement; homosexuality, abuse, and bizarre scenarios are strewn throughout this true-life account that somehow manages to just keep telling a great story.

The Lovely Bones by Alice Sebold

A murdered young teen narrates this heartbreaking story from heaven as she watches her family react to her untimely death. Despite the terrifying first chapter and the tragic events, this book is beautifully written and, ultimately, a family love story.

Sticky Situations

Wouldn't it be great if we could tell our teens that we never experimented with any drugs, alcohol, sex, or other unsavory behaviors? Wouldn't it be so much easier to tell them what not to do if we ourselves had "clean records"?

Some parents reading this may be able to do just that; but I'm betting that the majority of us will fear having out "little talks" turned on us. When it comes to our teens, talking about sticky situations can make us feel like we have just been caught with our hand inside the cookie jar. These are questions you may be avoiding: your own past.

Quick Picks

Don't forget, if your kids are making the right choices, let them know how happy you are for them. If a meaningful conversation happened in the car, write a note later expressing your appreciation or your pride. It's nice to end with, "I love you and I'm here for you." Then do both.

There are no easy answers when it comes to figuring out how much to say, when. The honesty-is-the-best-policy policy, may not work for every family. However much you decide to disclose about your own past is a personal decision, but avoiding any or all uncomfortable subjects could be extremely harmful. Just because you are not talking about tough topics doesn't mean everybody isn't. The following titles can help you get a better handle on how to start:

- *Staying Connected to Your Teenager: How to Keep Them Talking to You and How to Hear What They're Really Saying* by Michael Riera
- *Get Out of My Life, but First Could You Drive Me & Cheryl to the Mall: A Parent's Guide to the New Teenager, Revised and Updated* by Anthony E. Wolf
- *Yes, Your Teen is Crazy!: Loving Your Kid Without Losing Your Mind* by Michael J. Bradley, Jay N. Giedd
- *WHY Do They Act That Way?: A Survival Guide to the Adolescent Brain for You and Your Teen* by David Walsh

A Formula That Fits

Reading with your teen, like the rest of your activities together, is going to change and grow with your relationship. I do not know of any family where Mom and Dad are still tucking Junior into bed at night once he is a junior in high school. And this is probably a good thing; but it does mean that you will have to take advantage of different times throughout the day to touch base with your kids and keep your reading relationship on track.

In addition to the family-friendly strategies found here, seek out bookstores and libraries that appreciate your teen's patronage. Ideal locations will have separate Teen seating, shelves specifically for their materials, and employees who are knowledgeable about this genre. You probably prefer to do business in a place that appreciates and respects your time and preferences; help make the same favorable conditions open to your children.

Paired Reading

Paired reading is exactly as it sounds: a pair who is reading. Inherent is this combination is the idea of sharing in the reading experience, but how you go about achieving this is dependent on your family's preference. Because teenagers thrive on independence (good) and may be reluctant to want to share time with the family (not good), paired reading activities can be a great reason to get together for a few minutes, a few hours, or a few days. Looking at your schedule, you can decide how to best use books to your advantage. Your teenagers may be approaching their school graduation, thrilled at the prospect of autonomy, but as parents, it is important to teach your kids that they will never graduate from their family; they will always be an indispensable part of something bigger. These ideas can help drive that point home.

Quick Picks

Many libraries have teen groups that meet to do service projects, enjoy special events, and mingle with other kids in a safe place. Contact your library's YA librarian to find out if such a group exists.

- **Everyday Ideas** Buying or borrowing multiple copies of the same book is a great way to share a reading experience. Instead of having to pass a title back and forth, which can sometimes feel a lot like someone is reading over your shoulder, having your own book gives you the "right" to pick it up and put it down on your schedule. Each reader can first make the story his own, and then share it with others.

- **Extended Ideas** I am a huge fan of "running lists." In addition to keeping track of great movies to see or items to pick up at the store, keep a "Family Reading List" posted on the fridge. You can either jot down a title you heard being endorsed by someone else and pencil in your child's name next to it ("This sounded like something you might like") or keep track of books that are relevant to the whole family. For instance, if your family has just developed a taste for travel, *1,000 Places to See Before You Die* by Patricia Shultz could be a great addition to your home's library. Checking the list before heading out the door is a great way to remind yourselves what books to look for should you find yourself at the library or bookstore.
- **Holiday Ideas** I am a sucker for holiday traditions, but teenagers may need a bit more coaxing. Create some much-needed family-friendly time with a super-simple "time capsule" questionnaire that captures your family's interests. Print up a fun favorites list for the year that includes things like best friends, movies and books, and worst school disasters, trends and books. Don't forget to add a "Crystal Ball" section where each family member can make predictions about the future.
  Sweeten the deal with great coffee drinks and dessert. Reading and reflecting on the past year can be a great way to reconnect over memories. This is the kind of idea that will take a year to get off the ground, so be prepared for some resistance; however, once the first year's efforts are realized, it will no longer be such a hard sell.

Bookworms Beware

Timing is everything when it comes to teens. Making Friday night family night, when your daughter had already planned on going to the movies, will not a receptive audience make. Target "off" nights for such special events and you'll increase everyone's chances for enjoyment.

Pass It On

Everyone likes to get gifts and almost everyone enjoys giving them. Finding the perfect something for someone can be as exciting as receiving the perfect gift. But when we give reading gifts to our kids, we tend to want to follow up immediately, check in on how much they like the present, and complain if we don't see them using it to our satisfaction. Could you imagine giving someone a sweater and then insisting that they wear it everyday?

When passing a book, note, or article onto our kids, let's try to do so without any pressure. A gift given with an open heart means that the receiver may do with it what she likes, even if we don't like what she chooses to do with it. Sharing literature is a gift. So when you finish a great book, article, or magazine, by all means, pass it along to your children. Leave it on their bed, in their bathroom, or tuck it into their back pack. Then leave it alone. It is not required reading, it is a gift. The following excerpt from *Better Than Life* by Daniel Pennac, copyright 1999 Pembrook Publishers, can help drive this point home:

The Reader's Bill of Rights. Readers have …

- the right to not read.
- the right to skip pages.
- the right to not finish a book.
- the right to reread.
- the right to read anything.
- the right to escapism.
- the right to read anywhere.
- the right to browse.
- the right to read out loud.
- the right not to defend your tastes.

Quick Picks

If the "Reader's Bill of Rights" strikes a chord with you and your kids, print out a few copies and attach it to the cover of any reading materials you pass along, making the gift a choice, not a commitment.

What a difference our reading relationship with our children could be if we passed along a book with this "Bill of Rights" in mind. The same holds true for giving your children a card or note. Writing to your children is a wonderful way to express hard-to-vocalize feelings without putting everyone on the spot. Slipping a card under the bedroom door gives us a chance to deliver a message, without expecting the receiver to be responsible for C.O.D. (Conversation on Demand). Telling our children that we love them, we're sorry, or we're proud, without standing around and waiting for the obligatory "me, too" response, makes the message a true gift that your kids will want to read over and over again.

Your Home Library Grows Up

Many moons ago when you brought home your bundle of joy, you watched as your once-neat and orderly home was taken over by board books, squeaky toys, and stuffed animals. Nary a room was safe from your little one's treasures. Today, your teen's belongings are probably still all over the house, but we tend to see them as annoying, not endearing. You are not as likely to pick up their things and start playing together, so into the closet, out to the garage, and up to the bedroom they go. But often, what works in the beginning can work now. When it comes to books, the more the merrier.

Book nooks under sheet forts may not entice your kids off the couch, but keeping reading materials within reach is still an excellent way to inspire a few stolen moments for stories. When it comes to our teens, out of sight really is out of mind; in fact, right under their nose can often be out of mind, driving you out of your mind. If we want to help our kids keep reading, we have to make it as easy as possible to do so. Luckily, a little prep work and a bit of ingenuity make this idea easy on you.

Magazines and Newspapers

Subscribing to National Geographic for Kids may seem virtuous in comparison to inviting Vogue or Maxim magazine into your home, but when it comes to reading magazines, audiences read "up." This means that despite their titles, teen magazines are really targeted to a younger crowd. By the time your teenager reaches senior high school, he wants the real deal, not the watered-down versions implied with "Teen" versions. The nice thing about your teen requesting a subscription to a "real" magazine is that they are targeted toward you, the adult; the bad thing about these magazines is that they are targeted toward you, the adult. Keeping these magazines in the living room or kitchen gives you a much better chance of talking about the content, including advertising, trends, and sensitive topics, and gives you insight into what is considered "normal" for your kid's age. Like adult novels, magazines can be enjoyed together, providing another way to share reading.

Some families I know swear by newspapers. Delivered daily, everyone had their favorite section to look forward to. From sports, to horoscopes, to current events, having new material on hand makes for a great conversation opener. "Anything good in the paper today?" invites immediate sharing. The length of articles makes daily reading manageable for all reading levels and the Sunday paper, with its additional features, is often a great resource for interesting things to see, do, and talk about. A financially reasonable investment, newspapers may give you just the reading jumpstart you need.

Bookworms Beware

School assignments tend to rely heavily on current events. You may end up saving yourself time and money by having a daily paper delivered instead of having to hunt one down each time a project is given.

Around the House

Your home library is best considered a mobile montage. Treating reading resources as rotating inventory gives you the flexibility to make changes as you see fit. Instead of limiting yourself to bookshelves, which are aesthetically lovely, though not always hands-on inviting, think about where the bulk of your family's living is done and target these hot spots throughout your home. Here is a "Have on Hand" list to help encourage your family to get their hands on reading.

Someone's in the Kitchen (Reading!):

- Hang a wipe board on the fridge for quick notes.
- Use name magnets for holding reading specific materials for each family member.
- Put up magnetized pads for "running lists."
- Tape articles, movie reviews, or funny comic strips to morning cereal boxes and milk cartons.
- Dedicate a kitchen drawer to pens, pencils, blank note cards, stationery, and stamps.
- Prominently display the family calendar (and use it!).

Media rooms:

- Tape notes to your kids onto the remote.
- Keep television guides nearby.
- Subscribe to entertainment magazines and keep the updated issue spread out on the coffee table.
- Play board games such as Scrabble, Trivial Pursuit, and Cranium.

Behind closed doors—bathroom books:

- Keep magazine racks well stocked and updated.
- Hang a wipe board on the back of the door to reiterate quick messages.
- Dedicate a drawer for pads and pens (how many times have you had a great idea while sitting around?).

Quick Picks

If you are looking to raise savvy consumers and keep yourself on budget, consider keeping a running list of needed household items you are waiting to be featured in a sale. Check the paper for upcoming store events and make purchases at the best price. My in-laws passed along this great idea and it works like a charm.

In the Bedroom:

- Drop a book off on your child's pillow for her to use at her leisure.
- Give blank journals, stationery, stamps, and colorful new pens as presents.
- Provide an attractive bedside light to encourage bedtime reading.

Special Shelf Revealed

I hope that you have enjoyed using the Special Shelf with your children. It can be a fun and effective way to try new titles together, reiterate the value of reading in your home, and keep track of the reading progress your child is enjoying. But now it is time to turn the shelf over to your teenager. If we want our children to become readers for life, we have to give them the opportunity to do so independent of our efforts; therefore, instead of choosing what books go on the shelf, or even helping to decide, we can mark that spot off-limits and let our children become the sole proprietors of that literature ledge.

What the Special Shelf will hopefully reveal is that you have accomplished what you have set out to do: make reading a pleasurable passion to pursue. Of course you can give great new books as presents and hope they make it onto the shelf, but it is now up to your teen what titles make the cut. Yes, it is sad that your picture may be replaced by a new romantic interest, or a homemade holiday decoration discarded in preference of a CD collection; but this change is really bittersweet. Your teen's continued use of the Special Shelf, for treasures and titles, is your reward as much as his. Congratulations to both of you.

Success Story

Just as you hope your child will continue to use her Special Shelf, so should you continue to use yours. Modeling behavior is still the most important lesson you can ever give.

Communicating with your teenager may not always be easy, but with the right tools, it can be more effective. While there is no title that could ever claim, "How to raise your teenager in 10 easy steps," the ideas in this chapter can help you continue to raise a reader for life.

The Least You Need to Know

- Successful book talks require less talking and more listening. This means that you'll want to ask more questions and give fewer answers.
- Shared reading experiences can be light and lively. Take time to laugh at characters, and yourselves and never underestimate the bonding power of humor.
- Every room in your house provides reading opportunities. Try putting books and magazines in unexpected places so others may discover these treasures.

Chapter 20

Reluctant Readers and the Hard Sell

In This Chapter

- Winning back dissatisfied customers
- Managing mainstream influences
- The benefits of embracing reading trends together

I won't get into a lengthy discussion about how busy today's teens are, or how many different distractions they have beating down their door, except to say, the competition for their attention is fierce. Raising a reader for life takes staying power, yours and theirs, and when more-interesting, less-stressful activities make themselves available, it can be hard to convince your teen that reading is really terrific—especially when their own personal experiences are beginning to convince them otherwise. As parents of teens, we want to avoid a battle of wills, and instead have willing reading participants. For this to happen, we'll want to appreciate what we are up against and flex our creative and compassionate muscles. Let's first take a look at what drives tweens and teens away from reading and then look at some strategies for getting them back on the road to recreational reading.

How Schools Ruin Reading

Imagine having a plan to go to the movies with your friend, but before you walked into the theater, you were required to define all the unfamiliar words that you'd hear, read a detailed account of the director's life, and write a one-page prediction about what the movie may be about based on the title and time period. Reluctantly, you agree because you really like movies and are anxious to get on with it. Once inside, the movie starts and you are completely intrigued by what is happening, but your friend sees this as a good time to turn the movie off and talk about what you have learned so far, review the defined terms, and quiz you about some insignificant details, just to see if you were paying attention. See where this is going? How likely is it that you will love this movie, look forward to future movies, or speak to your friend ever again? Yet this is exactly how we teach novels in school.

I know that the above title sounds a bit harsh; but unfortunately, I have found it to be quite true. Schools are ruining reading for kids. Not all schools all the time, but enough to make it a real problem. Reading can teach us a ton of things, but if we don't find any pleasure in the learning process, what are the chances of us really becoming educated individuals? Continuing to make books a value at home can help put the focus back on pleasure and relieve some of the pressure associated with required reading.

Isolationism: Silencing Joyful Noise

While we have spent a great deal of time talking about shared reading experiences, this concept does not seem to translate well to high school classrooms. Yes, everyone is reading the same book at the same time, but everyone is also working toward the same end at the same time: a good grade. With the focus on the product, not the process, teens are less likely to enjoy the reading and more apt to approach assignments as just another thing they have to do. There may be some discussion about what is happening in the book, character motivations, or how the story relates to their own experiences, but because there are curriculum requirements to cover, these discussions are not the norm. More than likely, the teacher is explaining what the story means, reducing reading to an expert's opinion. To make matters worse, once the conversation gets going, the bell rings, bringing with it an abrupt end. As soon as the students are engaged, they are dismissed; how's that for a disappointing ending?

At home, reading for pleasure does not have to fit into a specific time period. We can provide quiet opportunities to unplug, but we certainly don't need to monitor page counts or hand out quizzes. We may even want to think about new ways to instigate book conversations. "What are you reading about?" will more than likely result in rote answers, "It's a book about a family who moves to a new town." Because all questions may be perceived as quizzes, it might be more beneficial for us to talk about what we are reading, modeling a more engaging approach. "In this new novel I'm reading, four women who are really close friends find out one of them has cancer. I can't decide if I would want to know if someone I loved was sick or prefer for it to be unexpected. Which way would you rather have it happen?" You are telling your son about what your book is about, but your question cannot possibly have a right or wrong answer because one doesn't exist. Not only do we want to be asking our kids open-ended questions about their reading, but we want to look for ways to bring about an open-ended discussion.

Quick Picks

If you get cut off mid-discussion with your teen because his bus is coming, make a quick note of where you were in the conversation, tape it to the bathroom mirror, and invite your son to pick up the conversation later. If he's interested, he will.

Irrelevance: Classic Mistakes

In each section I recommend "timeless tales" as opposed to "classics" because I myself have become so turned off by being told what to read, by being told "what counts." I had my fill of that in school, thank you very much. I know there are quite a lot of people who associate having read the classics with having been well educated; but I think it's more accurate to say if you have read the classics, then you are well educated in the classics. Is that even entirely necessary? I don't know. As an English major who graduated from a prestigious college with honors, I can tell you, reading the classics in high school and college did not make me want to be a reader or writer. Stephen King did that. (And his books weren't even allowed inside my parochial high school doors.) Sadly, I fear the goal of reading in high school is not to create readers for life, but to get kids into colleges where they brag (lament) about having read the classics.

> **Bookworms Beware**
>
> Once a book wins a prestigious award or is designated a classic, it is deemed "important," which we all-too-often associate with "required." Treat all designations as a recommendation, but try not to judge a book by the medal on its cover. For our purposes, it's more important to read what you like, and like what you read.

If you love the classics, that's great; but I'm betting you had one amazing teacher who made that book come alive for you. If we must teach the classics, and I'm not entirely convinced of this, then we must stop dissecting every metaphor, allegory, Christ-like figure, color, mood, and word and just let the kids read the darn story. I had one high school teacher who did this. Miss Hughes, my junior-year English teacher, introduced our new novel by writing a few simple questions on the board. One was, "Think about hosting a party at your house this weekend. Who would you invite and what would you do?" After a few minutes of brainstorming, she edited the question. "Now imagine your parents would be away for the weekend. Would anything about your party change?" Of course, the class erupted into a discussion about not having parents around, which led us to talk about the removal of authority from society, which ended with Miss Hughes passing out *The Lord of the Flies*. That's a classic that I could relate to and it is about adolescent boys stranded on a deserted island. I didn't even realize I was reading a classic; I thought it was just a good book. And I knew she was a good teacher.

My biggest beef with schools reading the classics is this: if it didn't have that coveted title, would you want to read it? Sometimes yes, sometimes no. But since we are interested in reading for pleasure, let's make sure our reading is pleasurable. If your kids are coming home with dense novels, lengthy writing assignments, and complex reading projects, now would be a good time to remind them that light reading is still available for their enjoyment. Magazines and newspapers are about as contemporary as writing gets and a good way to feel a sense of reading accomplishment. Are fashion articles and sports scores on par with literary masterpieces? No. And right now, that is probably their best-selling point.

Dissection: "Tell 'Em What They Want to Hear"

Throughout the school hallways of America there is one question that is heard each time a book is finished, "What did you get on the test?" Liking the characters, appreciating the author's point of view, or feeling a satisfied ending had been achieved all hinge on the almighty test score. If you ask your son, "Did you like the book?" he's likely to respond, "I'll tell you when I get the test back." Talk about a means to an end.

I am guilty of giving essay questions that asked for a student's opinion, knowing full well that I would be reading my opinion reworded. Even when I would try to have discussions about the book, I would catch my top students taking notes, convinced that I was giving clues to an impending test. Once, after finishing a novel that we had spent a great deal of time on, including quizzes, oral presentations, and projects, I did not give a cumulative final test. Some of those students still wake up in a cold sweat, certain that this oversight will affect their college entrance applications.

Success Story

Try to remember not to ask about the test before you ask about the book. Make time to talk about the reading for reading's sake; you'll find out about the grades soon enough.

Schools need a way to grade students; I just wish it didn't require such contrived methods. At home, we can reinforce that our readers have choices. If you have not already done so, post the "Reader's Bill of Rights" on your refrigerator and add to it as your family sees fit. Your teen may add that she has the right to "never has to appreciate an author's irony ever again." Your son may add that he "never has to read a book that weighs more than his hockey equipment." I hope that your kids read books in school, classic or otherwise, that they absolutely love; but if that isn't the case, let's make sure they know they are entitled to their opinion, even if it's one we would rather not hear.

When Writing Replaces Reading

Whenever parents ask what their children should be doing to become better writers, I answer "read." Nine out of ten times this is a completely unsatisfactory answer, and at first glance I would tend to agree. After all, if we become better readers by reading more, wouldn't it figure that we become better writers by writing more? But upon further thought it becomes clear that if a poor writer just keeps writing poorly, how will he get good? Practice does not make prefect. Practicing with better players who can mentor you makes you better. For this reason, I like to think of writing as the apprenticeship to reading.

The more you read, the more exposure you have to good, and hopefully great, writing. Reading an assortment of resources—novels, poetry, articles, and literature—can only strengthen your writing. But in school, we tend to teach formula writing. Start with a string opening sentence, write four or five supporting sentences, and close by reiterating the opening. Do that five times and call it an essay. Could you imagine reading that book?

Success Story

If your teen has dreams of being a writer, check out teen author Christopher Paolini of Eragon fame at www.randomhouse.com to read what inspired this author to self-publish his blockbuster book.

The last time someone asked me what I did for a living I answered simply, "I'm a writer." The response was, "Me, too!" My son's 14-year-old babysitter Amanda was working on a fantasy/adventure novel in her free time. Children, tweens, and teens are natural writers. Filled with passion, hope, and expectation, I bet we would have a lot more teen authors on our hands if we handed over lined paper or blank computer screens and told them to go for it; instead, we tell them what, how, and for how long to write. Under the guise of wanting our kids to be better readers, schools have even sacrificed reading time for writing time. That's like skipping practice for more games.

At home, everywhere you have books, have writing materials. Encourage journaling and diary writing with new stationary gifts and colorful pens. But most of all, encourage reading. Writers write because they have to. Given enough exposure to various reading, your teen may just find out that she, too, has a story that must be told.

Face the Competition

I have often fantasized that the Universal Calendar Committee will get together and decide that we now have 8 days in the week. On this eighth day, we would all be required to rest. No school, work, sports, shopping—just rest. Then maybe, I reason, I would have enough time to get done everything I needed to do. But I know full well that sooner or later this eighth day of rest would fall victim to my multi-tasking mania and I would be right back where I started.

Since there is no hope for additional calendar time any time in the future, we have to take a look at the time we have and budget accordingly. If you thought this was tough to do when the kids were little and on your schedule, imagine how much more challenging it will be once they have their own list of commitments they must fill (with the help of your car).

Despite all the advances to make our lives simpler, we seem to have found a way to further complicate them. The following suggestions fall just shy of the "if you can't beat 'em, join 'em" mantra. I prefer to stop insisting that there always has to be a fight at all.

Television and Computers

There are a few TV programs that I really enjoy. And I can always find something to do online. But unplugging from all electronics is necessary for me to relax, rejuvenate, and create. I'm not interested in eliminating media from my home, but I am committed to limiting it.

Instead of letting your children (or getting into the habit yourself) of turning on the television looking for something to watch, turn on the television when there is something to watch. This can help eliminate TV as your family's default activity. Not all television is bad, but television all the time can be. An easy way to limit everyone's tube time is by not letting your teens have a television in their room. This forces them to share the family set, giving you an opportunity to see what they like and give them an opportunity to find something else to do when you want to watch a program.

The same is true for computers. Yes, we read computer screens, but reading instant messenger ramblings and chat-room profiles should be filed under privilege, not value. If your teens are arguing that they are doing important research on the computer, pull up their history and see what constitutes important. Are they reading online journals and newsletters, or are they downloading music? There is nothing wrong with enjoying the Internet, and it can be a great source of information, but let's make sure that extended time "reading" on the Internet involves more than symbols and smiley faces.

If your teen is an avid computer user who is looking for an e-magazine worth reading, check out www.wildriverreview.com. Jonathan Maberry, author of *Ghost Road Blues*, has co-founded *The Wild River Review*, an online literary magazine that "seeks to create a community of writers and artists by showcasing the finest works of creative prose and poetry, and of contemporary visual artists." User-friendly links make reading fantastic essays and columns easy, and they welcome submissions. This is reading worth sitting in front of the computer for.

Quick Picks

If your teen loves e-mail, surprise her with a free e-card from hallmark at www.hallmark.com. When you care enough to e-mail the very best, do so. You will make her day (and yours).

Success Story

If you are looking for new timesaving tips, organization ideas, holiday features, and a free giveaway or two, check out www.momready.com. This free online magazine is geared toward busy moms who want quick, informative articles delivered to their e-mail. No fuss, all fun.

Parents often ask about reading e-books online and whether that counts. My answer is always another question, "What books are your kids downloading?" No one seems to know. This is really more of a hypothetical question than a real practice. While e-books may be the next big thing, right now it still remains a bit of a nonissue. With all we have to worry about, let's not go looking for new challenges; those will be here before you know it. Besides, printed books are more convenient, comfortable, and accessible; if it's not broke, don't fix it.

Sports and Clubs

I know parents now who spend more time in the car driving their kids back and forth to after-school activities than they do at home. I can't imagine what their lives are going to be like when their children reach high school and the time commitments increase exponentially. Most teens love the connection they make with teammates and cherish the time they can spend with friends. Instead of begrudging them their commitments, look for ways to sneak a little reading into their routine, and get to know your kids a little bit better as an added bonus.

While you are going to know your kid's closest friends, expecting to meet the whole team may not be realistic; but as you are likely to keep hearing the same names over and over again, why not put a name to the face? Give your daughter a disposable camera so she can capture her teammates, both in action and on the sidelines. After they are developed, encourage her to write names, dates, and messages on the back of the pictures, and then put together a scrapbook. If your son likes the idea, but feels scrapbooking is a bit too "girly," look for a photo album that has simple lines marked for a quick note. Talking about who's who and what's what is another way to stay connected with a busy teen using a simple book.

Success Story

You can also tap into your teen's competitive spirit with board games. Start a fun family tradition by buying a new game each holiday. Put kids in charge of reading the directions and getting game night going.

Fresh Approaches

When trying to reach a reluctant reader, we can look for ways to update things that have worked in the past—like keeping a variety of reading materials within reach—and come up with some new ideas that are specifically targeted for this tough group. Chances are, if your reader has come this far, he is not resistant to reading as a whole, but has probably found himself in a book slump. Even the most dedicated readers I know, including myself, have fallen away from daily recreational reading if business paperwork becomes too demanding. When it feels like all we are doing is reading, be it for career or the classroom, the last thing we want to do is relax with more "work."

What is needed at times like this is a kick start—something to pull you out of the slump. Whether it's getting back on the exercise treadmill or finally finishing that redecorating project or reading for pleasure, a new angle can be just the breath of fresh air you need to spark a renewed interest in a once-favored activity.

Book Clubs: Where Generations and Genres Meet

Thanks in large part to Oprah, book clubs are quite the rage right now. Although they have probably been around as long as books themselves, celebrity attention has made getting together over a book a trendy thing to do. Book clubs are all over the place: online, on TV, at the library, and at your neighbor's house. I had the pleasure of facilitating a book club for mothers and daughters when I was a middle school teacher and the experience had a lasting impression on me and the other members. For your kids, book clubs are really a great excuse to get together with friends on a school night; for you, they are a great opportunity to meet and mingle with other teens and their parents, in a comfortable, low-pressure situation. Plus, everyone gets to enjoy a great book along the way.

Our book club was mothers and daughters, but any parent/child or grandparent/child combination could work, and each will have its own unique dynamic. If you want to try a book club but don't know where to start, *The Mother-Daughter Book Club: How Ten Busy Mothers and Daughters Came Together to Talk, Laugh, and Learn Through Their Love of Reading* by Shireen Dodson is a practical handbook for getting your group off the ground. Loaded with great reading recommendations, the author and her daughter share their experience, noting what worked best. Although obviously not geared toward books that boys might love, the organization suggestions, staying committed to the group, and the benefits of sharing this important time together are not gender-specific and could be used as an outline for any group.

Since your teen may be hesitant to put herself in a potentially humiliating situation, make sure you include her in all of the details. Offer up your home to host, be open to her reading selections, and create the kind of atmosphere she wants—even if that means lighting every candle you own and sitting in virtual darkness. When your teen is engaged in the activity, she is much more likely to look forward to the event, making the planning as enjoyable as the party. And reading enjoyment is all we are about.

Here are a few suggestions to help get you started:

- **Be organized** While the last thing you may need is another commitment, if you want to get things going, you'll have to put in some extra time at the beginning. After brainstorming with your teen about who to invite, make up written invitations addressed to the parents that include details like when to meet, directions, and the first book to read. You may also like to invite participants to bring a book suggestion for an upcoming meeting. If you want to contact kids with their own e-vite or note, great; but make sure parents have their own copy of the invitation.
- **Be hospitable** If we want our kids to read for pleasure, let's make it pleasurable. Plan for some downtime as families arrive by having finger foods, desserts, and drinks available. While the kids are probably close, the parents may need some help with introductions and feeling more comfortable. Having pre-made nametags can really help, especially when they say "Patty—Heather's Mom."

Success Story

A great new addition to your kitchen and your reading club is *The Book Club Cook Book* by Judy Gelman and Vicki Levy Krupp. Filled with recipes inspired by favorite stories, this resource has some great ideas for making the most of your monthly meeting.

- **Be creative** As always, remember that recreational reading is not school. Stay away from teacher terms like "character" and "plot development" and talk about the story in the same way you would talk about a movie. It can help to have questions or conversation starters on hand to get things moving along. For instance, in Sharon Creech's *Walk Two Moons*, each chapter begins with a quote. I found a variety of famous quotes, taped them to the bottom of the chairs, and invited guests to read and comment on them. Some were moving, some were funny, but all gave us something to talk about.

- **Be enthusiastic** Start this club with the intention of keeping it going. Don't end the first meeting without deciding who and where the next meeting will be held, and what book should be read. Sticking to a regular date, such as "last Tuesday of the month," makes it easier to remember. If guests brought book recommendations, place the titles in a basket and pick your next read. A parting memento, like a new bookmark, can be a nice finishing touch.

Incentive Packages

I love a package deal, a free gift with purchase, and the punch card at my coffee shop where I can earn a free cup of caffeine. When we leave a store feeling like we got more than we bargained for, it can make us feel like we have won a prize. How many times have you actually spent more money than you intended just so you could walk away with the limited-time offer? I can't be the only one …. Bonus days don't have to be monopolized by big business; with a little preparation you can bring the same ideas home. Instead of bribing your teens, entice them with your own special brand of marketing.

I truly believe that children should have an interesting life, and quite frankly, the mall is just not that interesting. Putting your kids in charge of family outings, be it an afternoon for two or a full family weekend getaway, can help everyone reconnect and encourage reading. If, for instance, you have a Halloween aficionado on your hands, pick up a copy of *A Ghost in My Suitcase: A Guide to Haunted Travel in America* by Mitchel Whitington and have your teen plan a local, or not-so-local, visit to a haunted haven. If you are living with a history buff, try *Civil War Sites: The Official Guide to Battlefields, Monuments, and More* presented by the Civil War Preservation Trust. This book lists tons of relevant sites to see and visit, as well as any associated fees and hours of operation. Your kid gets to go where he wants to go, and gets to plan the trip using a cool new book you bought him. Now that is a package deal everybody can feel good about.

Build a Buzz

If there is one thing your teenager can relate to, it's gossip. There are few things more titillating than being the first to know. Having the inside scoop doesn't have to be limited to fashion or friends. Getting ahead of the reading game can carry just as much clout. Imagine being the one who discovered "Sex and the City" before it was a huge success, or knowing everything there is to know about an up-and-coming rock star? Get acquainted with these sites, and your reading recommendations could well become the hit of the season:

- **www.powells.com** An independent Oregon-based bookseller whose website is user-friendly, loaded with extras, and features a ton of used books for sale. Great recommendations, author interviews, and blogs.
- **www.authoryellowpages.com** A well-compiled resource to finding your favorite author's personal website and newsletter, publisher's information, and featured sites that often host book excerpts. A great way to find out what's on the horizon from your favorite writers.
- **www.bookreporter.com** This site is loaded with reading recommendations and contests, as well as "One to Watch" and "Coming Soon" sections to keep you ahead of the curve. With links to network sites www.kidsread.com and www.teensread.com you'll have a ton of exciting information at your fingertips.

Bookmark these sites to help keep your kids interested in the publishing market. With sites like these on your side, you'll never be left wondering what to read next.

A dissatisfied reader is not a lost cause, just a disappointed patron. Because we have helped give our teens pleasant reading experiences, we don't have to head back to the drawing board, but we do want to be aware of the effect a blackboard can have on our recreational readers. Regardless of what goes on at school, reading at home can be a pleasure when we choose to find pleasure in reading.

The Least You Need to Know

- Reading is about progress, not perfection. Make sure you let your child make her own reading mistakes, be it a poor library selection or a subscription to a dull magazine. Both can help refine taste.
- Writing is an extension of reading, not a replacement. Encourage your reader to journal and scrapbook but don't insist on checking his grammar when he's done.
- Teen-directed activities can engage, instead of enrage, a reader. This helps to give your child a sense of ownership when it comes to reading.

Chapter 21

Great Young Adult Titles to Try Together

In This Chapter

- The rewards of a job well done
- Living by the pleasure principle
- Readers for life read for life

When we first started this book, our emphasis relied heavily on establishing and promoting healthy reading habits. We talked about engaging our audience, following their lead, and enjoying the process; and today, those same ideas are still relevant. Reading for enjoyment is a learned behavior. It doesn't happen overnight and it cannot sustain itself without nurturing. Keeping reading a priority in your home is as important as it ever was; only now, you can hopefully look forward to your audience being as receptive to the ideas as you are.

Reading with your teen is such an exciting time because the books are as much yours as they are hers. Gone are the days when you toss yet another train book into the basket and go find your reading. Now, you are just as likely to ask your teen for a recommendation as you are to make one. This new aspect of your reading relationship is truly cause for celebration. And what better way to celebrate reading than by doing some?

Keep at It

With teens becoming more and more autonomous, it can seem increasingly difficult to connect with this socially conscious class of independent thinkers who want to be seen as equals, but have trouble realizing that responsibility. Busy making sure that everyone is getting where they need to go on time, we can find it hard to make time for the things that matter most. Reading can still be a valuable way to step back from our busy schedules and catch our breath.

What's interesting about the books written here are their familiar feel. Certainly, you may actually end up rereading titles you once called your own, but the stories reflect dynamics that are as relevant to teens as they are to adults. Being an adult is not without its own angst; making friends, feeling like we belong, and discovering one's true identity are not themes that we ever outgrow. There is no finish line when it comes to growing up, just as there is no finish line to reading together. Is it still worthwhile to read with your children? Absolutely, for you and for them.

The Big Payoff: Raising a Reader for Life

After all your hard work, you may be wondering if there is a way to be certain that your reading values have definitely gotten through to your child. It would be comforting to have your children say, "Wow, I really love reading. I consider myself a well-read individual. I look forward to reading more great books. I love my parents." But as that is not likely to happen, we can look for clues to give us that much-deserved sense of satisfaction. Yes, seeing your teen with a book in her hand is a good sign, but hearing your child talk about books is even more telling. When stories permeate our personalities and leave a lasting impression on the way we think, we have truly opened ourselves up to the power of books. Whether you take 5 minutes in the car to talk about an interesting article, compare someone you both know to a character in a story, or make a date to hit the bookstore together, reading is no longer just about words on the page; it is about the words imprinted on your lives. Make time to talk about books with your teen and you may find that your hard work has indeed paid off, and then some.

Apply the Pleasure Principle

The final selections recommended here were chosen because they are significant without being saccharine, entertaining without being empty. These books are a lot like a great dessert, sundaes that have been upgraded to soufflés. Both are sweet, but the latter is definitely more satisfying. For parents and teens, reading pleasure is likely to be characterized in much the same way. Instead of figuring out ways to apply the pleasure principle, we can enjoy having adopted it as a reading way of life.

I hope that your family has found a reading routine that works best for you, changes as you grow, and keeps readers coming back for more. When we like what we do, we do more of it. By building a literacy-rich home that values reading as an integral part of family life, you are likely to be surrounded by children who love to be surrounded by books. Continue to find new ways to experience books together and keep up the good work. Old habits are hard to break, and in this case, that couldn't be better news.

A Look Back: Five Timeless Tales

Some of the books recommended here would definitely be considered "classic" in academic circles, but I would read them regardless of any distinction. From titles that have been around for almost 200 years, to novels that my parents enjoyed in their day, the time spectrum certainly proves one thing: some stories are timeless in every sense of the word. It is always amazing to me that certain books become part of our collective psyche while so many others enjoy a limited blockbuster stint and are then never heard from again. I don't worry about anyone missing the opportunity to read a timeless tale, as its very nature tends to ensure that it will always be available; but I do hope that we continue to talk about what great stories these books are and attract a whole new audience to some older, but never dated, choices.

A Day No Pigs Would Die, copyright © 1994 Robert Newton Peck

An emotional powerhouse that pulls no punches, this realistic account of the work that must be done on a farm is brutal, and the young character's reaction to his role in its function is brilliant.

Little Women, first published 1868 Louisa May Alcott

This is the original "girls next door" story. The four March girls grow up in financial poverty, but are rich in spirit and family. Don't be put off by the length; the writing is clean and easy, making it easy to lose yourself in.

A Wrinkle in Time, copyright © 1963 Madeleine L'Engle

Not quite science fiction, more than just a fanciful superhero tale, this coming of age story has been captivating audiences with it's adventuresome journey through time and space. Winner of the 1963 Newberry Award, this allegorical story is multi-layered and compelling with plenty to talk about.

Animal Farm, copyright © 1946 George Orwell

A succinct, tightly woven tale of letting those with tails rule the roost. Sickened by their master, the animals unite and become rulers of themselves, even developing a creed of equal rights; but after the initial joy wears off, dissension among the ranks ensues and the animals are left in worse condition than when they started. A smart satire.

Emma, first published 1815 Jane Austen

Emma Woodhouse, born into privilege and prestige, has mistakenly assumed that she can do no wrong and insists that she is always just trying to help. Of course, this leads to quite a comedy of errors through which readers will find it hard not to side with the endearing, though thoroughly flawed heroine.

Quick Picks

The 1995 movie Clueless starring Alicia Silverstone is loosely based on the 1815 novel *Emma*. Now if that doesn't convince you that this story has staying power, nothing will.

Hot Off the Press: Five New and Improved Stories

I was introduced to most of the books listed here by teens themselves, which is one of the most hopeful signs that reading a hot topic is still a hot topic. Having grown up reading my own teenage angst novels, it is not surprising to find that while the players may have changed, the game is still the same. Some stories are darker and many reads are racier, but the coming-of-age emotions that make you self-conscious of every step you take haven't changed. Reading these books as a parent will no doubt remind you how glad you are that high school only lasts 4 years. Enjoy sharing your own stories with your teens, who no doubt are convinced that they are the only ones who feel this way.

Stargirl, copyright © 2002 Jerry Spinelli

Narrated by a 16-year-old high school student who falls somewhat reluctantly, but ultimately hopelessly, in love with a transfer student who is a self-assured anomaly. Stargirl is inspired and inspiring, until she becomes too threatening; high school can be an awfully fickle place for original characters.

Perks of Being a Wallflower, copyright © 1999 Stephen Chbosky

The tenth-grade narrator of this story flies just under the social radar, not too popular to be cool, not too much of a loser to be harassed, he is able to watch high school unfold from a safe distance, but he cannot avoid his own issues of loss, depression, and experimentation. Written in letters to an anonymous friend, the story is heartbreaking and hopeful, a lot like growing up.

10 Things to Do Before I Die, copyright © 2004 by Daniel Ehrenhaft

When a teenager becomes convinced that he has eaten poisoned fries, he and his friends come up with a list of things do with his remaining 24 hours. Ironic, funny, and definitely not sad, you'll be glad this kid makes it.

The Devil Wears Prada: A Novel, copyright © 2004 Lauren Weisberger

If your teen has any delusions about how rewarding it will be to work her way up the corporate ladder, then this book should help adequately squash those misconceptions. Everyone has a "boss from hell" story, but

Quick Picks

Megan McCafferty's debut novel has been followed up by *Second Helpings: A Novel* and *Charmed Thirds: A Novel.* Remember, if you or your children like a book, do yourself a favor and check out what else the author has out. You never know when your teen is going to hit her reading stride.

this one, set against the NYC fashion industry, truly takes the cake; a true guilty pleasure.

Sloppy Firsts: A Novel, copyright © 2001 Megan McCafferty

A completely relatable teenage angst story that reminds readers what it's like to hate everyone around you but still desperately want their approval. Filled with pop-culture references, this debut novel is sure to find a fast following.

Playground Picks: Five Mom-Approved Titles

In writing this book, I had asked friends what books they had passed back and forth in their families and was pleased to find out that such a practice is part and parcel of many homes. I love hearing, "My daughter told me I should read this," or "My son wouldn't stop talking about this book, so I read it." More than a mere recommendation, it is another way our children try to tell us to pay attention to them. If your kids hand you a book, read it immediately. If you hand them a book, be prepared to wait awhile for any reaction. This is a two-way street, but their side seems to be littered with detours. Be patient. Reading together can hopefully be done simultaneously, but thankfully, there is no statute of limitations imposed on the experience.

Read All About It!: Great Read-Aloud Stories, Poems, and Newspaper Pieces for Preteens and Teens, copyright © 1993 Jim Trelease

Trelease, author of *The Read Aloud Handbook*, has handpicked 50 age-appropriate reading selections that begin with an interesting author introduction and last long enough for a reading "fill in." Great for discussion or private enjoyment.

Seabiscuit: An American Legend, copyright © 2002 Lauren Hillenbrand

While the movie does the book justice, the eloquent writing truly captures each character, leaving readers to decide who the real hero is. A Cinderella story minus frilly dresses, this feel-good read leaves you feeling, well, good.

Bridget Jones' Diary, copyright © 1999 Helen Fiedling

This is the title that launched chick-lit into major mainstream status. This hilarious, obsessive book follows one women's quest to love her life as it is, just as soon as she can completely change it. You'll find yourself cheering for this relatable and likeable lady who is only 7 pounds (or is it 70?) away from her perfect self.

The Chocolate War, copyright © 1974 Robert Cormier

A groundbreaking book that dared to "disturb the universe," readers come face to face with mob mentality when a seemingly simple decision sparks an all-out war with clearly defined battle grounds mapped out on a high school campus. A psychological thriller with no easy answers.

Bookworms Beware

The Chocolate War has frequently come under fire for its graphic language and content, consistently landing on banned books list; naturally, this will be a huge selling point to your teens, but something you may want to investigate further.

Ties That Bind; Ties That Break, copyright © 2000 Lensey Namioka

Told in a series of flashbacks that bring readers head to head with 1911 China, the female narrator chronicles her journey from oppressed, but strong-willed young girl to fully realized adult. With just enough emphasis on history and culture, this page turner is a quick but effective read.

Award Winners: Five Critically Acclaimed Books

Most of the award-winning books I have recommended have been courtesy of the Newberry and Caldecott lists. While there are several prestigious awards for children's literature, I have found that these medal and honor books are consistently well received by their audiences and have therefore targeted a "sure thing." But now that we are reaching a more mature audience, we can broaden our spectrum a bit and look to two other reliable sources for relevant recommendations.

The Young Adult Library Services Association releases a yearly list of Best Books for Young Adults. "The books, recommended for ages 12 to 18, meet the criteria of both good-quality literature and reading appeal for teens." The YALSA is a division of the American Library Association, an organization committed to connecting reader and great reading. The Pulitzer Prize for Fiction is awarded "for distinguished fiction by an American author, preferably dealing with American life." Perhaps one of the highest honors a book can receive, the Pulitzer represents the best of the best. When you see the titles chosen, I hope you agree with these experts' opinions.

Nothing but the Truth, copyright © 1991 Avi

This Newberry Honor book does an excellent, and accurate, job of taking one detail and blowing it way out of proportion with the help of outraged (misinformed) citizens and appropriately edited media clips. Everyone has an opinion that is supported by his or her own version of the truth.

Out of the Dust, copyright © 1999 Karen Hesse

Hesse's Newberry medal winner, this story is told in poetry-like prose, which encourage the reader to linger over the language. The Depression and the Oklahoma Dust Bowl are perfect settings for this slow and stirring novel about a young girl whose hands and heart are permanently scarred.

To Kill a Mockingbird, copyright © 1960 Harper Lee

Winner of the 1961 Pulitzer Prize for fiction, many schools choose to read this book, but it a story that can also be embraced by your home. Tackling racism in the deep South during the Depression, this poignant novel is made accessible through the eyes of an adolescent girl who struggles to make sense of her increasingly complicated world.

Success Story

The elusive Harper Lee never published another book, detests publicity, and has avoided interviews since the early 1960s. In a www.teenreads.com article we learn that when asked to write an introduction to the book on its thirty-fifth anniversary, she refused, saying, "It says what it has to say." The book clearly stands on its own merit.

Looking for Alaska, copyright © 2005 by John Green

A high school boy looks to relocate and reinvent himself, only to find that wherever you go, you take yourself with you. An original coming-of-age story that is immediately engaging, with just the right amount of deviant behavior to keep your teen hooked. A YALSA Best Books for Teen 2006 recommendation.

As this book comes to an end, I hope that your reading routine does not. I encourage you to continue looking for ways to connect with your children through stories. Your literacy-rich home need never roll up the welcome mat; everyone can be invited inside.

The Least You Need to Know

- Talking about books is as important as reading them. Make sure you don't miss out on these special opportunities by incorporating down time discussions into your reading routines.
- Enjoy continuing to nurture your family's reading experience by sharing stories you grew up with and asking your children for book recommendations.
- A literacy-rich home always has an open door. And that means welcoming all sorts of reading materials into your home; and then deciding how long they get to stay.

Appendix A

Titles to Share—A Compilation

Here is a compiled list of some reading titles you and your children can share together. This list just begins to scratch the surface of great literature and is best used as a starting point for generating your family's personal reading list.

"More, More, More" Said the Baby: Three Love Stories by Vera B. Williams

1,000 Places to See Before You Die by Patricia Shultz

10 Things to Do Before I Die by Daniel Ehrenhaft

500 Hilarious Jokes for Kids by Jeff Rovin

A Day No Pigs Would Die by Robert Newton Peck

A Family of Poems: My Favorite Poetry for Children compiled by Carolyn Kennedy

A Ghost in My Suitcase: A Guide to Haunted Travel in America by Mitchel Whitington

A Light in the Attic by Shel Silverstein

A Potty for Me: A Lift-the-Flap Instruction Manual by Karen Katz

A Series of Unfortunate Events by Lemony Snicket

A Terrible Thing Happened—A story for children who have witnessed violence or trauma by Margaret M. Holmes, Sasha J. Mudlaff, Cary Pillo

A Tree Is Nice by Janice May Udry, Marc Simont

Al Capone Does My Shirts by Gennifer Choldenko

Alex Rider Adventures by Anthony Horowitz

Alexander and the Terrible, Horrible, No Good, Very Bad Day by Judith Viorst, Ray Cruz

Amelia Bedilia Goes Camping (I Can Read Book 2) by Peggy Parish, Lynn Sweat

And Tango Makes Three by Peter Parnell, Justin Richardson

Animal Farm by George Orwell

Anne of Green Gables by L. M. Montgomery

Are You My Mother? By P. D. Eastman

Are You There, God? It's Me, Margaret by Judy Blume

Artemis Fowl by Eoin Colfer

Arthur's Underwear (Arthur Adventure Series) by Marc Brown

Baby Einstein's Water, Water Everywhere: A Splash and Giggle Bath Book by Julie Agner-Clark

Bailey Goes Camping by Kevin Henkes

Barking Mouse by Antonio Sacre and Alfredo Aguirre

Barnyard Dance by Sandra Boynton

Better Than Life by Daniel Pennac

Black on White by Tana Hoban

Brave Irene by William Steig

Breastmilk Makes My Tummy Yummy by Cecilia Moen

Bridget Jones' Diary by Helen Fiedling

Brown Bear, Brown Bear, What Do You See? by Bill Martin and illustrator Eric Carle. Available in Spanish *Oso Pardo, Oso Pardo, ¿Qué Ves Ahí?*

But Not the Hippopotamus by Sandra Boynton

Captain Underpants series by Dav Pilkney

Changes, Changes by Pat Hutchins

Charlie and the Chocolate Factory by Roald Dahl

Charlotte's Web by E. B. White

Chicka, Chicka, Boom Boom copyright by Bill Martin, Jr., John Archambault

Chronicles of Narnia by C. S. Lewis

City of Ember by Jeanne Duprau

Civil War Sites: The Official Guide to Battlefields, Monuments, and More presented by the Civil War Preservation Trust

Click, Clack, Moo: Cows That Type by Doreen Cronin, Betsy Lewin

Clifford the Big Red Dog by Norman Bridwell

Cloudy with a Chance of Meatballs by Judi Barrett, Ron Barrett

Coin Collecting for Kids by Steve Otfinoski, Jack Grahamm Compilation

Crafts for All Seasons, copyright © 2000 Kathy Ross

Crinkleroot's Guide to Walking in Wild Places by Jim Arnosky

Dare to Dream!: 25 Extraordinary Lives by Sandra McLeod Humphrey

Dear Mr. Henshaw by Beverly Cleary

Define "Normal" by Julie Anne Peters

Different Seasons by Stephen King

Discover America State by State: Alphabet series, published by Sleeping Bear Press

Doll People by Ann Matthews Martin, Laura Godwin, illustrator Brian Selznick

Don't Laugh at Me by Steve Seskin, Allen Shamblin, and Glin Dibley

Don't Let the Pigeon Drive the Bus by Mo Willems

Emma by Jane Austen

Esperenza Rising by Pam Munoz Ryan

Everyone Poops (My Body Science series*)* by Taro Gomi and Amanda Mayer Stinchecum

Falling Up by Shel Silverstein

Family Fun Homemade Holidays by Deanna Cook

Field Trips: Bug Hunting, Animal Tracking, Bird Watching, Shore Watching by Jim Arnosky

Fire in My Heart, Ice in My Veins: A Journal for Teenagers Experiencing Loss by Enid Samuel Traisman

Follow the Drinking Gourd by Jeanette Winter

For Better, For Worse: A Guide to Surviving Divorce for Pre-teens and Their Family by Janet Bode

Freight Train by Donald Crews

Frindle by Andrew Clements

From the Mixed-Up Files of Mrs. Basil E. Frankweiler by E. L. Konisburg

George by Kate Kiesler

Go Away Big Green Monster by Edward R. Emberly

Go, Dog, Go by P. D. Eastman

Goodnight Gorilla by Peggy Rathman

Goodnight Moon by Margaret Wise Brown

Green Eggs and Ham by Dr. Seuss, available in Spanish *Huevos Verdes Con Jamón* by Aida E. Marcuse

Guess How Much I Love You by Sam McBratney

Harold and the Purple Crayon by Crockett Johnson

Harriet the Spy by Louise Fitzhugh

Harry Potter series by J. K. Rowling

Help Me Say Goodbye: Activities for Helping Kids Cope When a Special Person Dies by Janis Silverman

Hippos Go Berserk by Sandra Boynton

Holes by Louis Sachar

Hoot by Carl Hiaasin

How I Spent My Summer Vacation by Mark Teague

How to Be a Friend: A Guide to Making Friends and Keeping Them (Dino Life Guides for Families) by Laurie Krasny Brown, Marc Brown

I Froze My Mother and Other Seriously Funny Family Poems by Ted Scheu, Peter Lourie

I Love You as Much by Laura Krauss Melmed, Henri Sorensen

I Love You, Stinky Face by Lisa McCourt

I Miss You: A First Look at Death by Pat Thomas, Leslie Harker

I Spy Books by Jean Marzallo

If I Were In Charge of the World and Other Worries: Poems for Children and Their Parents by Judith Viorst, Lynne Cherry

If You Give a Mouse a Cookie by Laura Numeroff, Felicia Bond

In the Small, Small Pond by Denise Fleming

Ira Sleeps Over by Bernard Waber, Larry Robinson

Island of the Blue Dolphins by Scott O'Dell

It's Not the End of the World by Judy Blume

It's Not Your Fault, Koko Bear: A Read-Together Book for Parents and Young Children During Divorce by Vicki Lansky

It's Our World, Too! by Phillip Hoose

Joey Pigza Swallowed the Key by Jack Gantos

Join In and Play (Learning to Get Along) by Cheri J. Meiners

Joseph Had a Little Overcoat by Simms Taback

King of the Playground by Phyllis Reynolds Naylor, Nola Langnor Malone

Lily's Purple Plastic Purse by Kevin Henkes

Little Bunnies Pacifier Plan by Maribeth Bolts and Kathy Parkinson

Little Women by Louisa May Alcott

Looking for Alaska by John Green

Lovely Bones by Alice Sebold

Magic for Kids by Kay Presto

Magic Tree House series by Mary Pope Osborne

Mouse's First Halloween by Lauren Thompson and Buket Erdogan

My Big Boy Potty Lap Edition by Joanna Cole and Maxie Chambliss

My Big Girl Potty Lap Edition by Joanna Cole and Maxie Chambliss

My First Farm Board Book: English/Spanish by DK Publishing

My First Taggies Book, copyright © 2003 by Kaori Wantanabe

My Parents Are Divorced, Too: A Book for Kids by Kids by Melanie Ford

Nate the Great Marjorie Weinman Sharmat, Marc Simont

Night Sounds (Play the Sounds, Pull the Tabs) by Frank Gallo, Lori Lohstoeter

Nobody Knew What to Do: A Story About Bullying by Becky Ray McCain, Todd Leonardo

Nothing but the Truth by Avi

Number the Stars by Lois Lowry

Oh Yikes!: History's Grossest Moments by Joy Masoff, Patricia Polacco's

Oh Yuck!: The Encyclopedia of Everything Nasty by Joy Masoff

Olive's Ocean, copyright © by Kevin Henke

Olivia by Ian Falconer

One Fish Two Fish Red Fish Blue Fish by Dr. Seuss

Out of the Dust by Karen Hesse

Owl Babies by Martin Waddell

Pajama Party: All Aboard Reading (Level 1) by Joan Holub, Julie Durrell

Pancakes for Breakfast by Tommy dePaola

Pat the Bunny by Dorothy Kunhardt

Pearl's Eight Days of Chanukah: With a Story and Activity for Each Night by Jane Breskin Zalben

Perks of Being a Wallflower by Stephen Chbosky

Play and Find Out series by Janice Van Cleave

Politically Correct Bedtime Stories: Modern Tales for Our Life and Times by James Finn Garner

Read All About It!: Great Read-Aloud Stories, Poems, and Newspaper Pieces for Preteens and Teens by Jim Trelease

Recycle!: A Handbook for Kids by Gail Gibbons

Roll of Thunder, Hear My Cry by Mildred D. Taylor

Running with Scissors: A Memoir by Augusten Burrows

Sammy Keyes series by Wendelin Van Draanan

Say Something by Peggy Moss, Lea Lyon

Saying Goodbye to a Pet (Saying Goodbye series) by Nicola Edwards

Seabiscuit: An American Legend by Lauren Hillenbrand

Sing a Song of Popcorn: Every Child's Book of Poems by various contributing authors and award-winning illustrators

Sisterhood of the Traveling Pants by Ann Brashares

Sloppy Firsts: A Novel by Megan McCafferty

Spike It by Matt Christopher

Stargirl by Jerry Spinelli

Stone Soup by Jon Muth

Stop Picking on Me (A First Look At series) by Pat Thomas, Lesley Harker

Summer (Beginner Books) by Alice Low, Roy McKie

Ten, Nine, Eight by Molly Bang

That Was Then, This Is Now by S. E. Hinton

That's Mean by Francesco Pittau, Bernadette Gervais

The Agony of Alice by Phyllis Reynolds Naylor

The Bully Blockers Club by Teresa Bateman

The Butterfly by Patricia Polacco

The Chocolate War by Robert Cormier

The Devil Wears Prada: A Novel by Lauren Weisberger

The Diary of Anne Frank by Anne Frank

The Dot by Peter H. Reynolds

The Family Book by Todd Parr

The Foot Book by Dr. Seuss

The Girls by Amy Goldman Koss

The Jumbo Book of Outdoor Art by Irene Luxbacher

The Kid Who Only Hit Homers by Matt Christopher

The Kids Book of Questions: Revised for the New Century by Gregory Stock

The Kissing Hand by Audrey Penn

The Little House on the Prairie by Laura Ingalls Wilder

The Little Mouse, the Red Ripe Strawberry, and the Big Hungry Bear by Don Wood, Audrey Wood

The Magic School Bus series by Joanna Cole

The Middle School Survival Guide: How to Survive from the Day Elementary School Ends Until the Second High School Begins by Arlene Erlbach, illustrator Helen Flook

The Outsiders by S. E. Hinton

The Phantom Tollbooth, copyright © 1961 Norton Juster

The Polar Express, copyright © 1985 by Chris Van Allsburg

The Red Book, copyright © 2004 Barbara Lehman

The Scrambled States of America by Laurie Keller

The Snowy Day, copyright © by Ezra Jack Keats

The Start to Read! Books by Barbara Gregorich

The Thorn Birds by Colleen McCollough

The Ugly Duckling by Hans Christian Anderson

The Wizard of Oz by L. Frank Baum

Ties That Bind; Ties That Break by Lensey Namioka

Time for Bed by Mem Fox

To Kill a Mockingbird by Harper Lee

Toasting Marshmallows: Camping Poems by Kristine O'Connell

Too Old for This, Too Young for That!: Your Survival Guide for the Middle-School Years by Harriet S. Mosatache, Karen Unge

Trip-Tracker: Travel Journal and Gamebook, published by Rand McNally

Tuck Everlasting by Natalie Babbit

Two Homes by Claire Masurel, Kady Macdonald Denton

Velveteen Rabbit by Margery Williams

Wayside School Is Falling Down by Louis Sacher

We Have a Baby by Cathryn Falwell

We Were There, Too! Young People in U.S. History by Philip M. Hoose

What Mommies Do Best by Laura Numeroff

What Was I Scared Of? by Dr. Seuss

Where Is Baby's Belly Button? copyright © 2000 Karen Katz

Where the Sidewalk Ends by Shel Silverstein

Where the Wild Things Are by Maurice Sendak

Where's Spot? (Little Spot Board Books) by Eric Hill

Wiley and Grandpa's Creature Features by Kirk Scroggs

Wind in the Willows by Kenneth Grahame

Wringer by Jerry Spinelli

Yoko by Rosemary Wells

Appendix B

Titles for Parents to Try

Here is a compiled list of titles that were recommended throughout the book as reading resources for parents. There are many more books available, but these I find to be the most user-friendly and practical.

10 Conversations You Must Have with Your Children by Shmuley Boteach

Better Than Life by Daniel Pennac

Book Club Cook Book by Judy Gelman, Vicki Levy Krupp

Get Out of My Life, but First Could You Drive Me & Cheryl to the Mall?: A Parent's Guide to the New Teenager, Revised and Updated by Anthony E. Wolf

How to Talk So Kids Will Listen and Listen So Kids Will Talk by Adele Faber and Elaine Mazlish

Reclaiming Childhood: Letting Children Be Children by Dr. William Crain

Staying Connected to Your Teenager: How to Keep Them Talking to You and How to Hear What They're Really Saying by Michael Riera

The Mother-Daughter Book Club: How Ten Busy Mothers and Daughters Came Together to Talk, Laugh, and Learn Through Their Love of Reading by Shireen Dodson

The Read-Aloud Handbook by Jim Trelease

The Rollercoaster Years by Charlene C. Gianetti and Margaret Sagarese

WHY Do They Act That Way?: A Survival Guide to the Adolescent Brain for You and Your Teen by David Walsh

Yes, Your Teen is Crazy!: Loving Your Kid Without Losing Your Mind by Michael J. Bradley, Jay N. Giedd

Index

Numbers

A

B

C

D

E

F

G

H

I

J-K

L

M

N

O

P

Q-R

S

T

U–V

W–X

Y–Z